Appreciating the Art of Television

Ted Nannicelli's *Appreciating the Art of Television* is a signal intervention into the burgeoning field of television aesthetics. Nannicelli draws on contemporary analytic philosophy of art to advance compelling, often original, arguments about the authorship and ontology of television works, television's distinctiveness as a medium, the role of authorial intentions in the audience's interpretation of television works, and the evaluation of television as an art. His theorizing is characterized by impeccable clarity and rigor, and he mounts formidable challenges to arguments that are commonplace in TV studies: that fans determine the meanings of television works, for example, or that there is nothing objective about the evaluation of television as an art. These claims will have to be reckoned with by anyone seeking to understand the nature of television as an art and our appreciation of it, and this book is therefore required reading for those interested in the aesthetics of television.

Malcolm Turvey, Tufts University, Massachusetts

This is an exciting and valuable book project, in which Nannicelli brings together two lines of inquiry—analytical aesthetics and philosophy of film on the one hand and television studies on the other. Specifically, he explores how an intentionalist approach can solve a series of philosophical problems indirectly evident in many accounts in television studies. Through careful discussion he disentangles these philosophical problems and presents an original contribution to the emerging field of television aesthetics. Philosophically minded media scholars and philosophers interested in television will learn from and enjoy this book.

Margrethe Bruun Vaage, University of Kent, UK

Contemporary television has been marked by such exceptional programming that it is now common to hear claims that TV has finally become an art. In *Appreciating the Art of Television*, Nannicelli contends that televisual art is not a recent development but has in fact existed for a long time. Yet despite the flourishing of two relevant academic subfields—the philosophy of film and television aesthetics—there is little scholarship on television, *in general*, as an art form. This book aims to provide scholars active in television aesthetics with a critical overview of the relevant philosophical literature, while also giving philosophers of film a particular account of the art of television that will hopefully spur further interest and debate. It offers the first sustained theoretical examination of what is involved in appreciating television as an art and how this bears on the practical business of television scholars, critics, students, and fans—namely the comprehension, interpretation, and evaluation of specific televisual artworks.

Ted Nannicelli is Lecturer in Film and Television Studies at the University of Queensland, Australia. He is the author of *A Philosophy of the Screenplay* (Routledge, 2013). He is co-editor, with Paul Taberham, of *Cognitive Media Theory* (Routledge, 2014), and associate editor of *Projections: The Journal for Movies and Mind*.

Routledge Advances in Television Studies

1 Parody and Taste in Postwar American Television Culture
  Ethan Thompson

2 Television and Postfeminist Housekeeping
  No Time for Mother
  Elizabeth Nathanson

3 The Antihero in American Television
  Margrethe Bruun Vaage

4 American Militarism on the Small Screen
  Edited by Anna Froula and Stacy Takacs

5 Appreciating the Art of Television
  A Philosophical Perspective
  Ted Nannicelli

Appreciating the Art of Television
A Philosophical Perspective

Ted Nannicelli

NEW YORK AND LONDON

First published 2017
by Routledge
711 Third Avenue, New York, NY 10017

and by Routledge
2 Park Square, Milton Park, Abingdon, Oxon OX14 4RN

Routledge is an imprint of the Taylor & Francis Group, an informa business

© 2017 Taylor & Francis

The right of Ted Nannicelli to be identified as author of this work has been asserted by him in accordance with sections 77 and 78 of the Copyright, Designs and Patents Act 1988.

All rights reserved. No part of this book may be reprinted or reproduced or utilised in any form or by any electronic, mechanical, or other means, now known or hereafter invented, including photocopying and recording, or in any information storage or retrieval system, without permission in writing from the publishers.

Trademark notice: Product or corporate names may be trademarks or registered trademarks, and are used only for identification and explanation without intent to infringe.

Library of Congress Cataloging-in-Publication Data

Names: Nannicelli, Ted, author.
Title: Appreciating the art of television: a philosophical perspective / by Ted Nannicelli.
Description: New York: Routledge, 2016. | Series: Routledge advances in television studies | Includes bibliographical references and index.
Identifiers: LCCN 2016015659
Subjects: LCSH: Television—Philosophy.
Classification: LCC PN1992.55 .N235 2016 | DDC 791.4501—dc23
LC record available at https://lccn.loc.gov/2016015659

ISBN: 978-1-138-84078-2 (hbk)
ISBN: 978-1-315-73263-3 (ebk)

Typeset in Sabon
by codeMantra

For my parents, Paula and Tom Nannicelli, with love and gratitude for their boundless support, including viewing companionship during episodes of *Quantum Leap, Picket Fences, The Commish, The X-Files, Seinfeld,* and innumerable Red Sox games.

Contents

List of Figures xi
Acknowledgments xiii

Introduction: Appreciating the Art of Television 1

1 Authorship and Agency 18
2 The Medium 51
3 Ontology 88
4 Interpretation I 122
5 Interpretation II 156
6 Evaluation 181

Bibliography 209
Index 225

List of Figures

4.1	"Made in America," the final episode of *The Sopranos* (HBO 1999–2007). Tony's first glance up at the door of Holsten's, motivated by the sound of the bell.	146
4.2	Tony's point of view: A female customer entering the restaurant.	146
4.3	A "reverse shot" matching 4.1 and emphasizing the subjectivity of 4.2.	146
4.4	Tony glances up at the door of the restaurant, again motivated by the sound of the bell.	146
4.5	Tony's point of view: A male customer entering the restaurant.	146
4.6	A "reverse shot" matching 4.4 and emphasizing the subjectivity of 4.5.	146
4.7	Tony glances up at the door of the restaurant, again motivated by the sound of the bell.	146
4.8	Tony's point of view: Carmela enters the restaurant.	146
4.9	A "reverse shot" matching 4.7 and emphasizing the subjectivity of 4.8.	146
4.10	Tony's point of view: Carmela approaches and makes eye contact.	146
4.11	A "reverse shot" matching 4.9 and 4.7, a gain emphasizing the subjectivity of 4.10 and 4.8.	146
4.12	Tony's ostensible point of view of the "Members Only man," although likely not a literal POV shot because the door has yet to open and ring the bell, cuing Tony's glance.	146
4.13	A "reverse shot" of Tony's gaze, ostensibly revealing the source of the apparent POV.	146
4.14	A "true" point of view shot of the "Members Only man" and of A. J. from Tony's perspective.	146
4.15	A "reverse" shot indicating the source of the point of view in 4.14.	146
4.16	A wide shot, revealing the men's room, which the "Members Only man" is entering, in relationship to Tony.	146

xii *List of Figures*

4.17	Tony glances at the restaurant door, cued by the sound of the bell.	146
4.18	The final "shot"; arguably Tony's "point of view."	146
4.19	An earlier shot of the "Members Only man" looking (at Tony's table?).	147
4.20	A shot of Tony following 4.19, ostensibly revealing what the "Members Only man" is looking at.	147

Acknowledgments

Like my first book, this project began in some sense when I was a graduate student at Temple University. In 2004, I arrived back in the United States after two years abroad, during which time I had no exposure to television in my native language. It was then that Jeff Rush and Noël Carroll introduced me to the riches of *The Sopranos*, a show that rekindled my interest in the art of television. I am grateful for their many conversations with me and their supportive feedback on my eager but ingenuous work from that time. So, too, am I grateful to Murray Smith, who was yet to become my Ph.D. supervisor, for sharing with me his work-in-progress on *The Sopranos* from across the Atlantic. But my greatest debts from Philadelphia are to my friends: Matthew Morrow, who demanded I watch *The Wire*, Russell Rochestie, who awoke me to the drama of the NFL draft, Alexis Adorno and David O'Connell, who helped me transition back to American life, and Aliza Nimon, for countless hours of television-watching companionship and conversation and much, much else.

Writing on the project began at the University of Waikato, where I received valuable feedback and support from my colleagues in Screen and Media Studies, especially Gareth Schott, Alistair Swale, and Bevin Yeatman. I owe special thanks to Geoff Leland for the insight and generosity he provided in our co-taught course on television, as well as for his tutelage in rugby matters. It was not until I arrived at the University of Queensland that the project really took shape for me, and this is largely a result of extensive, helpful discussions with my new colleagues. In particular, I would like to thank Lisa Bode, Frances Bonner, Elliott Logan, Jason Jacobs, Tom O'Regan, and Jane Stadler, all of whom gave feedback on the ideas in this book, whether in conversation or in writing.

At the institutional level, I must thank the University of Queensland's Faculty of Humanities and Social Sciences for a New Staff Start-Up Grant and the Institute for Advanced Studies in the Humanities for a Faculty Fellowship, both of which lent the project significant financial support. The writing process was also supported by helpful feedback from audiences at a 2014 aesthetics conference at the University of Auckland, at which I was generously hosted by Stephen Davies, a research seminar in the Philosophy Department of Lingnan University, at which I was generously hosted by

Paisley Livingston, and a research seminar at the University of Kent, at which I was generously hosted by the members of the Aesthetics Research Centre. Earlier versions of Chapter 3 and Chapter 6 were published in *Screen*, and I am grateful to Oxford University Press for allowing authors to retain copyright of their work for the purposes of republication.

Jason Jacobs and Tom O'Regan read the entire manuscript, as did Sarah Cardwell, Paisley Livingston, Malcolm Turvey, and Margrethe Bruun Vaage, and I owe them a particular debt of gratitude. Their patient and generous feedback improved the book immeasurably and saved me from innumerable mistakes, not to mention some of my worst tendencies as a writer. To quote Flint Schier, any shockers that remain are of my own doing.

Finally, I am most grateful to my family: my boys, Leo and Vin, not least for their valuable "research assistance" on children's television, and my wife, Aliza, for her support, sense of humor, and love.

Introduction
Appreciating the Art of Television

Although the title of this book is not intended as a provocation, I am aware it could be taken as one, oddly enough, by two groups of people with quite disparate views.[1] Noël Carroll has documented and analyzed a philosophical tradition of resistance to mass art, including television, whose exponents include critics and theorists such as Dwight MacDonald, Clement Greenberg, R. G. Collingwood, T. W. Adorno and Max Horkheimer.[2] I expect that, on the one hand, those who are aligned with this tradition will scoff at the idea that television can afford and reward sustained appreciation, let alone that it can be art. Every once in a while I briefly convince myself that Carroll's analysis, while excellent, is merely of historical interest … but then I am proven wrong.[3] However, I could not improve upon Carroll's rebuttal if I tried and will not undertake to sway cynics here. This is also partly because, in my own experience, hostility to mass arts like television tends not to be grounded in the sort of argumentation Carroll challenges, but rather in snobbery.[4] That's not to dismiss snobbery as a problem, but merely to acknowledge that snobs tend not to be moved by reasons and arguments.[5]

On the other hand, I imagine that the title of the book is also likely to elicit skepticism from some cultural studies theorists in television studies.[6] For the scholars I have in mind, asseverating an art of television is an insidious, "pre-structuralist" effort to "legitimate" a set of preferred (bourgeois) values at the expense of others, thus reifying a hierarchy of cultural values that poststructuralist thought has putatively demolished.[7] Such are the charges that have been leveled at recent contributions to the recent "aesthetic turn" in television studies to which this book attempts to contribute. While some of my colleagues have, quite ably, responded to specific objections, my own view in preparing this book was that a more sustained account of the appreciation of television as an art form was needed.[8] In part, this is specific to television studies: It seems to me that in a pluralistic field, which has successfully prosecuted arguments for taking television seriously as a cultural form, there ought to be space for taking television seriously as an art form.[9] Moreover, I believe that making more explicit the assumptions that underlie such an approach, and arguing for them at length, will show that cultural studies scholars have fewer objections to the television aesthetics project that it appears at first sight.[10]

However, I also have broader reasons for offering an account of the appreciation of the art of television. One is that appreciation involves concepts and activities that are central to most forms of engagement with television, regardless of whether one bristles at the concept of artistic (or aesthetic) appreciation. So, readers who are steadfast in their opposition to an art of television are nevertheless likely at some point to think or write about television as something that is authored, as something that has a particular ontology, as something that is interpreted, or as something that is evaluated. This book attempts to clarify the concepts involved in identifying authorship, individuating instances of television, interpreting television, and evaluating television—a task that I hope will facilitate television criticism and theorization, whether or not one conceives of television as an art form.

Another reason is that although I do not imagine I will pique the interest of philosophers who are outright dismissive or hostile to mass art, I believe that there are many contemporary philosophers of art who would be more interested in television and would be able to make rich contributions to our understanding of it if only their awareness of it was raised.[11] More specifically, one of my goals here is to demonstrate that a philosophical perspective on appreciation of the art of television simultaneously dovetails with work that is already being done in parts of philosophical aesthetics (in particular, the philosophy of film) but also raises both old and new puzzles. For example, how do we (if we can) theorize authorship in a context that is, arguably, more subject to industrial constraints than filmmaking? Speaking of filmmaking, what exactly is the medium of television, and what, if anything, makes it distinctive? What is *the* work of television? What determines and how do we know what is in and outside of the work? These are just some of the questions this book tries to answer.

Such questions indicate, I hope, that with regard to the book's title, "appreciation" figures more centrally than "art." However, this idea, as well as the sense in which I am using these terms, demands further explanation, and much of the rest of this introductory chapter will be dedicated accordingly. I will also briefly characterize and defend the philosophical perspective I take before turning to a brief summary of the chapters and the book's overarching arguments.

Art

Unsurprisingly, the attempt to define art has been a central occupation of contemporary philosophical aesthetics. Also unsurprisingly, there is little agreement, let alone a consensus, about what defines art.[12] It is important to acknowledge this latter point up front because, if passed over, it is sometimes then pounced upon as if it self-evidently entails that any further use of the term "art"—in particular, the classification of some things as art or non-art—is illicit. However, such skepticism about our ability to use the term overlooks the fact that we rarely, if ever, take consensus about the definition of a concept as a necessary condition for the successful or appropriate use of the term that refers to it. What an unreasonably high standard that would be! As Carroll has argued, for everyone except philosophers, being able to identify art is much more important than being able to define it.[13] And while there is hardly consensus about the identification of all art, identifying art and distinguishing art from non-art are activities that we tend to get on with relatively easily.

For the purposes of this book, I do not need a definition of art. I do need agreement on *some* points about what art is, but I hope to show that there is actually little that is controversial about these points. First, though, let me say something about how I do not conceive of art. I do not think that "art" is an essentially honorific term. In particular, I do not think that art-hood is a matter of possessing a certain level of aesthetic value.[14] In my view, numerous ready-mades, conceptual pieces, and instances of bad art have negligible aesthetic value, yet are plausibly art. The works I have in mind here range from ready-mades like Marcel Duchamp's *In Advance of the Broken Arm* (1964) to the television program *WWE Raw* (USA 1993–2000; 2005–present). Neither do I think that art status is essentially institutionally conferred.[15] Institutions can and often do help us identify art, but in my view something can be art in the absence of an institution having conferred that status upon it. Furthermore, institutions sometimes incorrectly identify non-art artifacts as art.

Given that I deny art-hood is a matter of achieving aesthetic or institutional status, I also reject the idea that identifying art (correctly and for the right reasons, that is) involves the expression of taste or the attribution of value in anything other than this minimal sense: When one identifies something as art, there is some basic attribution of value in so far as the work becomes a candidate for appreciation as the result of human efforts to achieve something. However, I would deny that the attribution of value in this case is distinct from that which is involved in identifying any object as an artifact or other sort of human creation. Identifying an object as, say, a chair, similarly makes the object a candidate for appreciation (a point which I shall explain more fully in a moment) and thus attributes value in this same, minimal sense.

Despite this admission, I maintain that the sense in which I use the term "art" is a descriptive, classificatory one, which refers to a cluster of quite heterogeneous cultural practices and their products.[16] If I were advancing a definition of art, I would be obliged to say something about what all of those practices and products have in common that is sufficient for them to be *art* practices and *art* works. Because my aims are much narrower, though, it will suffice to mention two features that I assume are necessary for art-hood. The first, I hope, will be relatively uncontroversial: In my view, art-hood is necessarily a matter of standing in the right sort of relation to history—more specifically, tradition. Art practices and artworks are not timeless, but historically and culturally contingent. Not just anything can be art at any time; art practices take shape and evolve (or mutate), as do any cultural practices, against the backdrop of custom and tradition.[17]

Obviously, this claim and its implications bear much more elaboration than I can give here, so let me emphasize just two general points and comment specifically about their application to the study of television. One consequence that falls out of this view of art is that, in light of the centrality of cultural practices, art forms are not to be strictly identified with their physical or vehicular media. Being in a particular vehicular medium, such as photography, radio, film, or television, for example, is insufficient for being an artwork. In all of these cases, there are instances of art and non-art that, importantly, have to do *not* with aesthetic value, institutional status, or taste formations, but rather with the development of particular practices for working with these vehicular media. Second, the boundaries of art do exist, but are unstable and difficult to track owing to the diversity and variability of cultural practices.

The consequences for my study of the art of television are these. First, my view is neither that all television is art, nor that only good or aesthetically meritorious television is art. I think there is plenty of bad television art, just as there is plenty of bad film art and musical art. For pragmatic purposes—that is, for making the writing of the book tolerable—most of my examples are of television art that isn't bad, although I do refer to some instances of bad television, in a sense to be explained in due course, where necessary to my argument. Second, I am happy to acknowledge that the boundary of television art and non-art is not particularly clear and certainly subject to dispute.[18] Again, for pragmatic purposes, I draw heavily upon instances of television drama and television comedy—two noncontroversial (I hope) instances of television art. (One can, at least, point to practices of dramatic and comedic art in other media.)

To put my cards on the table, I take a rather inclusive view of television art. I think it includes soap opera, most reality television, and documentaries, even though I don't discuss those forms very often. Hard cases, in my view, involve instances of television in which, roughly speaking, the form seems incidental to the content because the programs aren't intended to be appreciated *as* television but merely give us access to the actual object of interest or appreciation. I have in mind here broadcasts of live concerts, sportscasts, broadcasts of legislative activity in parliaments and the like, so-called "courtroom TV," weathercasts, and *some* newscasts (a particularly knotty category).

In most instances of these forms, I think we are *not* dealing with television art, but, again, not because such forms lack aesthetic value or cultural cachet. Here is a very loose rule of thumb for sorting out the art television from non-art television in my view: If you can get the information you need by listening to *just* the audio track, or an equivalent radio broadcast, you are probably not engaging with television art. Clearly this does not approach anything like a sufficient condition for something to be television art, but I really do mean to suggest that it be thought of as a rule of thumb. Importantly, this book's central arguments do not depend on a clear boundary between television art and non-art, much less upon readers' agreement with me about where the boundary lies.

Why focus the inquiry upon the appreciation of television *art*, then, rather than upon television *simpliciter*? The answer to this question, as well as to the above question (about what forms of television are non-art), relates to the other condition I maintain is necessary for art-hood. Art practices are, in my view, necessarily intentional activities—in a sense of "intentional" to be clarified in the next chapter.[19] This is a moderate thesis, which should not be taken to endorse frequently lambasted "myths" about fully rational, wholly autonomous individuals—genius or otherwise.[20] Rather, the idea here is merely that participation in a cultural practice against a background of custom and tradition requires a rather modest sense of intentional agency. This is true, I believe, of any cultural practice, including those that comprise the concept of art.

However, these two moderate, necessary conditions have far-reaching consequences for shaping an approach to the appreciation of television as art. To appreciate instances of television as artworks is to treat them as special sorts of artifacts—the results of human agential activity performed within a tradition of television-making. As such, it is to approach them as shaped, expressive, usually communicative objects whose natures, meanings, and values all need to be conceived as standing in relation to the conventions, norms, and aims of that tradition and its history. Furthermore, it is to approach them as attempts—often but not necessarily successful—to achieve various goals, such as communicating meanings, eliciting emotions, and expressing ideas.[21]

These points are rather general because they apply to television *qua* art and so are necessarily applicable to all artworks. For the present purpose, however, they bear significant explanation and elaboration because they entail consequences that have received little acknowledgment from television studies. One such consequence, I shall argue, is that the nature, meanings, and values of television artworks are significantly more determinate than much of the field has thought them to be. Much of the book will be dedicated to supporting this claim in detail, but first I need to say something more about what I mean by "appreciation" and "a philosophical perspective."

Appreciation

Somewhat surprisingly, appreciation is a concept that has attracted relatively little explicit attention in philosophical aesthetics, let alone in television studies.[22] As a starting point, it is worth the risk of stating the obvious and noting that the term "appreciate" has at least three common, distinct senses. The first sense of the term, which we can quickly put aside, is to increase in value, as in: "I'll never be able to buy a house at the rate my paltry investments are appreciating." The second two are more closely connected by a common reference to recognition or apprehension: On the one hand, to appreciate may be to recognize in the sense of understanding. For example, one time the host of a conference told me, in correspondence, "I appreciate that you don't eat meat," which did not constitute an affirmation of an ethical stance, but merely an acknowledgement of his understanding that I required vegetarian catering.

On the other hand, to appreciate may be to recognize in the sense of apprehending value. When I used to visit the home of a colleague who happened to be a connoisseur of single-malt Scotch, I, normally a drinker of middling beer, would tell him: "Don't waste the good stuff on me; I can't appreciate it." Here is a television example: For the two years I lived in Cabo Verde, the only fictional television programs I watched were telenovelas. My friends had reasoned opinions about the relative artistic merits and flaws of particular telenovelas. However, I was unable to perceive these differences because of my unfamiliarity with the genre and my poor Portuguese; I wasn't able to appreciate the telenovelas as my friends were. My focus will be on this value-laden sense of appreciation, but it is important to see that understanding is still part of the concept; it's just that in this latter case, appreciation goes beyond understanding.

Before going further, it will be helpful to distinguish potential objects of appreciation. As the example of single-malt Scotch indicates, appreciation need not take artworks as its objects. Indeed, in philosophical aesthetics, there is a significant literature on the *aesthetic* appreciation of nature.[23] However, the examples of single malt Scotch, telenovelas, and nature should *not* be taken to indicate that all appreciation is aesthetic appreciation. It is plausible that single malt Scotch, telenovelas, nature, and, to take more obvious examples, architecture, furniture, pottery, and clothing, can be appreciated aesthetically and non-aesthetically regardless of how one wants to draw the perennially contested aesthetic/non-aesthetic distinction.[24]

So, too, I am going to assume that television can be appreciated aesthetically and non-aesthetically, and, furthermore, this does *not* map on to the distinction between television art and non-art. That is, non-artistic instances of television, including newscasts and even pure electronic noise or "snow," can be appreciated aesthetically. And artistic instances of television, such as music videos, can be appreciated non-aesthetically. Again, I think this is a plausible claim regardless of how one conceives of the aesthetic or distinguishes between aesthetic and non-aesthetic.

My focus in this book will be on appreciation *simpliciter* rather than aesthetic appreciation. As I have just noted, my primary focus is on the appreciation of television art, which does not necessarily demand aesthetic appreciation. Why not? I am a pluralist about the aims, functions, and values of art. As I see things, art pursues various aims, fulfils a number of functions, and bears a plurality of values, which are not reducible to the generation of aesthetic experience. A television documentary, for example, may have the primary aim of changing its viewers' political views and, indeed, if it fulfils this function successfully, its primary value may be characterized as cognitive rather than aesthetic. This is not to deny that much television art has an aesthetic function and aesthetic value; surely it does. My only claim here is that appreciating the art of television necessarily involves attending to an evident diversity of aims, functions, and values that extend beyond the aesthetic. Therefore, a broader sense of appreciation is needed than merely aesthetic appreciation, although the former should clearly encompass the latter.

Yet while aesthetic appreciation is a narrower sense of appreciation than we need here, it would still be helpful to specify, more precisely, what the appreciation of artworks involves. One helpful starting point is to review what Gary Iseminger identifies as "five key notions involved in the idea of appreciation."[25] I think the first four of these are plausible.

1. "Qualitative specificity" describes appreciation's focus on the constitutive properties of the object rather than the object in toto. Television studies folks might think about this as analogous to an insistence upon the sort of close analysis that is sensitive to the details of an episode, program, and so forth.
2. "Objectivity" refers to the idea that "one appreciates in a thing only the properties that it *actually* has or does not have." Some scholars who work in reception studies might immediately bristle at this notion; they would point to the heterogeneous uses to which television can be put. Yet this point is compatible with the claim that the properties of a work of television are not wholly indeterminate and, moreover, *one* of our interests in television is discerning what properties a particular work actually does have—in many cases, for example, what meanings a work actually has.
3. "Experientialist," sets down a kind of "acquaintance principle," demanding that the appreciator have direct contact with the object (or an adequate copy of it in the case of multiple-instance works). Again, this is not to deny the significance of the myriad ways in which people engage with television, including, for example, participation in paratextual activity around television works themselves.[26] However, it is to insist that for the purpose of appreciation, it is an experience of the artwork that is crucial. Note also, that it follows from point 2, above, that the work can be identified and individuated apart from other works and/or surrounding para-texts.
4. "Cognitivity" says "that *in* experientially taking something to have a property that it actually has, one does come to know that it has that property."[27] In the context of television studies, we might think

about this as opposing "false consciousness" theses in the vein of the Frankfurt School—or, at least, as insisting that "false consciousness" and appreciation are incompatible. Appreciation, in this view, takes a more optimistic view of the cognitive powers of television enthusiasts. For on this account, (adequate) appreciation involves belief that television artworks have certain properties because they actually do have those properties—not because someone's experience of the work has resulted in a false belief about its properties.

I recognize that in another context, in which the primary aim was really to give an analysis of appreciation, more would need to be said in defense of these ideas. For now, though, just one proviso related to the above point: Appreciation is a normative concept, and these are all features of *proper* or *adequate* appreciation. Arguably, appreciation is scalar—it is an activity that can be performed more or less successfully.[28] It is possible for faulty or inadequate appreciation to mistake the properties of what's being appreciated and/or involve false beliefs. The features described by Iseminger obtain in instances of proper or adequate appreciation. One might justifiably wonder about the nature and source of that normativity—particularly in the context of appreciating television—and this is a query to which I hope to address "on the hoof" as the book proceeds.

Iseminger's fifth feature of appreciation raises the somewhat more complicated issue of how evaluation figures into things. According to Iseminger, appreciation involves "favorable evaluation." That is, he claims, "If one appreciates a quality of something one takes it that that quality as exemplified in that thing is good."[29] But while I endorse the idea that the relevant sense of appreciation involves value, it is not clear to me that it necessarily involves favorable evaluation.[30] On the contrary, appreciating, say, beer seems to usually involve the discrimination of values—apprehending the relative merits or demerits of constitutive properties like hops, malt, and sometimes herbs or fruits, as well as how these are integrated. So, too, I would suggest it goes with the appreciation of television.

On a different view in the literature, evaluation is to be conceived as related to appreciation, but distinct from it. According to this view, appreciation involves an apprehension or appraisal of value in one's *experience* of the object. In contrast, evaluation renders value judgments that are abstracted from experience. Thus, appreciation may lead to evaluation, but does not necessarily do so, for the former is an end in its own right.[31] Perhaps this is a plausible account of aesthetic appreciation. However, I suspect it is too narrow a characterization of appreciation *simpliciter*. One potential worry about this proposal's adequacy as an account of the latter is specific to a particular formulation of it in the literature, according to which "appreciation involves an experience of value, positive or negative, that does not come into understanding. The experience of value *constitutes* appreciation ... Appreciation *is* the apprehension of a type of value and the experience *consists in* and *is defined in* the apprehension."[32] If one accepts an account of aesthetic experience and aesthetic judgment that is divorced from understanding, then perhaps this is a plausible characterization of aesthetic appreciation.[33] But I am skeptical of the idea that, beyond the realm of the aesthetic, values are "apprehended" in a way that does not involve understanding. Furthermore, whether one arrives at a sense of value via apprehension or judgment, it seems to me that, prima facie, appreciation is not wholly constituted by an experience of value. Surely in a variety of appreciative contexts, it is proper to take an interest in what is being represented and how or what is being expressed and how. In short, while the relevant sense of appreciation here involves value, it seems unlikely that the concept boils down to the experience of value, much less an experience of non-aesthetic values that are divorced from understanding. This is an important point because, in my view, appreciating the art of television involves much more than apprehending value.

Even from a less contentious view of how value is experienced in appreciation, this general account of appreciation works for aesthetic appreciation rather than appreciation *simpliciter*. For example, in his discussion of the appreciation of popular music, Theodore Gracyk denies there is a sharp distinction between aesthetic value and cognitive value and characterizes the appreciative experience of value as an "appraisal" rather than an "apprehension."[34] Yet Gracyk's conception of appreciation is admittedly oriented towards aesthetic experience rather than the work from which that experience arises, and he rejects "the proposal that an aesthetic appreciation of [the work] necessarily incorporates an appeal to its *artistic* value, that is, an explicit or even implicit understanding of it as a work of art." That is, Gracyk's focus is really on aesthetic appreciation, which is narrowly concerned with the aesthetic experience and aesthetic value to which a work gives rise rather than the understanding and evaluation of the work itself.[35]

In contrast, I am after a broader sense of appreciation—one that I would maintain is manifest in common usage—that involves the logically distinct (if often contingently intertwined) activities of perception, comprehension, interpretation, and evaluation of instances of television as *artworks* in the classificatory sense explained above.[36] The sense of "appreciation" I have in mind here is thus closer to that described by James Grant, who summarizes his view thus: "Appreciating an artwork involves having appropriate perceptual, cognitive, cogitative, affective, or conative responses to the right aspects of the work for the right reasons."[37] While Grant's account might require more development as an analysis of artistic appreciation, I hope it will suffice for the present purpose of clarifying the sense of the term as I use it in the title and throughout this book. For Grant's characterization of appreciation includes the perception of both aesthetic and non-aesthetic properties, the cognitive tasks of comprehension and judgment—the former in relationship to both the artists' aims and the content of their creations and the latter in relationship to both interpretation and evaluation, the cogitative activity of imagining what is true of the fictional world, the affective engagement central to much of our experience of television, and, last but not least, the conative or desire-oriented responses into which we could plausibly group aesthetic pleasure.

Neither is it plausible that any individual activity on this list is, by itself, sufficient for appreciating television as an art, nor is it likely that every activity is necessary for such appreciation. Yet I doubt we need a definition comprising necessary and sufficient conditions to get on with the task of investigating the artistic appreciation of television. For that purpose, we can, instead, make do by thinking of artistic appreciation as a kind of cluster concept that involves many of these activities, but with some variation from case to case.[38]

A Philosophical Perspective

Having glossed the senses in which I am using the terms "art" and "appreciation," it is time to say something about the book's "philosophical perspective." (This is not to imply that the term "television" is self-explanatory; far from it. Chapter 2 takes up this topic in depth.) The book is intended primarily as a contribution to the field of television studies and secondarily to the philosophy of art. Despite the book's interdisciplinary ambitions, I am cognizant of the ways in which the approach taken to the subject matter could be seen as the imposition of the aims, methods, and standards of one field onto another.[39]

Nevertheless, I see the book as being located within an established—if a minority—tradition within television studies, namely "television aesthetics." "Television aesthetics" is a term that, to be best of my knowledge, Sarah Cardwell coined in ground-breaking work first published almost exactly ten years ago.[40] Cardwell characterized one of her papers' contribution to the study of television aesthetics like this: "I wish to capture something of the individuality and distinctiveness of the programmed [*Almost Strangers* (BBC, 2001)], evaluate its achievements and also address the more 'theoretical' questions that the programme raises."[41] In my initial attempt to add something to this research program, I emphasized the importance of Cardwell's description of the twofold nature of "aesthetics" as a field: It is concerned with criticism and appreciation as well as theoretical questions at a high level of generality that are raised by our critical and appreciative practices.[42]

With a few exceptions—Cardwell's ongoing work constituting the main one—most work within television aesthetics (before or after the term for it was coined) has tended to focus on criticism and appreciation. This is unsurprising and, indeed, basically as it should be, as most scholars working within the television aesthetics research program are justifiably interested in with getting on with the business of criticism and appreciation. Here one only need look to instances of outstanding work such as Jason Jacobs's *Body*

Trauma TV and *Deadwood*, Greg M. Smith's *Beautiful TV*, Elliott Logan's *Breaking Bad and Dignity*, Jason Jacobs and Steven Peacock's *Television Aesthetics and Style*.[43]

This book does not contribute to the study of television aesthetics in the sense that the above titles do; it is not an instance of television appreciation and does not explore the appreciation of television as an art by doing it. Instead, as with my initial foray into this research program, I try here to explore the central concepts and ideas that underwrite our appreciation of television as an art form. The book thus foregoes criticism and appreciation of television in favor of an investigation of the general, meta-theoretical issues involved in those activities. This is the sense in which the book attempts to contribute something to the television aesthetics research project and the way which I see the book as situated within the field of television studies rather than unjustifiably imposing upon the field the concerns and methods of philosophy.

More specifically, the book draws upon the literature in both fields as well as traditional philosophical tools like conceptual analysis and dialectical argumentative structure to analyze what I take to be foundational concepts comprising the activity of appreciation in the broad sense outlined above. These foundational concepts, which roughly map onto the book's chapters, include authorship, the medium, ontology, interpretation, and evaluation. I will offer a brief summary of the chapters presently. First, though, a quick word about those "traditional philosophical tools." The sort of approach I take, which can be roughly characterized as "analytic," can rub non-philosophers the wrong way. I know, because this was my original experience with philosophy.

I have done my best to write the book for open-minded television studies scholars, but a few words of warning are still in order. First, the book is critical of a number of extant claims and positions in the field. Most of the chapters begin with extensive critiques of competing views. I am neither defensive nor apologetic about this, but do want to make a couple of things clear. The emphasis on criticism does not spring from a desire to personally attack others (if I have done my job well, readers will find no *ad hominem* arguments in these pages) or an attempt to "prove" that everybody else is wrong. Rather, the philosophical approach I adopt here is concerned first and foremost with the details of arguments that are made to support claims, so critique is one of a philosopher's most important tasks.

Furthermore, this point relates to the structure of argumentation in the book, which strives to be dialectic in the classical sense of that term. As such, what could be mistaken for a glorified literature review is an attempt, at least, to successively refine the concepts and claims under discussion. I need to warn non-philosophers that this manner of writing is not to everyone's taste. In fact, in trying to think about how to make my approach explicit, I took *The Philosopher's Toolkit* off my bookshelf and was immediately thrown by the first sentence: "Philosophy is for nitpickers." I was struck not because I disagree; as the authors qualify, "That's not to say it is a trivial pursuit."[44] Rather, it was because "nitpicking" and various synonyms for it were words that several candid and helpful reviewers used to describe the book's style. I do not think this anecdote completely insulates me from criticism; the line between nuance and tedium can be a fine one, and there is no question that one can err too far in the direction of the latter. But I would ask for a bit of forbearance from television studies scholars who are unfamiliar with the methods and standards of philosophical argumentation.

Finally, let me briefly outline the book's chapters and arguments. The first chapter takes on the puzzling question of authorship in television production, but in doing so also establishes the book's conceptual foundation. The approach I advocate emphasizes the agency of television creators, seeking to reconcile conflicting views according to which authorship is completely abstracted (i.e., an author function), a matter of being an autonomous *auteur*, or dispersed among *all* members of the creative team. According to my answer to the question, "What is an author?" the subsequent question, "Who is the author?" is an empirical one that varies on a case-by-case basis and that those with expertise in production studies are best equipped to investigate. In Chapter 1, I address the former question by arguing that there is a basic way in which our appreciation of the art of television essentially involves reference to human agency whether such agency is embodied in an individual author, joint authors, or the non-authorial collaborators in a production collective. Part of my aim is to establish a foundation for the book's subsequent arguments, according to which agency features fundamentally in the analysis of central elements in the appreciation of television artworks. Of these, this book will examine the television medium (Chapter 2), the ontology of television and individual television artworks (Chapter 3), the interpretation of television artworks (Chapters 4 and 5), and the evaluation of television artworks (Chapter 6). Insofar as agency is centrally involved in these domains, the overarching argument of the book is that the appreciation of television must necessarily refer to the agency behind a work of television.

Chapter 2 argues for a distinction between the medium of television and the art of television. I advance an account of the medium according to which the medium is not constituted simply by a set of materials (physical or otherwise), but by what practitioners do with clusters of materials. Furthermore, I claim that appreciating the achievements of television artworks necessarily depends upon understanding what agents have done in the medium.

Recognizing the necessity of identifying an object of appreciation, Chapter 3 offers a focused response to the perennial question, "What is television?"—that is, it addresses the ontology of television. Although I acknowledge that conceiving of television as "textual" was a crucial part of arguments for taking it seriously as a cultural form and emphasizing the activity of viewers, I claim that continued use of the textual model in our theorization has muddled matters and led us badly astray. I urge that we embrace a descriptive metaphysics and identify the relevant object of appreciation by unearthing the tacit ontological assumptions embodied in our creative and appreciative practices. My suggestion is that we discard the term "text" in favor of the more precise lexicon already at our disposal, which includes terms to refer to discrete objects of appreciation: "episode," "season," "series," "program," and so forth.

Chapters 4 and 5 are both dedicated to interpretive matters. There is a lot to say, because television studies has historically focused on interpretation and because interpretation raises a host of difficult theoretical questions. The chapters divide up the work along these lines: Chapter 4 initiates the discussion by looking at the question of fictional truth—that is, what is true *in* the fiction with which we engage. Here too, I emphasize agency and argue that when there are determinate facts about what is true in the fiction (for many things are, plausibly, simply left indeterminate) these facts are wholly established by the successfully realized intentions of the creators of the television works. That is neither to say that creators can never fail to realize their intentions nor that they can never be wrong about what is true in a fiction they created. Nor still does it mean that creators can generate fictional truths after the work is completed, simply by declaration. But it is to say that fictional truths are not established in reception practices, even if we admit (as we should) that viewers are free to imagine anything they like about a given program. I argue that discerning fictional truths is an interpretive activity and, moreover, since higher-order interpretations necessarily depend upon fictional truths, there is an important way in which television meanings are objective and interpretations of those meanings are evaluable for truth and falsity.

Chapter 5 takes up these well-trodden questions about the nature of higher-order interpretations. One central claim in this chapter is that a general doctrine of critical pluralism, according to which interpretation has heterogeneous aims and functions, is compatible with the idea that television works have determinate, objective meaning, the discovery of which is one admissible interpretive aim. My hope is that this recognition dissolves a number of problems raised by competing "readings" of television series. Nevertheless, I argue that if one's aim is to appreciate a television work as art, then it is with what the work actually means, as a matter of fact, and that this is constrained in significant ways by the successfully realized intentions of television creators.

The link between Chapter 5 and Chapter 6 is this: It seems extremely plausible that evaluative judgments of television works often, if not necessarily, depend upon interpretive claims about the shows. If interpretive claims are, as I argue, evaluable for truth or falsity, then there is at least one important way in which evaluative judgments of television are objective and truth evaluable: Such judgments can be right or wrong about the interpretations upon which they are based. I argue that this had better be the case for anyone who is interested critiquing television from an ideological, political, or ethical perspective; this sort of criticism is incoherent unless the claims it makes are based upon meanings that television works actually possess.

Chapter 6 addresses the vexed topic of the evaluation of television—a matter over which there has been rich debate in recent years. Here I supplement the above points with additional arguments regarding the objectivity of evaluative judgments of television artworks. Once again, agency is central here. A key idea in this chapter is that as *works*, instances of television have been designed to fulfil certain functions or to achieve certain effects. This, I claim, is an objective matter, as is the extent to which a function is successfully fulfilled and an effect is successfully achieved. It follows that there is another important sense in which evaluative judgments of television works are objective—to wit, they track (or should track) the work's success relative to its aims or purposes. And the work's aims or purposes are established by its creators.

In sum, what I hope emerges from these chapters is an overarching argument that foregrounds the importance of agency in our appreciation of television as an art. So, too, I hope readers are somewhat persuaded by the unorthodox view that television works have at least some meanings and values objectively as a result of the successfully realized intentions of their creators. It is the objectivity of those meanings and values that underlies the emphasis upon sensitivity and discrimination that we see in practical instances of appreciation of television or any of the arts.

Notes

1. After drafting this Introduction, I re-read an excellent paper by Sarah Cardwell and found that she makes a similar observation about the sources of opposition to the idea of television as an art form. For her take on the issue, see "Television amongst Friends: Medium, Art, Media," *Critical Studies in Television* 9, no. 3 (Autumn 2014).
2. Noël Carroll, *A Philosophy of Mass Art* (Oxford: Clarendon Press, 1998). Also see on this topic Richard Shusterman, *Pragmatist Aesthetics: Living Beauty, Rethinking Art* (Oxford: Blackwell, 1992).
3. See, for recent examples, Jane M. Shattuc, "Television Production: Who Makes American TV?," in *A Companion to Television*, ed. Janet Wasko (Malden, MA: Blackwell, 2006); Christina Berchini, "A Critical Scholar with a Dirty Little Secret (or Two)," *Inside Higher Ed* (September 25, 2015). Accessed December 7, 2015. https://www.insidehighered.com/views/2015/09/25/scholar-says-academics-shouldnt-apologize-popular-entertainment-they-personally.
4. An exception, however, is a sympathetic view of the cultural forms Carroll calls "mass art" that bypasses the question of art-hood in favor of defending the aesthetic value of those forms. See, especially, Theodore Gracyk, *Listening to Popular Music: Or, How I Learned to Stop Worrying and Love Led Zeppelin* (Ann Arbor: University of Michigan Press, 2007).

5. See Matthew Kieran, "The Vice of Snobbery: Aesthetic Knowledge, Justification, and Virtue in Art Appreciation," *The Philosophical Quarterly* 60, no. 239 (April 2010).
6. I am painting with a broad brush for the moment; there are exceptions. See, for example, Stuart Hall and Paddy Whannel, *The Popular Arts* (London: Hutchinson Educational, 1964).
7. See Matt Hills, "Television Aesthetics: A Pre-Structuralist Danger?," *Journal of British Cinema and Television* 8, no. 1 (April 2011); Michael Z. Newman and Elena Levine, *Legitimating Television: Media Convergence and Cultural Status* (New York: Routledge, 2012).
8. See Sarah Cardwell, "Television Aesthetics: Stylistic Analysis and Beyond," in *Television Aesthetics and Style*, ed. Jason Jacobs and Steven Peacock (London: Bloomsbury, 2013), 23–44.
9. I hasten to add, emphatically, that this is not to say that nobody in the field takes television seriously as an art form, for obviously a number of us do (even if few scholars explicitly refer to television as an art). In addition to the relevant work already cited, recent scholarship I have in mind includes Jeffrey Sconce, "What If? Charting Television's New Textual Boundaries," in *Television After TV: Essays on a Medium in Transition*, ed. Lynn Spigel and Jan Olsson (Durham, NC: Duke University Press, 2004); Greg M. Smith, *Beautiful TV: The Art and Argument of Ally McBeal* (Austin: University of Texas Press, 2007); Jason Jacobs, *Deadwood* (London: BFI, 2012); Jason Mittell, *Complex TV: The Poetics of Contemporary Storytelling* (New York: New York University Press, 2015); and Elliott Logan, *Breaking Bad and Dignity: Unity and Fragmentation in the Serial Television Drama* (Basingstoke, UK: Palgrave Macmillan, 2016).
10. Again, see Cardwell, "Television amongst Friends," for a helpful discussion.
11. For rare examples of philosophical discussion of television outside of the *X and Philosophy* mold of book, see Stanley Cavell, "The Fact of Television," *Daedalus* 111, no. 4 (Fall 1982); and Ted Cohen, "Television: Contemporary Thought," in *Encyclopedia of Aesthetics*, vol. 4, ed. Michael Kelly (Oxford: Oxford University Press, 1998), 369–70.
12. See, for a start, Stephen Davies, *Definitions of Art* (Ithaca, NY: Cornell University Press, 1991); and Robert Stecker, "Definition of Art," in *The Oxford Handbook of Aesthetics*, edited by Jerrold Levinson (Oxford: Oxford University Press, 2003), 136–154.
13. Noël Carroll, "Identifying Art," in *Beyond Aesthetics* (Cambridge, UK: Cambridge University Press, 2001), 75–100.
14. For a recent, sophisticated attempts to define art in aesthetic terms, see Gary Iseminger, *The Aesthetic Function of Art* (Ithaca, NY: Cornell University Press, 2004); and Nick Zangwill, *Aesthetic Creation* (Oxford: Oxford University Press, 2007).
15. See, for a classic statement of the institutional view, George Dickie, *The Art Circle* (New York: Haven Publications, 1984).
16. Some such practices may comprise loose institutions. However, my claim is that this is not strictly necessary for art-making. My thinking about the definition and nature of art is influenced by Noël Carroll and Jerrold Levinson. See, especially, Noël Carroll, "Art, Practice, and Narrative," in *Beyond Aesthetics* Cambridge: Cambridge University Press, 2001), 63–75; Noël Carroll, "Art, Creativity, and Tradition," in *Art in Three Dimensions* (Oxford: Oxford University

Press, 2010), 53–73; Jerrold Levinson, "Defining Art Historically," in *Music, Art, and Metaphysics* (Ithaca, NY: Cornell University Press, 1990), 3–25; Jerrold Levinson, "Refining Art Historically," in *Music, Art, and Metaphysics*, 37–59; and Jerrold Levinson, "Extending Art Historically," in *The Pleasures of Aesthetics* (Ithaca, NY: Cornell University Press, 1996), 150–71.
17. Two astute readers have wondered whether "custom and tradition" do not simply amount to the broad view of art world institutions Dickie has in mind. This objection has been made in the literature—indeed, by Dickie himself. See Stephen Davies, *Definitions of Art*; George Dickie, *Art and Value* (Malden, MA: Blackwell, 2001), 45. Responding here would take me beyond my present concerns—nothing much of what follows depends on the institutional theory being incorrect—but see my comments in Ted Nannicelli, *A Philosophy of the Screenplay* (New York: Routledge, 2013).
18. See David Novitz, *The Boundaries of Art : A Philosophical Inquiry into the Place of Art in Everyday Life*. (Philadelphia: Temple University Press, 1992).
19. On this point, from which much of the book's subsequent thinking and argumentation stems, I have been influenced by Paisley Livingston. See, especially, *Art and Intention: A Philosophical Study* (Oxford: Oxford University Press, 2005).
20. That said, I am not sure who propounds such myths anymore ...
21. Some readers may be wondering if some of my earlier examples of non-art television (e.g., newscasts) might meet these conditions in certain cases. I am happy to admit they might. I am laying out two *necessary* conditions here—not sufficient conditions.
22. According to Dominic McIver Lopes, "nobody has a theory of appreciation". See his "True Appreciation," in *Photography and Philosophy: Essays on the Pencil of Nature*, ed. Scott Walden (Malden, MA: Blackwell, 2008), 210.
23. See, for a start, Malcolm Budd, *The Aesthetic Appreciation of Nature* (Oxford: Oxford University Press, 2002). For an excellent discussion of other examples of "everyday" sorts of aesthetic appreciation, see Yuriko Saito, *Everyday Aesthetics* (Oxford: Oxford University Press, 2007).
24. For a seminal discussion, see Frank Sibley, "Aesthetic and Non-Aesthetic," in his posthumously published *Approach to Aesthetics*, ed. John Benson, Betty Redfern, and Jeremy Roxbee Cox (Oxford: Oxford University Press, 2001).
25. Gary Iseminger, "Aesthetic Appreciation," *Journal of Aesthetics and Art Criticism* 39, no. 4 (Summer 1981): 389.
26. For a seminal discussion of paratexts, see Gérard Genette, *Paratexts: Thresholds of Interpretation*, trans. Jane E. Lewin (Cambridge, UK: Cambridge University Press, 1997). For application of these ideas in television studies, see Jonathan Gray, *Show Sold Separately: Promos, Spoilers, and Other Media Paratexts* (New York: New York University Press, 2010).
27. Iseminger, "Aesthetic Appreciation," 389–90.
28. See Kieran, "Vice of Snobbery"; and Lopes, "True Appreciation."
29. Iseminger, "Aesthetic Appreciation," 390.
30. Stein Haugom Olsen, "Value Judgments in Criticism," *Journal of Aesthetics and Art Criticism* 42, no. 2 (Winter 1983): 133; and Gracyk, *Listening to Popular Music*, 111.
31. See Stein Haugom Olsen, "Criticism and Appreciation," in *Philosophy and Fiction: Essays in Literary Aesthetics*, ed. Peter Lamarque (Aberdeen: Aberdeen University Press, 1983); Olsen, "Value Judgments in Criticism"; and Gracyk, *Listening to Popular Music*, 109–14.

32. Olsen, "Value Judgments in Criticism," 133; 134.
33. In fact, if my aim here were an analysis of the concept of aesthetic appreciation, I would want to raise objections to Olsen's proposal in this context too. Briefly, it is plausible that the perception of various aesthetic properties depends upon contextual knowledge of art-historical context in which the work was created. See, for example, Kieran, "Vice of Snobbery," but this is a claim that has enjoyed increasing acceptance, at least since the publication of Kendall Walton's seminal essay, "Categories of Art."
34. Gracyk, *Listening to Popular Music*, 110.
35. It is perhaps worth noting that the way Gracyk conceives of aesthetic value here bears little resemblance to the straw man of "autonomous," "inherent," or "intrinsic" value as it is variously constructed in some of the television studies literature. For Gracyk, aesthetic value "can refer to instrumental value that adheres to public objects, or to non-instrumental value that adheres to the experiences offered by those public objects." *Listening to Popular Music*, 106. For a clear survey discussion that casts doubt upon the idea that anyone actually takes the position that the value of art is intrinsic, see Robert Stecker, "Value in Art," in *The Oxford Handbook of Aesthetics*, ed. Jerrold Levinson (Oxford: Oxford University Press, 2003), 307–24. I return to this issue in more detail in the final chapter.
36. Compare with Olsen, "Criticism and Appreciation": "Discrimination in literary appreciation is constituted by the identification of textual features as aesthetic features through the application of interpretive descriptions (48). Also see Olsen, "Value Judgments in Criticism."
37. James Grant, *The Critical Imagination* (Oxford: Oxford University Press, 2013), 173.
38. If one really wanted a definition, then we could, from here, try to develop a disjunctive one. See the discussion in Berys Gaut, "'Art' as a Cluster Concept," in *Theories of Art Today*, ed. Noël Carroll (Madison: University of Wisconsin Press, 2000).
39. For a measured, cogent response to this worry, see Cardwell, "Television amongst Friends."
40. See, especially, Sarah Cardwell, "Television Aesthetics," *Critical Studies in Television* 1, no. 1 (2006), and Cardwell's below-cited essay. Also see Jason Jacobs, "Television Aesthetics: An Infantile Disorder," *Journal of British Cinema and Television* 3, no. 1 (2006).
41. Sarah Cardwell, "'Television Aesthetics and Close Analysis," in *Style and Meaning: Studies in the Detailed Analysis of Film*, ed. John Gibbs and Douglas Pye (Manchester, UK: Manchester University Press, 2005), 180.
42. Ted Nannicelli, "Ontology, Intentionality, and Television Aesthetics," *Screen* 53, no. 2 (Summer 2012).
43. Jason Jacobs, *Body Trauma TV: The New Hospital Dramas* (London: BFI, 2003); Jason Jacobs, *Deadwood* (London: BFI, 2012); Greg M. Smith, *Beautiful TV: The Art and Argument of Ally McBeal* (Austin, TX: University of Texas Press, 2007); Elliott Logan, *Breaking Bad and Dignity: Unity and Fragmentation in the Serial Television Drama* (Basingstoke: Palgrave Macmillan, 2016); Jason Jacobs and Steven Peacock, eds., *Television Aesthetics and Style* (New York: Bloomsbury, 2013).
44. Julian Baggini and Peter S. Forsi, *The Philosopher's Toolkit: A Compendium of Philosophical Concepts and Methods* (Malden, MA: Blackwell, 2003), 1.

1 Authorship and Agency

Introduction

My aim in this chapter is twofold: I want to argue for a number of conditions that should be met by any successful account of television authorship. However, through the analysis of authorship that I develop in arguing for these conditions, I aim to show that what is really central to our appreciation of television as an art is not authorship *per se,* but agency. Thus, my aim is to make do with *agency* in a sense to be explained presently. This chapter constitutes the groundwork for an "agential" approach to the appreciation of television.

"Authorship" is, of course, an ambiguous term that connotes various things in different contexts. To give just one simple example, anyone at all familiar with the history of writing for the screen will agree that authorship in a legal sense (i.e., who gets credited as a writer) often does not correspond with authorship as we commonly use the term (i.e., to indicate who has contributed to the creation of screenplay, book, and so forth). In analyzing the concept of authorship as it is relevant to the appreciation of television as an art, I think we ought to be somewhat less legislative than in legal contexts, yet somewhat more stipulative and technical than we are in common usage.

The question is: What sort of concept of authorship do we need to account for our appreciative practices? Our appreciative practices are not entirely uniform, of course, but I assume they at least include activities such as attributing praise for achievements and blame for failures. When the achievements of an artwork, taken as a whole, are significant, it is often the authors who receive awards. When the failures of an artwork, taken as a whole, are significant, it is often the authors who bear responsibility—sometimes financial, sometimes even legal. In the context of artistic appreciation, then, authorship is a causal concept, which centrally involves control over the work as a whole and, in relation, responsibility. Or so I shall argue, building upon plausible proposals along these lines that have been advanced by film theorists such as V. F. Perkins and philosophers of art like Paisley Livingston.

The difficulty is that television complicates things in a number of ways. Given the collaborative, industrial context in which television is produced over an extended duration, control and responsibility are usually dispersed across multiple agents and across time. If we consider a long-running soap opera, for example, it is not clear that anyone has control over the work as a whole. Of course, the field of television studies has devised a number of strategies to accommodate such challenges, but none, I believe, that sufficiently accommodates our needs as appreciators of television as an art form.

What I have in mind here are various authorship constructs ranging from implied authors to author functions.[1] Borrowing Livingston's term, we can think of these as attributional conceptions of authorship, distinct from the sort of causal conception of authorship that I am advocating here.[2] I am happy to accept that such constructs serve a variety of useful purposes in myriad contexts. For example, it seems plausible, as Jason Mittell claims, that many of us casually infer a single authorial force, such as that of Chris Carter, Jill Soloway, or Louis C. K., when watching an episode of *The X-Files* (Fox 1993–2002; 2016), *Transparent* (Amazon 2014–), or *Louie* (FX 2010–).[3] Even if such inferences are empirically wrong, say because the episode has multiple authors, they can be useful psychological short cuts for viewers.

However, it seems to me that viewers also can (and do) make use of such psychological short cuts without inferring a specific author (hence students' ubiquitous use of the pronoun "they" to describe what has been done in a work of television); on the contrary, the real necessity here, and in many other cases, is simply agency.[4] Furthermore, my contention is that in cases when we do need to make reference to authorship for the purpose of appreciating the artistic achievements (or failures) of an instance of television, the conception of authorship we require is a causal one. This is because, in the context of appreciation, we are interested in what has been done in the creation of the work—that is, how the work came to be just as it is and who is responsible.[5] Another way of putting it is that, in the context of appreciation, the sort of authorship in which we are interested necessarily involves real agents.[6] Therefore, this chapter will simply set to the side the various attributionist accounts of authorship prevalent in television studies.[7]

My attempt at an intervention acknowledges that, in the context of television appreciation, there are some cases in which authorship obtains, but there are many in which it does not. In the latter cases, I claim, appreciation can get by with reference to agency more broadly—a category in which authorship is a specific subset. That is, when we want to assign praise or blame for the achievements or failures of a particular instance of television, we can do so by identifying the responsible agents, even if those individuals are not the work's authors in the sense glossed above. However, I also want to claim something stronger and, I hope, more original. Even in cases in which we *can* identify the author(s) of a television artwork, there are some appreciative contexts in which our focus still needs to be on agency more generally—that is, on agents who are not the same as the work's author(s). In these cases, which I will outline in due course, focusing on agency more broadly allows us to more accurately assign praise and blame where they are deserved. In short, I will argue that, in the context of television appreciation, authorship is best conceived as involving control over the work as a whole, so it will usually be limited to a few individuals or simply not obtain at all. As such, the broader category of agency is much more useful for the practical purposes of lauding or holding responsible key creative contributors who, in most cases, are not authors.

Agency and Intentions

Before beginning in earnest, I want to gloss two terms that I will be using in this and subsequent chapters, both for the purposes of clarity and of keeping the flow of my arguments moving. By "agency," I mean in particular, "individual human agency," unless I explicitly speak of "group agency," "collective agency," or "shared agency."[8] There is a vast philosophical literature on the nature of agency, but for the purposes of clarity, I will simply stipulate what I take to be a plausible account of individual, human agency—one that is intended to be noncontroversial. In the present context, we can think of "agency" as, roughly, an exercised capacity for acting or causing things to happen, which is underwritten by rational reflection upon one's own mental states—that is, by deliberative reasoning about one's own beliefs, desires, and intentions.[9]

Of such mental states, the one that is most salient in the present context is "intention." As with authorship, which I discuss presently, intention is a concept that has engendered a good deal of controversy and suspicion in the humanities in general and in literary, film, and television studies in particular.[10] My view is that much of the wariness of intentions is overstated. This is not to deny that appeal to intentions in our appreciative engagement with art raises some difficult philosophical questions—particularly in the context of collaborative, commercially produced art like television series.

It might be assumed, for example, that the vicissitudes of film and television production fundamentally undermine our ability to offer intentionalist explanations of the presence of particular artistic properties or effects. For example, it may be the case that a scene in a series like *Friday Night Lights* (NBC 2006–11) looks a certain way because the actors improvised a moment and, perhaps, the hand-held camera operator had to make a sudden, unorthodox move to capture it. It seems implausible, so the argument goes, that such moments and the properties of film and television works in which they result have any intention behind them.

I am happy to acknowledge that, in fact, many things that happen on film and television sets are indeed unplanned, thus resulting in finished works having certain features that are also unplanned. But preliminarily, at least, perhaps some of the skeptical worries about intention can be diffused by being clear about the sense(s) in which one uses the term. Drawing on the literature in philosophy of action, one preliminary distinction we can make is between what Michael Bratman calls "present-directed intentions" and "future-directed intentions."[11] In cases like the one described above from *Friday Night Lights*, there is an important kind of intention that is significantly diluted or, perhaps, even absent—to wit, future-directed intention.

But it does not follow that, in such contexts, talk of intentions is illicit or misguided. This claim erroneously assumes that future-directed intentions are completely constitutive of intentional action. On the contrary, we can avail ourselves of the literature in action theory and point out that while such "off-the-cuff" moments derail intentions characterized by planning, the actors' improvised behavior, and the camera operator's reaction are not merely happy accidents either. Rather, they are the results of a different kind of intention—namely, present-directed intention. This sort of intention is successfully realized *in* the execution of the action itself and, furthermore, does not require conscious awareness of it on the part of the agent.[12] For example, I have, undoubtedly, been typing intentionally for the past few minutes, but until just now I was not consciously intending to type.

The distinction between present-directed and future-directed intentions is an important step towards reinserting intentions in the analysis of television production and appreciation. Still, I suspect that much, if not most, television production is marked by future-directed intentions—that is, by intentions characterized as planning states. Although researchers of production know this well, it bears emphasizing that television (and film) production are so time- and labor-intensive, so expensive, so financially risky, that it is hard to think of many instances or moments of commercial television—even live television—that are plausibly *not* the result of successfully executed intentions (understood as planning states).[13] So, henceforth, unless I am specifically discussing present-directed intentions, I will follow Michael Bratman in understanding intentions (distinguished from intentional actions) as "plan states": "They are embedded in forms of planning central to our internally organized temporally extended agency and to our associated abilities to achieve complex goals across time."[14] Furthermore, according to Bratman, "as elements in such partial plans, future-directed intentions play important roles as inputs to further reasoning aimed at filling in or modifying these plans, as well as in the more direct motivation of action when the time comes."[15] It is this sort of future-directed intention we typically have in mind when invoking intentions in our appreciation of television artworks—that is, for example, when we say of a television series something such as "the creators intended *Deadwood* (HBO 2004–06) to be four seasons, but HBO cancelled it after three" or "the brilliance of *Breaking Bad* (AMC 2008–13) is that Walt is intended to be both sympathetic but also deeply morally flawed."

One final preliminary point about intention that I hope will at least temporarily assuage skeptical concerns: Oftentimes anti-intentionalists appeal to the putatively inaccessible nature of intentions in order to discount the relevance of intentions to the appreciation of a work. But this is among the least convincing of the anti-intentionalist's various arguments. For one thing, this claim typically underestimates the extent to which successfully realized intentions are manifest in the work and can justifiably be inferred from a careful inspection of it. In relation, the anti-intentionalist's insistence that the relevant intentions cannot be known with *certainty* sets an unreasonable standard to meet. As E. D. Hirsch points out, it is a simple truism that *certainty* about relevant creative intentions is impossible (in the absence of some sort of Vulcan mind-meld, that is). But why should that matter? As Hirsh writes, "this obvious fact should not be allowed to sanction the overly hasty conclusion that the author's intended meaning is inaccessible and therefore useless as an object of interpretation."[16] That is, the anti-intentionalist unfairly sets up a false either/or dynamic. In the absence of certainty, we can and often do avail ourselves of concepts like "reasonable inference," "plausible hypothesis," and "warrant," to advance well-supported hypotheses approximating creators' actual intentions. As Hirsch observes, "It is a logical mistake to confuse the impossibility of certainty in understanding with the impossibility of understanding. It is a similar, though more subtle, mistake to identify knowledge with certainty."[17]

To Hirsch's points, I would add one more, which is that it is also a logical mistake to conflate metaphysical questions regarding the nature and function of intentions with epistemological questions about how we can know "for sure" what various agents actually intend or what collectively held intention agents jointly realize in the production process. Even if actual artistic intentions *were* epistemologically inaccessible, this would not show that that they do not figure into the creation of works of television in various ways. The epistemic claim that intentions may, as a matter of fact, be inaccessible, is compatible with various metaphysical claims—for example, that intentions determine the category (e.g., genre or mode) of a work, what is fictionally true of a work, or what a work means (where this is distinct from what significance it has for particular socially situated viewers, as I will explain presently). Furthermore, the anti-intentionalist's "inaccessibility argument" is also compatible with at least one specific intentionalist account of interpretation—namely, hypothetical intentionalism, which, as the name indicates, takes the meaning of a work to be constituted by the most plausible hypothesis about what its creator(s) intended. I will have more to say about this, not to mention both intention and agency more generally, in what follows, but hopefully this is sufficient as a starting point.

The Material Conditions of Television Production and the Place of Production Studies

The first condition for which I want to argue is that any account of television authorship needs to respect the material conditions of television production. By this I simply mean that a plausible characterization of television authorship must be consistent with how television is actually made—that is, with the industrial, social, cultural, and economic factors that shape production practices. Burgeoning research in production studies has already begun to give us a valuable sense of what the material conditions of television production look like.[18] This subfield is currently thriving, and it seems likely that the scholars who are active in it will produce additional work that helps clarify and articulate the subtleties of television production practices. For our present purposes, however, it is enough to bear in mind one truism that production studies has established beyond a doubt: television production is an inherently collaborative enterprise. The thought behind the first condition is that any plausible account of television authorship must be consistent with this and other salient facts established in production studies research.

Now, I take the first condition to express a noncontroversial claim, and I suspect that some scholars might even find it mundane. But part of what is interesting about it is that, in the literature, it tacitly motivates several different kinds of views, all of which attempt to reconcile collaborative production and authorship. Following Berys Gaut, we can characterize the first of these views as *restriction strategies*, which are often combined with *sufficient control strategies*.[19] Roughly speaking, the former class of strategies attempts to restrict ascriptions of authorship to the individual(s) responsible for those features of a film relevant to our appreciation, whether they are conceived as artistic properties in general or, more narrowly, the relationships that obtain between such properties. The strategies in the latter class attempt to attribute authorship on the basis not of the creation of the entire work (i.e., the creation of all of its constitutive elements) but rather on the basis of one's control over the creative work of others and, thus, the overall shaping of the work.

As Gaut explains, perhaps the best-known versions of these two strategies have been advanced, in combination, by V. F. Perkins.[20] In his influential book, *Film as Film*, Perkins writes, "If the film's form embodies a viewpoint, explored in depth and with complexity, it is almost certain to be the director's. He is in control throughout the period in which virtually all the significant relationships [between various elements of the film] are defined. He has possession of the means through which all other contributions acquire meaning *within* the film. The director's authority is a matter not of total creation but of sufficient control."[21]

Restriction strategies and sufficient control strategies seem close to what Jason Mittell has in mind when he glosses the terms "authorship by responsibility" and "authorship by management" in a chapter on television authorship from his recent book.[22] Following Horace Newcomb in observing that in the context of television the director is typically less important than the producer in shaping the overall look of a series, Mittell sketches, without committing to, the rough outlines of a combined restriction / sufficient control approach to television authorship in terms of "a model of authorship by management."[23] As far as I can see, this sort of strategy tacitly underwrites *all* claims for individual authorship in the context of television, most notably to well-known "show-runners" such as Aaron Sorkin, David Chase, Joss Whedon, David Milch, and Vince Gilligan.[24]

Two interesting questions thus arise here: What would a plausible sufficient control strategy for the identification of (individual) television authors look like? And would this be consistent with our condition that we respect the material conditions of television production? Here we can benefit from drawing upon the work of Livingston, who has developed a subtle and plausible sufficient control account of cinematic authorship. In Livingston's view, "the word 'authorship' is best used in the context of aesthetics and elsewhere to classify accomplishments that we evaluate as instances of expressive or artistic behavior in various media, where authorship also involves exercising sufficient control over the making of the work as a whole."[25] Note that this proposal is neutral with regard to whether authorship is to be identified in an individual or a collective; in fact, Livingston argues that his account covers instances of both individual and "joint authorship," but for now I want to focus on the case for individual authorship.

Can Livingston's account of cinematic authorship be adapted such that we might be able to identify individual authorship in the context of television? The challenge, as I see it, is to say something more specific about the notion of "sufficient control"—particularly in the context of television production. Yet if one could provide an adequate characterization of sufficient control, then whether individual televisual authorship ever obtains would be an empirical question—one that could not be settled a priori by appealing to facts about the collaborative nature and commercial constraints that characterize television production.[26] For, in principle at least, it could be the case that in some instances "respecting the material conditions of production" amounts to acknowledging that, as a matter of fact, a single individual has nearly complete creative authority—enough, anyway, that it could be regarded as "sufficient control" on a plausible account of that concept. As such, I think it is wise to remain agnostic about the *possibility* of individual televisual authorship, while also admitting that, however the idea of sufficient control is analyzed, the empirical work of identifying an instance of television production that meets the conditions for individual authorship looks like a tall order. Still, simple claims that the nature of commercial television production precludes individual authorship are too hasty. As I discuss below, such claims often simply conflate collaborative production with collaborative authorship without actually arguing that the latter is reducible to the former.

Collaborative Production versus Collective Authorship

As indicated above, one way of attempting to square collaborative production with authorship is to assert that the inherently collaborative nature of production necessarily vitiates individual control and disperses it among members of the production team, resulting in what theorists have variously called collective authorship, multiple authorship, or joint authorship. For example, writing of film, Gaut claims, "In light of the fact of artistic collaboration, we should admit that mainstream films have multiple authors."[27] Similarly, writing about television, John Thornton Caldwell asserts, "Viewing television as an industrial—rather than merely artistic—practice shows television authorship to be inherently protracted, collective, and contested."[28] The plausibility of these claims depends on what explanatory work "authorship" is supposed to do in these two sentences. Caldwell, for example, is using the term "authorship" in a way that tracks the creative contributions of various agents as a kind of important corrective to the ways in which such contributions have historically been overlooked. Indeed, both Gaut and Caldwell's accounts are subtle and cogent. It is because these accounts get so much right, especially with regard to respecting the material conditions of production, that I want to try to build upon them.

Nevertheless, I want to argue that if one accepts the prima facie claim that, in the context of appreciation, authorship involves control over the work as a whole and responsibility, then there are good reasons to retain a distinction between collaborative production and authorship *per se*. Furthermore, it should be clear that, even if no single individual exercises sufficient control over a production as to be identifiable as the author, it does not follow that every contributor must therefore be among the work's multiple authors. In such cases, it may instead be the case that nobody is properly regarded as an author of the work. And here is one way in which agency could help us: Supposing, again, that authorship does, in fact, involve a certain degree of control over the whole of a work, we are likely to need another means of praising creative contributions and talking about achievement in the context of television, where authorship in this sense simply does not obtain in the majority of cases. The broader concept of agency provides those means.

However, we should also recall that, on Livingston's account of cinematic authorship, sufficient control is necessary, but not sufficient, for authorship. Also necessary—and, together with sufficient control, sufficient—is "the intentional realization of another type of goal in a work—namely, "expression," where "expression" is to be understood in the broad sense of "intentionally making an utterance or work that provides some indication that some psychological state or attitude, broadly defined, obtains in the author."[29] As Livingston explains, his proposal is motivated by our creative and appreciative interests in art: "People are often interested in expressing their attitudes and feelings in an utterance or work and in this accomplishment being recognized by an audience. Audiences often have a corresponding interest in trying to find out what the maker of a work was trying to convey ..."[30] And, in fact, Gaut accepts this assumption in arguing that films are necessarily multiply authored inasmuch as *many* different individuals, from actors to set designers, "express their attitudes through their contributions."[31] The problem for Gaut's account is, as Livingston indicates, that although expressing an attitude (broadly speaking) may be necessary for authorship, it is not sufficient.

Indeed, there are good reasons to doubt that either the intentional expression of attitudes or, more broadly, the performance of various activities that contribute to the artistic (or artistically relevant) properties of a work are sufficient for authorship. Although Gaut is surely right in characterizing cinema as involving "qualities of images and sounds, dependent on the particular individuals who generated them, which are crucial to a film's artistic features," he errs in assuming this entails the multiple-authorship view he endorses.[32] Contribution of *any* artistic or artistically relevant properties, let alone the audiovisual qualities on which such properties depend, seems far too broad to be sufficient for authorship. For example, in both film and television production, the type of lenses and film stocks used are often artistically relevant. Consider the noticeable darkening of color palette from Season 1 to Season 2 of *Breaking Bad*, which was partly achieved by switching from Fuji film stocks to Kodak film stocks. Surely in cases such as this we would not be tempted to credit manufacturers like Kodak as some of the "multiple authors" of films or television series despite their evident contribution to the audiovisual qualities and artistically relevant properties of those works. Rather, more plausible is the idea that having the power to choose particular lenses and film stocks might, at least in part, be sufficient for authorship. In the *Breaking Bad* example, the power to switch film stocks lay with the cinematographer from Season 2 onwards, Michael Slovis.[33]

What about more proximate contributions from individuals who are members of a production collective charged with the assignment of making a specific work of film or television? Again, we ought to resist the idea that the contributions of such individuals are sufficient for authorship. Consider the camera operators on the series *Friday Night Lights*. The dizzying hand-held camera work is undoubtedly one of the series' distinctive audiovisual features and is, plausibly, artistically relevant. But surely it would be a mistake—or, at least, a radical revision of our present concept of authorship—to list the camera operators as (some of) the authors of the series. Perhaps, this claim has less intuitive pull than the rejection of Kodak employees' claims to authorship. But it is grounded in the idea that authorship, properly so-called, must involve more than simply doing one's part in the absence of knowledge of how one's contribution fits within the work as a whole and in the absence of any control over that part/whole relation (not to mention the very circumscribed space in which one performs one's part in the first place).

As has been argued by Livingston recently and by V. F. Perkins before him, a plausible account of cinematic (and, for our purposes, televisual) authorship must attend to the ways in which commercial production generates complex relationships amongst a work's constitutive parts and the work as a whole. In Perkins's words, "Style and meaning are twin products of synthesis; they do not result from a simple accumulation of independent statements by actors and technicians."[34] In other words, although we surely ought to acknowledge the artistic and expressive contributions from actors and technicians, those contributions take on new stylistic qualities and new significance within the work as a whole. Given the disconnect between style and meaning of an artistic or expressive contribution to a part of a television work and the style and meaning of the work overall, which results from the coordination of parts contributed by a variety of different people, it seems rather premature to conclude that all such contributors are among the work's multiple authors. Livingston puts the point succinctly: "Given a prevalent and relatively uncontroversial idea about the importance of certain types of relational properties amongst a work's artistic and expressive properties ... the appreciation of a work *qua* work of art or *qua* expressive utterance leads us inevitably from the various parts and elements to relations between these parts, and, ultimately, to the person (or persons) who can be understood as potentially responsible for the work's design, which is taken as including such relations between the parts."[35]

More generally, then, it seems plausible that television authorship must essentially involve the power to make decisions that determine the artistically relevant properties of television artwork in a global sense, where those properties are not shaped discretely, in isolation from other artistically relevant properties of the work, but rather in coordination with the shaping of those other properties and in view of additional artistic properties that are likely to emerge out of the relationships established in this process. Importantly, this claim is neutral on the matter of the titular role(s) of such decision makers and how many of them there might be in any particular case.

In offering an example here, I will stick with Gaut's (and subsequently Livingston's) focus on the contributions of actors.[36] Perhaps, as Gaut claims, it is plausible that some actors are able, through their performances, to express their own attitudes about the characters they embody. Still, the general problem here is inescapable: Any attitudes the actors express are ultimately situated in a context over which someone else has ultimate control. Although we don't often think about it, one such person is almost always the editor, who has varying degrees of authority in different production contexts.[37] Thus, the editor (and, perhaps, the director and show-runner) may shape the overall organization of the work in such a way that their attitudes mesh with those expressed by the actor, or, alternatively, in such a way that the attitudes intended to be expressed by the actor are undermined. In an interview with television critic Alan Sepinwall, Bryan Cranston memorably described the radical edit of his performance in the final scene of *Breaking Bad's* Season 3 finale, "Half Measures."[38] Cranston recalled playing the scene, in which Walter White runs over two drug dealers with his car, gets out, and shoots one of them in the head, with a good deal of impulsiveness and uncertainty—another instance of Walt reluctantly succumbing to extenuating circumstances before making a morally dubious decision. Yet in the final cut of the episode, Walter's actions are cold and calculated; the edit of the scene clearly shows that Walt is farther down the path of evil than Cranston thought or, indeed, intended in his performance. In any case, whether an actor's intended attitudes are successfully expressed is ultimately a matter of power that, in typical cases, is held by some person(s) other than the actor himself. Thus, *pace* Gaut, the intentional expression of attitudes is insufficient for authorship.

There is one more objection to make to the suggestion that collaborative production essentially entails multiple authorship—one that, to my knowledge, no one else has made, but that I think is very important. Part of the initial attraction of regarding television as *essentially* collectively authored is, I think, that this view seems, laudably, to secure approbation for *all* of the contributors.[39] However, not all television productions have happy results. As I argued in the previous section, some television artworks deserve condemnation—not only for artistic reasons, but for ethical or ideological reasons—and in such cases their authors deserve blame. Surely in these cases, we do not want to commit to the view that, by virtue of the idea that television is essentially collectively authored, all of the contributors to the creation of a morally flawed episode deserve to be blamed. On the contrary, we want to identify the person(s) who are ultimately responsible for the properties of the episode that make it flawed.

Consider, for example, the artistic and ethical failings of HBO's *The Newsroom* (HBO 2012–14). The series' artistic demerits plausibly include forced expository dialogue, contrived scene structure, bad acting, saccharine music (or, at least, a saccharine *use* of music), feeble attempts at humor, heavy-handed use of cinematographic/televisual conventions such as slow-motion and dolly-in to close up to indicate "seriousness," and, above all, sententiousness and didacticism.[40] In fact, the series' artistic flaws are so copious that it is hard to find any element of the program that is not somehow marred. Now, if the contributors to the production of the series were, in fact, co-authors, they would deserve blame for these failings. But it seems right that when we lambast the show, the targets of our attacks are *not* people like the composer, the focus puller, the camera operator or even the actors or individual writers. For although it is the case that all of these individuals contributed to the creation of artistically relevant properties in an artistically flawed work, they are not *responsible* for the way their individual contribution was situated in the overall work or, indeed, the overall failure of the work.

This idea, that television authorship is partly a matter of responsibility as well as power or control, seems to me frequently overlooked, but of crucial significance when we think about television from the perspective of ethics. In the case of *The Newsroom*, frequently voiced and, in my view, sound, complaints regarding the series' ethical flaws tend to cluster around two problems: The first is the stereotypical and/or cursory representation of "token" characters of color like Neelamani Sampat (Dev Patel) and Kendra James (Adina Porter). The second is the depiction of women as unable to function professionally without being distracted by romantic worries and, thus, as basically tolerated for the purpose of supporting men who can get the job done.

Importantly, ethical criticism does not stop with the identification and description of ethical flaws. On the contrary, it is standard practice in popular, if not academic, criticism to assign blame to the person(s) who appear responsible for the moral failing(s).[41] And, although arguing for it here would take me beyond my current aim, it seems plausible that critics are rationally warranted to do so. For the purposes, of ease and clarity, let us just focus on the charge of sexism. Several critics have noted the series' gender politics are all the more shocking in comparison with its competition (e.g., *The Good Wife* (CBS 2009–16)) and HBO compatriots (e.g., *Veep* (HBO 2012–) and *Girls* (HBO 2012–)), and this observation tends to motivate the assignment of blame to individual agency. More specifically, critics tend to single out show-runner Aaron Sorkin for criticism, sometimes claiming that a broader pattern of sexism is evident across his career.[42] I think the charge of sexism and the blame of Sorkin is basically right, although I think it's possible that on an episode-by-episode basis, there might be other key creative members that deserve a share of the blame.

However, the point of this example is that whether one thinks that Sorkin alone is responsible for the series' sexism or whether he shares blame with a few other individuals, we do not want to embrace a conception of authorship by which *everyone* who contributed to the series' artistically relevant features is partly responsible and, thus, partly blameworthy for the series' sexism. And this is why we should resist identifying all of the series' contributors as among its multiple or collective authors. For authorship is not simply a matter of contributing to the artistically relevant features of a work, nor even having sufficient control over a work, but also being responsible for a work's failings, whether artistic, moral, or of any other sort.

The collectivist accounts of film and television authorship advocated by Caldwell and Gaut are significant contributions. They have, in slightly different ways, given us a much subtler understanding of the nature of film and television production, and they have rightly emphasized the importance of developing a concept of authorship that respects the empirical facts about production. I believe we should build upon these accounts. My claim in this section is that part of this work necessarily involves further refining collectivist accounts of authorship, for, as I have indicated, some of the logical extensions of these accounts could lead to unintended consequences—in particular, burdening the wrong people with the responsibility for artistically and ethically flawed television artworks.

Another way of putting the general point here is to say that, for appreciating the art of television, we need a concept of authorship that correctly ascribes praise and blame for television artworks' artistic (and moral) successes and failures. To be clear, this does not preclude the common practice of praising the artistic merit of specific contributions (or contributors) to a television artwork. In other words, the idea is *not* that we put a moratorium on evaluating and praising particular contributions like performances. Rather, the idea is just that these contributions are to be distinguished from authorship properly so-called, which entails a certain degree of responsibility for the artistic and moral features of a work as a whole. Emily Mortimer's performance on *The Newsroom*, for example, is part of what makes that series what it is—it is a constitutive feature and it is an artistically relevant feature. But Mortimer's artistic contribution no more makes her an author of *The Newsroom* than it makes her responsible for the series' ethically dubious representation of women.

Sufficient Control Revisited

The question of responsibility for the moral failings of television series brings us back to the thorny matter of sufficient control, which must now be explored in depth. I have emphasized that responsibility for a work as a whole, in particular, is central to authorship, whether it is responsibility for artistic success or responsibility for moral failure. However, responsibility for such things is ultimately dependent upon control. Without a certain amount of control over a work, one cannot correctly be regarded as being responsible for it. In addition, I have stressed the significance of control in terms of the closely related concept of power. The mere contribution to some of a television work's constitutive and artistically relevant qualities does not suffice for authorship. Rather, what is needed is the power (usually held in terms of the authority of one's role on a production) to determine how such constitutive parts will relate to other constitutive parts—how they will be integrated into the work as a whole. In most cases, this requirement also entails that television authors possess the power to shape the work as a whole—that they are able to control the creation of the overall work.

So, we must now address the issue of sufficient control head on. But, of course, there are several obstacles. One is, as Livingston notes, that control and coercion (which undermines control) are scalar concepts: perhaps no single individual or even team of individuals is ever in complete control of the production of a television program, but we assume that some person(s) has enough control such that we typically regard neither artistic successes nor moral failures as unfortunate accidents. Another task is to say something more specific about what is actually involved in the exercise of sufficient control; what does the process of exercising sufficient control look like? So, the difficult challenges are, from my point of view, to say how *much* control is sufficient for authorship and in what more specific terms can sufficient control be analyzed. If we can do this, the payoff should be a clearer sense of when sufficient control obtains in television production and how it is shared (if it is) among members of a production collective.

A helpful place to begin is with C. Paul Sellors's proposal, regarding cinematic authorship, for analyzing sufficient control in terms of intentionally making what he calls, following Livingston, a "filmic utterance." That is, for Sellors, control over the making of a filmic utterance is not, in itself, essential to authorship, but rather is important, because "not to be in control would result in a failure to intentionally make or token an utterance."[43] Moreover, Sellors maintains that his account avoids conflating collective production with collective authorship because filmic utterances are not to be strictly identified with films themselves. Creating the film itself is, for Sellors, "manifesting the work materially," which is, in principle, distinct from "communicating an utterance." Thus, on Sellors's account, the production collective shares a collective intention to make a film, but "this collective's interest is not directed towards producing an utterance, so this collective is not authorial." Rather, the authorial collective comprises those individuals who participate not only in "manifesting the work materially" but also intentionally create a filmic utterance by virtue of this. Formally, then, Sellors's claim is this:

> Filmic author = the agent or agents who intentionally token(s) a filmic utterance, where "to token" refers to any action, an intended function of which is to make manifest or communicate some attitude(s) by means of the production of an apparently moving image projected on a screen or other surface and a filmic utterance is the result of the act of tokening in this medium.[44]

Obviously, Sellors's account crucially depends on the notion of a filmic utterance, which he defines as the result of any action that has the intended function of expressing some attitude(s) through the creation of a filmic work. The central idea here, borrowed from Livingston's work, is worth preserving. Although some television studies scholars may take issue with the "utterance model" of the intentional expression of attitudes, I think it is plausible so long as it is understood broadly, in Livingston's words, as "anything that has a certain kind of expressive function, or, in Paul Grice's terms, 'non-natural meaning.'"[45]

Despite Sellors's claims to the contrary, however, his account does not provide sufficient means for distinguishing contributors from authors properly so-called. Putatively, members of the production collective are distinguished from members of the authorial collective in virtue of not having an interest in making an utterance. The problem is that authorship is not merely a matter of having an interest in making an utterance, whether filmic, televisual, or whatever, but is, again, a matter of having the power to do so and successfully acting on that power. Sellors's claim that authors are to be understood as those who "intentionally token a filmic utterance, where 'to token' refers to any action, an intended function of which is to make manifest or communicate some attitude(s)" allows that *any* production member is able to contribute to the creation of the filmic utterance. But this proposal will not do because, in fact, not just any contributor has the power to shape the utterance.

Sellors's appeal to John Searle's conception of collective intentionality does not help matters. For Sellors, the people who count as members of the authorial collective, that is, as authors, are "those that adopt and are able to realize the relevant collective intention" to make a filmic utterance.[46] But Sellors understands collective intention as "do[ing] away with the need for singular authority over intention [and] accept[ing] that others can contribute to shaping and achieving the shared will."[47] So, it appears that, by his account, *any* contributor is able to adopt and realize the collective intention to make a filmic utterance. Once again, the problem is that this proposal ignores the fact that power is partly constitutive of authorship. A given collaborator's ability to contribute to the realization of a filmic utterance crucially depends upon that collaborator having the requisite power to do so. In addition, a number of commentators have pointed out that Searle's account of collective intentionality does not actually require intentions to be shared.[48] Putatively, a "we-intention," to use Searle's term, can obtain in the mind of any individual who intends to perform an action with others. Yet surely we do not want to allow that any given member of a film or television production can simply contribute to shaping and achieving "the shared will" in virtue of intending to do so. Finally, it is not clear what Sellors takes "the shared will" to actually comprise, since he emphasizes the possibility of dissention and disagreement within the authorial collective.

Livingston has advanced a more compelling analysis of sufficient control, which underpins what I take to be the most plausible extant account of cinematic authorship. Although Livingston maintains his theory can accommodate both individual authorship and what he calls "joint" authorship, I will narrow my focus to the latter, given the above-mentioned considerations militating against—although not necessarily precluding—individual authorship in television production.

Livingston proposes the following conditions on joint authorship, generally: "First of all, if two or more persons jointly author an utterance or work, they must intentionally generate or select the text, artifact, performance, or structure that is its publicly observable component: in so doing, they act on meshing sub-plans and exercise shared control and decision-making authority over the results; furthermore, in making the work or utterance, they together take credit for it as a whole ..."[49] Although Livingston explicitly acknowledges the possibility of joint authorship involving a kind of hierarchy of contributions, his analysis (in both *Art and Intention* and *Cinema, Philosophy, Bergman*) focuses primarily on joint authorship among equals.

As we saw in Sellors's account of authorship, which is indebted to Livingston, the requirement on sufficient control, in the latter's words, "follows from the more basic assumption that authoring utterances or works is a species of intentional action."[50] Working with the assumption that undertaking intentional action "entails the exercise of sufficient control" and with a focus on joint authorship among equals, Livingston's appeal to Michael Bratman's work on shared intentions and shared cooperative activity is apposite. For the object of Bratman's analysis is what he calls "modest sociality"—that is, "the shared intentional activities of small, adult groups in the absence of asymmetric authority relations within those groups, and in which the individuals who are participants remain constant over time."[51]

What I want to point out here is neither a problem with Bratman's account of modest sociality nor with Livingston's use of it in his analysis of joint authorship among equals in the context of cinema and other art forms. Rather, it is simply that neither is suited for understanding *most* kinds of contemporary television authorship—a kind of social phenomenon that, in stark contrast with Bratman's conception of modest sociality, typically involves the intentional activity of institutionally embedded large groups of adults organized in hierarchical authority relationships, and whose memberships frequently change over the course of a single season (and sometimes even episode) let alone a multi-season series. I should add, however, that in some forms of television art, things are less complicated. It may simply be the case, for example, that Livingston's model of individual authorship or joint authorship amongst equals can account for one-off television plays such as *Marty* (1953), *Patterns* (1955), and *Requiem for a Heavyweight* (1956), or "TV movies" such as *The Laramie Project* (2002), *Saraband* (2003), *Normal* (2003), and *Too Big to Fail* (2011). My point is just that any full account of television authorship must also account for the more theoretically troublesome television miniseries, anthology series, and long-form serial—to mention just a few other kinds of television.

Still, faced with challenges posed by these latter forms of television, we should not give up on an analysis of sufficient control (or the intentional actions underlying it) in joint or co-authorship in television production too quickly. As we have seen, there are good reasons to think that power and responsibility are central components of television authorship, and it is plausible that control—and, more basically, intentional action—underlies both. What might sufficient control look like in the institutionally embedded, hierarchically organized, and fluid collectives that create television? It seems to me that one key consideration is this: In virtue of television's extended and shifting temporal boundaries as well as the changing nature of its production collectives, control on a television series is typically both more dispersed and more subject to change over time.

That is, unlike most film shoots of several months, the creation of a television series over several years often involves key contributors such as producers, writers, cinematographers, and directors coming and going, being promoted and given more control in some cases and being demoted or fired and given less control in other cases. Consider, for example, the vicissitudes of the writers' room on *The Sopranos* (HBO 1999–2007), which featured the young writer Todd Kessler's rapid ascent, abrupt firing, re-hiring, and permanent firing, as well as Matthew Weiner's climb from writer to co-executive producer. In addition, the temporally prolonged nature of television series entails that, in comparison with film production, there are typically more ebbs and flows of institutional control vis-à-vis the control of members of the production collective. Here *The Sopranos* is atypical in as much as HBO reportedly took an exceptionally hands-off approach to overseeing production. On the other side of the spectrum, AMC displayed an unusual assertion of control by firing *Walking Dead* (AMC 2010–) show-runner Frank Darabont. In between these two poles, there are all manner of ways in which the control over a television series shifts between the production collective and corporate executives. My conjecture is that what sets television apart from film here is the duration of production, over which such power relationships between the production collective and corporate executives shift and shift again—just as they do within the production collective itself.

Given these considerations regarding the typically protean nature of control in television production, I am skeptical that sufficient control in this context is analyzable in terms of the shared intentions, involving meshing sub-plans, that Bratman argues are central to modest sociality and Livingston argues are central to joint authorship among equals. I suspect the problem is actually not, as it may initially appear, a lack of mesh in the sub-plans by way of which individuals intend to jointly create a televisual work. For as both Bratman and Livingston point out, the "meshing condition" does not require strict agreement between sub-plans (although it does involve practical consistency in the form of mutual realizability). The idea is, rather, that a *mesh* of sub-plans, understood as obtaining "just in case there is some way that we could [perform a joint activity] that would not violate either of our sub-plans but would, rather, involve the successful execution of those sub-plans," is necessary for joint action.[52] Instead, I think this model will not give us an accurate picture of television authorship because the relevant intentions in this context do not have the same content and are hierarchically structured.

Let me try to make these ideas a bit more concrete. We can start by reflecting further on what goes wrong with Sellors's account of film authorship. As I indicated earlier, Sellors's proposal holds that any member of the production collective—from caterer to sound recordist—is a coauthor of a film if he or she has a "we-intention" that matches the we-intentions of other members to make a certain kind of filmic utterance. As we saw, one of the problems is that caterers and sound recordists do not have the requisite power to share such an intention. In other words, an intention to create a filmic utterance is not the content of an intention that a caterer or sound-recordist *could* rationally have because it is not something that they could reasonably act upon; there would be a kind of means/ends incoherence in such a case.

The content of the intentions of *most* members of the production collective is much more modest in scale and ambition precisely because their power and control are narrowly limited by their specific roles. There is, thus, rational pressure on such contributors to formulate intentions—whether individual or shared—of much more modest content. For example, the focus puller of a static camera might formulate and act upon an intention to properly rack focus from the foreground to the background. Or, on a Steadicam set-up, the focus puller and Steadicam operator might formulate and jointly act upon the shared intention (of the Bratmanian model) to keep the image in focus as the camera approaches the subject. The vast majority of roles on television and film sets are of this nature, and although we ought to admit, as Livingston does, that the individuals who perform these roles do essential work—literally, labor that is partly constitutive of the television work's identity—nevertheless, there are no good reasons for thinking that they are coauthors of the work as a whole.

Taking a cue from Christopher Kutz, we can think of the sorts of intentions of focus pullers, camera operators, and the like as subsidiary intentions, and we can contrast them with what Kutz calls executive intentions. Kutz puts the distinction this way:

> An executive intention is an intention whose content is an activity or outcome conceived as a whole, and which plays a characteristic role in generating, commanding, or determining other intentions and mental states in order to achieve that total outcome. A subsidiary intention is an intention generated and rationalized by an executive intention, whose content is the achievement of part of the total outcome or activity.[53]

I hope that salience of this proposal is immediately clear. Given the ways in which power and control centrally figure in the concept of authorship, it seems plausible that what is distinctive about authorial intentions is their content; authorial intentions are aptly characterized as a particular kind of executive intention. In contrast, most other intentions are best characterized as non-authorial precisely because they are subsidiary in the way that Kutz describes. (There are also, on this account, some executive intentions that are non-authorial.)

Thus, I agree, with Sellors and Livingston, that the best way to analyze sufficient control is, indeed, in terms of intentions and the successful realization thereof. However, my conjecture is that, in the context of television authorship, the relevant authorial intentions are, typically, neither Searlean we-intentions (since non-authors may formulate and act upon such intentions just as much as authors) nor Bratmanian intentions, with meshing sub-plans, which are shared among equals. Rather, my proposal is that part of what constitutes authorship is the ability to formulate and successfully realize executive intentions about the outcome of the work as a whole. Moreover, intentions regarding the outcome of the work as a whole are successfully realized in large part by determining (through the exercise of power) the relevant subsidiary intentions of the production collective. In short, television authors are necessarily those members of a production collective who successfully realize executive intentions regarding a work (although this is not sufficient for authorship because, as I argue below, not all executive intentions are properly characterized as authorial).

Importantly, my account is neutral with respect to what member(s) of a production team may be regarded as authors. In principle, single authorship is a possibility, but as indicated earlier, it remains unlikely. More commonly, several contributors formulate and act upon executive intentions, and this may happen in at least a couple of different ways. One possibility is that multiple individuals share several executive intentions with the same content and act upon them accordingly. So, for example, it may be the case that Trey Parker and Matt Stone jointly decided that they would make an episode of *South Park* (Comedy Central 1997–) that referenced *The Human Centipede* (2009) and satirized Steve Jobs and Apple. Or, perhaps, the Kessler siblings and Daniel Zelman decided that the narrative structure of *Damages* (FX 2007–10; Audience Network 2011–12) would be constructed around flashbacks, and that those flashbacks would be distinguished visually through the use of a higher-contrast, grainier film stock. Or, perhaps, in planning and writing *The Wire* (HBO 2002–08), David Simon, Ed Burns, and Robert Colesberry acted upon an intention to make a series about the decay of America—to express certain attitudes regarding institutional dysfunction, political corruption, the failed war on drugs, and racial and economic inequality. In all of these cases, the intended outcome was achieved by virtue of successfully realized executive intentions, which were, in turn, partly achieved by virtue of the successful realization of the subsidiary intentions of other collaborators.

In the cases above, the salient executive intentions likely have something like the structure of Bratmanian shared intentions. But my central point here is that in the vast majority of instances of television production, even if some executive intentions are shared, other executive intentions are not shared because their content differs. In the above cases, *South Park* (or at least many episodes of it, if not the series in its entirety) is probably the best contender for being an outcome of Bratmanian shared cooperative activity and, thus, joint authorship because of Stone and Parker's well-known creative control over the series and the control afforded by animation more generally.

However, when we turn to live-action, long-form television, the situation looks very different because there is a rotating cast of writers, producers, and directors. In cases like *Damages* and *The Wire*, there may still be a hierarchy of authority, whereby the executive intentions of the show-runners could, in principle, trump those of, say, head writers, directors, and cinematographers (where the show-runners are not themselves occupying those roles). Nevertheless, it should be clear that head writers, directors, and sometimes even cinematographers still formulate and execute their *own* executive intentions with regard to individual episodes, if not series as wholes. In many, if not all, cases, this happens with minimal interference from show-runners or other individuals with greater power. And although head writers and directors need to fit their episodes within a show-runner's overall plan for a season or series arc, this collaboration does not entail that the content of their intentions is the same. For the former direct their intentions at an individual episode, while the latter direct their intentions at the overall series.

The upshot is that the identification of television authors depends on the specification of the relevant "work." The general point is an obvious one, but it bears emphasis because in the present context it means we need at least some tacit conception of the ontology of television—in particular, how television works are individuated. Here, matters are not so straightforward. As I have already indicated, television's temporal prolongation raises some interesting questions here insofar as in many cases the temporal boundaries of one work expand gradually over time. Yet it is also important to observe that this gradual expansion of one work—the series—occurs by virtue of the completion of distinct works. Although my sustained arguments on the ontology of television will have to wait until Chapter 3, let us suppose for now that the appreciation of television involves attending to a number of different kinds of work, which are often intimately connected: episodes, seasons, and series. Plausibly, these works are all unified wholes of various sorts, but episodes and seasons also comprise series. Again, the salience of this proposal is that analyzing sufficient control in terms of executive and subsidiary intentions suggests that the authors of episodes are unlikely to be the authors of series and vice versa.

Thus far, then, I have focused on the fact that executive intentions often take different objects, such as episodes and series. But an additional complication for television authorship (and cinematic authorship, in my view) is that it seems plausible that even within a single episode (or an individual film), the executive intentions of key creative figures may differ in content. It is important to recall here that executive intentions and subsidiary intentions are distinguished by virtue of function and that this distinction is relative. With this principle in mind, we ought to resist the thought that forming and executing executive intentions in the context of television production is a matter of just one or two persons taking a single global attitude towards the work—for example, that they intend to create an episode of television or that they intend that the episode express cynicism regarding the prospects of social equality in the United States. On the contrary, it seems more plausible that several individuals form and execute executive intentions with more specific content—say, regarding the soundscape or the lighting of the episode overall *and* regarding how a particular component of the episode relates to the others. My conjecture is that executive intentions at *this* level—executed, perhaps, by people like set designers, cinematographers, sound designers, head-writers, and directors—support and interact with higher-order executive intentions regarding both the style and content of the episode but also, of course, the overall series.

It is this interaction between executive intentions directed at an episode and/or season and executive intentions directed at a series that raises especially difficult questions about television authorship. In almost all cases, the key creative members who form and act upon executive intentions vis-à-vis an episode do so as part of the realization of higher-level executive intentions regarding *another* work—to wit, the season or the series. For example, whatever executive intentions were realized with regard to the narrative structure of *The Sopranos* Season 3 episode "Pine Barrens," they had to align with different executive intentions regarding the narrative arc of Season 3 and, more broadly, the development of the relationship between Paulie and Chris across the overall series. Although I do not think this consideration suggests that the control of key creative roles on an individual episode is coerced is any substantive sense, it certainly raises questions about the extent to which (and how) executive intentions can be formed and executed vis-à-vis a series.

Turning our attention to the question of authorship of television series, then, we can identify several difficult puzzles. One puzzle stems from the fact that sometimes key creative figures other than show-runners are given the power to direct executive intentions not only at an individual episode, but at a series as a whole. Consider, for example, a show-runner like Vince Gilligan, whose leadership style is marked by the delegation of authority. On *Breaking Bad*, Gilligan gave cinematographer Michael Slovis enormous latitude in shaping the show's visual style. Insofar as Slovis had the power to determine the visual style of the overall series (and how that "look" related to other parts of the series and the series overall), in large part by delegating specific duties to other collaborators who would help assist in realizing them by acting upon subsidiary intentions, his artistic intentions are correctly characterized as executive and *pro tanto* authorial. Moreover, there is some degree of overlap between Slovis's executive intentions vis-à-vis the series and vis-à-vis individual episodes: Slovis was cinematographer for every episode following Season 1, so he essentially realized his own executive intentions regarding the series by virtue of forming and executing executive intentions regarding those episodes. And this constitutes a good prima facie reason to think that, whoever the authors of *Breaking Bad* and its individual episodes are, Slovis is one of them.

But things are significantly more complicated in the many cases where such an overlap fails to obtain because individuals do not have the same role—and thus do not possess the same degree of power and control. In less complicated cases, there is a single show-runner who acts upon various executive intentions vis-à-vis the series over its entire run. But even in these cases, of course, show-runners accomplish this in a variety of different ways. Some show-runners are actively involved in the production of individual episodes, acting upon their executive intentions vis-à-vis the series by virtue of acting upon executive intentions vis-à-vis those episodes. In other situations, though, show-runners may prefer to delegate a great deal of authority, trusting that their executive intentions vis-à-vis the series will be realized via the execution of others' executive intentions vis-à-vis various episodes. In such cases, where the show-runner (and anyone else who has executive intentions directed at the series) acts upon very few or no executive intentions vis-à-vis an episode, we should resist attributing to that person or persons authorship over that episode.

But now we are on a slippery slope: Evidently episodes (and their arrangement) partially constitute overall series. Can, then, one be an author of a series without being an author—analyzed in terms of the successful realization of executive intentions--of *any* episodes? Such an idea has the air of paradox. But if the answer is "no," then it seems like we ought to be able to say that authorship of some number of episodes would be sufficient for authorship of a series—but how many? Specifying a number would appear arbitrary. One thing, at least, seems clear: Suggesting that authorship of a series requires authorship of *every* episode sets the bar too high. Plausibly, an individual can be a co-author of a work—whether an omnibus film, a book of short stories, or an academic paper—without authoring all of the work's constitutive parts. Indeed, this is one of the key lessons to be drawn from our analysis of sufficient control. Yet the unattractiveness of the other options—admitting authorship of a series in the absence of authorship of *any* episodes or simply stipulating some definite amount that is sufficient—should give us pause.

Here is another puzzle for television authorship. As we saw above, key creative roles, in which the power to formulate and act upon executive intentions are embodied, tend to be occupied by several different individuals over time. This point is closely connected to my earlier one regarding the way in which the temporality of television series results in an ebb and flow of institutional control. Another effect of television's unusual temporality is that, farther down the hierarchy, power and control are also fluid to the extent that such key creative roles go through cycles of being occupied and vacated. In some cases, there is an abrupt change in staffing—someone is hired, fired, or dies—during the production of the series that necessarily changes the hierarchy of authority simply because someone who did not previously formulate and execute executive intentions now does, or someone who did no longer does. For example, during the third season of *The Wire*, co-executive producer Robert F. Colesberry died, and Nina K. Noble was promoted to co-executive producer for the duration of the series. In other cases, like that of *The Sopranos* writers' room, some individuals were entrusted with more power over time, while others were stripped of it. The point here is that in as much as a series experiences such personnel changes, its hierarchy of authority is fluid. And to the extent that its hierarchy of authority is fluid, so too is the formulation and execution of executive intentions. In particular, some individuals attain the power to act upon executive intentions only after a significant amount of a series has already been created, while others lose the power to act upon executive intentions before the series is concluded.

Such considerations should not cast doubt upon the analysis of sufficient control in terms of forming and executing executive intentions, but they do raise questions about whether sufficient control can actually be achieved when the power relations among the production collective are so protean. In such cases, the relevant executive intentions to shape a series in a particular way seem only partly realizable. For the successful realization of executive intentions requires a certain amount of power, and where one does not have that power (whether as a result of death, job loss, or some other change), one is unable to formulate and act upon such intentions. Thus, control over the work is vitiated to the degree that an individual is not in a position to execute executive intentions vis-à-vis the work even while the work progresses temporally. At other points in the work's temporal progression the individual *may* be able to execute executive intentions, but it seems natural to say that, in such cases, those executive intentions are no longer authorial since they no longer have claim over the work as a whole.

The sort of situation I describe here bears a resemblance to what Paisley Livingston refers to as a "traffic jam" movie, which he characterizes as a case of (intentional) collective production resulting in "an undesirable and unintended collective consequence of actions that members of a group undertake with wholly different ends in view."[54] In such cases, Livingston denies that joint authorship among equals obtains, because "there is no system of widespread mutual belief with regard to the [contributors'] plans, and the absence of such beliefs converts *de facto*, emergent meshing of efforts [if there is a mesh] into a happy accident."[55] Therefore, according to Livingston, "traffic jam movies" are best characterized as authorless or unauthored.

As I indicated earlier, I suspect that joint authorship among equals is rare in television production, and thinking about the fluid nature of personnel and authority along the lines of a "traffic jam movie" may provide more support for that idea. Now, Livingston may be a bit too quick in declaring "traffic jam movies" to be authorless—since he does not rule out the possibility that such movies may be instances of joint authorship among *unequals*—but even if he is, our analysis of sufficient control in terms of executive intentions would seem to render many television series authorless, where authorship is construed as joint among equals *or* as joint among unequals.

Some theorists find the idea of authorless works counterintuitive. Sondra Bacharach and Deborah Tollensen point out that, unlike traffic jams, films do not come about by accident; they are the result of some intentional activity.[56] And Sellors objects to Livingston's view on the grounds that, putatively, "where we have an instance of an intentional utterance, no matter how poor, we also have an instance of authorship."[57] Objections to authorless works also threaten my own account, so I want to respond here. The first thing to say is that both of these objections appear to rest on mistakes. In the first case, it is evident that even though traffic jams occur by accident, they are nevertheless brought about by intentional activity; Bacharach and Tollefsen have not identified a disanalogy but simply changed the level of analysis. In fact, traffic jams are the accidental results of intentions to get home as soon as possible after work ends, just as incoherent films are the accidental results of intentions to make a box-office success. Meanwhile,

Sellors's claim suffers from the problem identified in earlier discussion of his proposal: insisting that all utterances have authors simply collapses the distinction between (intentional) production and authorship.

Authorship is a causal notion, to be sure, but it is also a normative one (even when the term is not used honorifically). This was a point I tried to emphasize at the beginning of the chapter: In clarifying the concept of authorship that is relevant for the appreciation of television, we cannot simply defer to common usage. We need to strike a balance between tracking actual practice and stipulating a more technical concept that suits the purpose for which we want it—namely, appreciation. But, as I noted, authorship is also a concept that we necessarily legislate or stipulate to some extent outside of appreciative contexts as well. For authorship is not a natural kind, about which there are certain mind-independent facts. Rather, it is a cultural kind—a concept we have devised for a variety of human purposes and interests. It is in large part because authorship is a cultural kind that I doubt the notion of authorless works is really as counterintuitive as Livingston's critics suggest. Why should we worry about not being able to identify this *human* concept, something of our own invention, behind the creation of television artworks?

As far as I can discern, the claim that the idea of an authorless work is counterintuitive boils down to the worry that it makes little sense to regard something as a *work*—or, even an utterance—in the absence of some agent undertaking intentional activity. The premise is correct, but the conclusion doesn't follow: The counterintuitive notion is not of an authorless work, but of an agentless work. What we need, logically speaking, for causal explanations of the creation of artworks, is the mind-independent concept of agency—not the mind-dependent, cultural concept of authorship. The worry about authorless works thus arises as a result of conflating agency and authorship. Therefore, I maintain, we should not be unduly worried about proposals according to which a significant number of collaboratively produced works—whether films or television series—turn out to be authorless. Newman and Levine, among other television scholars, are right to note that thinking about television as something that can be authored is a relatively recent development.[58] That doesn't mean that there were no authored instances of television before we had the means to describe the concept. But it does remind us that our appreciation of unauthored instances of television was apparently no poorer for *not* having the term "authorship" at our disposal.

Concluding Remarks: Making Do with Agency

I have claimed that in many cases television works will turn out to be authorless. I would also maintain that, in many other cases, we may simply not have the means at our disposal to find out who the authors of a work are—or whether the work even has any authors. This may seem like an anticlimactic conclusion and, furthermore, one that threatens the very phenomenon this book sets out to explore—the appreciation of television art. However, my conjecture is that the appreciation of television as art actually requires identifying authorship rather rarely; in much of our appreciative engagement with television artworks, we can simply make do with agency—a more general category of which authorship is a particular subset.

To be sure, identifying authorship is a component of what we sometimes do in our appreciative practices. When a television work *is* authored (individually or jointly), a full appreciation of it may necessitate that we identify the author(s) and understand their roles in creating the work. For example, it matters to our evaluation of the second season of *True Detective* (HBO 2014–) that at least one of its prima facie authors is Nic Pizzolato and not David Milch, because it matters that some of the stilted dialogue is a poor imitation of Milch's style rather than Milch churning out some weak pages. It matters to our understanding and evaluation of *Fanny and Alexander* (1982) that the joy and, even, optimism of the work are due to Ingmar Bergman's authorial voice, since Bergman's prior oeuvre indicates his understanding that such sentiments aren't cheaply bought. It matters to our appreciation of the magnitude of such sprawling works as *The Decalogue* (1989) and *Berlin Alexanderplatz* (1980)—and to our understanding of the social and philosophical themes underlying them—that they were authored, prima facie, by Krzysztof Kieslowski and Rainer Werner Fassbinder, respectively—two prolific artists who revisited similar themes and problems in different ways throughout their careers. And it matters to our assessment of how *Top of the Lake* (BBC Two 2013–) depicts New Zealand society, particularly in terms of gender relationships, that Jane Campion is, along with two Australian men, Gerard Lee and Garth Davis, one of the work's prima facie joint authors.

However, I contend we can make do with agency for appreciating most television art. In one sense, the plausibility of this claim will be defended in the book's subsequent discussions. But my claim also finds support in the terrain covered thus far. Recall that I am thinking of "agency" in a fairly robust sense of human agency, roughly characterized as an exercised capacity for intentional action. At this point we are in a position to appreciate an additional reason why intention and agency are so important in this context: Arguably, an agent that acts without intention, like an infant, is open neither to praise nor blame and is not a moral agent.[59] At the other extreme, think of someone who plans and exercises control over a crime as a whole—the *author* of a crime—who bears the lion's share of responsibility and deserves the most punishment. (Since we are talking about television, just think of Tony Soprano or Gus Fring.) Yet cases like this often involve other moral agents who have some lesser degree of responsibility and thus deserve some lesser degree of punishment. In such cases, we are concerned with the "authors" of the crime but need the concept of moral agency to make the appropriate gradations of moral responsibility when considering the fates of the collaborators or conspirators.

A key virtue of the agential approach to the appreciation of television (and in other art contexts) is its analogous function of finely attributing credit and responsibility for a work's artistic merits and moral flaws amongst the relevant contributors, including its authors (if it has any). Earlier I resisted embracing collective or multiple authorship because of the undesirability of burdening all of a work's contributors with the responsibility for morally flawed works. I argued that we do not want to incorrectly assign responsibility to individuals who are merely doing their part as contributors and are not themselves guilty of any moral failing. Rather, in *most* cases, the person who is responsible and who should be assigned blame is the author(s), and this is by virtue of the author(s) having sufficient control over the work as a whole.

This is right, as far as it goes, but there are some important cases where moral responsibility is neither correctly assigned to *all* contributors, nor exhausted by being assigned to a work's authors. Here, the concept of agency may prove valuable by providing us with finer gradations of moral responsibility.[60] Consider, first, an extreme example in the context of film: *A Serbian Film* (2010). Suppose, just for the sake of argument, that this film has only one author: Srdan Spasojevic. Assume, too, that the film is deeply morally flawed insofar as it glamorizes child rape—or, at least, gratuitously and explicitly depicts child rape for the sole purpose of scandalizing the audience. From these assumptions, it follows that Spasojevic is morally responsible, indeed blameworthy, for the film's moral flaws. This is right, but moral responsibility is not like a pie that has a definite number of pieces to be parceled out.

Although Spasojevic clearly bears most moral responsibility and deserves most of the blame, there are plausibly other members of the production collective who are morally responsible to lesser degrees. The camera operator, for example, had the ability to refuse filming the child-rape scenes, and the sound recordist had the ability to walk off the set rather than complete his job. That is, some non-authorial agents within the production collective had the power to control the morally relevant components of the film. Because they could have taken action, but did not, they too bear some responsibility for the film's moral flaws. Thus, we are justified in assigning them blame. The excuse, "I was just doing my job," would ring hollow and be unacceptable coming from the camera operator and sound recordist, whereas it might be perfectly acceptable if it were tendered by a caterer who was entirely unaware of the film's content.[61] The concept of authorship is insufficient to capture the necessary distinctions between degrees of responsibility and blame, because not all of the agents had control over the work as a whole. But *authorship* is not the concern here; rather, we are interested in intentional action: Who intentionally contributed to the film's immoral character and to what extent? We want to know what *agents* are responsible and to what degree.

How might this work in the context of television? Just assume, for the sake of argument, that the charges of animal cruelty lodged against *Luck* (HBO 2012) are valid—whether or not they actually are.[62] Also assume, for the sake of argument, that David Milch and Michael Mann are correctly regarded as equal joint authors of the series. Again, it follows that Milch and Mann are morally responsible for not taking the measures they could have to minimize risk to animals—say, for example, simulating the horse racing rather than recreating it. Now, most members of the production collective probably had little or no awareness, let alone power and control, of how the horses were treated and, therefore, are blameless. But, if Gary Baum's exposé is accurate *some* (non-author) contributors could have undertaken various actions that would have at least diminished the probability of animals being injured on set. That is, the agents that could have refused to comply with salient parts of production share moral responsibility with Milch and Mann. In this case, then, moral responsibility lies not just with the authors and not with all of the contributors to the work. The concept of agency allows us, in principle, to sort out who bears responsibility and who doesn't; it also allows that some individuals bear more responsibility than others—prima facie, those with more agency on the set.

Of course, this is all rather speculative, but my concern in the present context has to do not with the individual cases, but with the general point regarding the distribution of moral responsibility among contributors. While we certainly do not want to unduly saddle *all* contributors with moral responsibility for harms over which they had no control, there are plausibly some cases where a film or television work's authors are not the *only* members of the production collective that bear responsibility—even if responsibility is not borne in equal measure. The upshot is that there may be some cases where a focus on authorship could have the negative consequence of effacing or obscuring the responsibility of non-author contributors for the moral flaws of a work. And for this reason, it may be an advantage to talk of agency, rather than authorship, since the concept of agency gives us the various gradations and distinctions we will sometimes require to correctly analyze moral responsibility in the context of collective production. True, in some cases, we can also, in principle, identify gradations of moral responsibility in cases of authorship amongst unequals. But in such cases, we may also need to assign moral responsibility to some (but not all) non-authorial contributors. Focusing on agency gives us the means to do so.

I have stressed that responsibility for a television work's merits and flaws, whether artistic or moral, depends crucially upon having control over the work—or, at least, relevant parts of the work. In this sense, focusing on agency rather than authorship might be beneficial not only to analyzing responsibility in the context of collaborative television production, but also to analyzing control itself. If my earlier analysis of control in terms of executive and subsidiary intentions has some plausibility, then a focus on authorship and authorial intentions limits our view to a particular set of executive intentions. But, I argued, it seems natural to admit that in television production, some executive intentions are non-authorial. Such intentions will often be relevant to our appreciation of television works—to our interpretation of, say, what a writing staff intended to communicate in a certain narrative structure or line of dialogue. Moreover, as suggested in the above-mentioned cases of morally flawed works, both non-authorial executive intentions and, perhaps, some subsidiary intentions are relevant to the process of assigning moral responsibility and blame.

In addition, a focus on agency in the analysis of control might achieve what the model of collective or multiple authorship unsuccessfully attempts. That is, analyzing control not just in terms of authors and authorial intentions, but also in terms of the agency of non-authorial collaborators, should allow us to more precisely assign credit for a television work's artistic merits. I doubt anybody involved in authorship debates actually wants to deny the valuable contributions of various below-the-line workers or, indeed, those of actors or cinematographers. An emphasis on agency provides a cogent way of affirming the value of those contributions and assigning credit for them in a nuanced way without misidentifying contributors as authors. A focus on agency gives us the tools to talk about the exquisite design of a costume, the subtleties of a sound mix, the beauty of a gesture, or the technical brilliance of a camera move as artistic merits and contributions to a work's overall artistic value without becoming embroiled in debates about authorship.

In sum, my proposal is *not* that we do away with the notion of television authorship altogether. I would happily assent to a theory of television authorship that met the conditions for which I have argued. And I think that, even in the absence of a general theory of television authorship, these conditions and the analysis of sufficient control can help us identify television authors on a case-by-case basis. And I believe that there could be various situations in which identification and discussion of authorship might enhance our appreciation of a television work. But my conjecture is that the *basic* necessity for the appreciation of television as an art is recognizing agency, and that in cases in which authorship does not obtain (and perhaps some in which it does), a focus on agency is also sufficient for appreciation. Furthermore, I have averred that shifting our analysis in this way seems likely to be beneficial both in terms of our ability to precisely assign moral responsibility and artistic credit. Thus, in most of what follows, I shall eschew reference to authorship and attempt to make do with agency.

Notes

1. On the topic of implied authors, the *locus classicus* is Wayne C. Booth, *The Rhetoric of Fiction* 2nd ed. (Chicago: University of Chicago Press, 1983); on the topic of author functions, it is Michel Foucault, "What Is an Author?" in *Language, Counter-Memory, Practice: Selected Essays and Interviews*, ed.

Donald F. Bouchard, trans. Donald F. Bouchard and Sherry Simon (Ithaca, NY: Cornell University Press, 1977).
2. Paisley Livingson, "Authorship," in *The Routledge Companion to the Philosophy of Literature*, ed. Noël Carroll and John Gibson (New York: Routledge, 2016), 173.
3. The examples are my own. On "the inferred author function," see Jason Mittell, *Complex TV: The Poetics of Contemporary Television Storytelling* (New York: New York University Press, 2015), 105–17.
4. See Torben Grodal, "Agency in Film, Filmmaking, and Reception," in *Visual Authorship: Creativity and Intentionality in Media*, ed. Torben Grodal, Bente Larsen, and Iben Thorving Laursen (Copenhagen, Denmark: Museum Tusculanum Press, 2005). The idea that such psychological short cuts are useful in typically less collaborative art forms, like literature, is somewhat less compelling. See David Herman, *Storytelling and the Sciences of Mind* (Cambridge, MA: MIT Press, 2013), especially 57–63.
5. On this point, see Aaron Meskin, "Authorship," in *The Routledge Companion to the Philosophy of Film*, ed. Paisley Livingston and Carl Plantinga (New York: Routledge, 2008), 12–28; and C. Paul Sellors, *Film Authorship: Auteurs and Other Myths* (London: Wallflower, 2010), especially Chapters 2 and 5.
6. Berys Gaut offers a helpful outline of the various ways in which authorship theses can be formulated. In his terms, one option has to do with the ontology of the author: an actual person or a critical construct. My contention is that for the purposes of artistic appreciation, we need actual people. See Berys Gaut, *A Philosophy of Cinematic Art* (Cambridge, UK: Cambridge University Press, 2010), 99–102.
7. See, for recent examples, Michael Z. Newman and Elena Levine, *Legitimating Television: Media Convergence and Cultural Status*. (New York: Routledge, 2012), 38–58; and Jonathan Gray, "When Is the Author?" in *A Companion to Media Authorship*, ed. Jonathan Gray and Derek Johnson (Malden, MA: Wiley-Blackwell, 2013), 88–111.
8. I do not, by the way, deny that nonhuman animals have agency. I am merely attempting to offer a rough-and-ready characterization of human agency in particular.
9. This gloss has been influenced, in particular, by J. David Velleman, "What Happens When Someone Acts?" *Mind* 101, no. 403 (July 1992); Michael E. Bratman, "Reflection, Planning, and Temporally Extended Agency," *The Philosophical Review* 109, no. 1 (January 2000): 35–61; and Lynne Rudder Baker, *Naturalism and the First-Person Perspective* (Oxford: Oxford University Press, 2013), 183–98.
10. The *locus classicus* on this topic is, perhaps needless to say, W. K. Wimsatt Jr. and M. C. Beardsley, "The Intentional Fallacy," *The Sewanee Review* 54, no. 3 (July–September, 1946): 468–88. For a fairly recent example in television studies, see Glen Creeber, "The Joy of Text?" Television and Textual Analysis," *Critical Studies in Television* 1, no. 1 (2006): 81–88. For example, Creeber writes, "Despite [Stuart] Hall's crucial insight that there are various ways in which a TV program can be interpreted, his concept of a 'preferred meaning' [...] still betrays a dangerous assumption about readership: i.e., the belief that we can ever be sure of what meaning is 'preferred' or how a TV program was originally 'encoded' (echoing aspects of the 'Intentional Fallacy')" (82).

11. Michael E. Bratman, *Intention, Plans, and Practical Reason* (Cambridge, MA: Harvard University Press, 1987), especially 54.
12. For arguments along these lines, see Alfred R. Mele and Paul K. Moser, "Intentional Action," *Noûs* 28, no. 1 (1994): 39–68; Alfred R. Mele, "Conscious Intentions and Decisions," in *Effective Intentions: The Power of Conscious Will* (Oxford: Oxford University Press, 2009), 21–48; Paisley Livingston, *Art and Intention: A Philosophical Study* (Oxford: Oxford University Press, 2005), 42–49; and, in a somewhat different vein, the discussion of Babe Ruth in Stanley Cavell, "A Matter of Meaning It," in *Must We Mean What We Say?* Updated Edition (Cambridge, UK: Cambridge University Press, 2002), 23–35. I am grateful to Elliott Logan and Steven Peacock for this latter reference.
13. Thanks to Paisley Livingston for encouraging me to emphasize this point.
14. Michael E. Bratman, *Shared Agency* (Oxford: Oxford University Press, 2014), 15. This is Bratman's most recent statement of his planning theory of intention, initially advanced in *Intention, Plans*, and *Practical Reason*.
15. Bratman, *Intention, Plans, and Practical Reason*, 107–8.
16. E. D. Hirsch, *Validity in Interpretation* (New Haven, CT: Yale University Press, 1967), 17. This is not to endorse Hirsch's positive account of interpretation and meaning, which, as will be clear in Chapters 4 and 5, I do not.
17. Ibid.
18. See, for example, John Thornton Caldwell, *Production Culture* (Durham, NC: Duke University Press, 2008); Vicki Mayer, *Below the Line* (Durham, NC: Duke University Press, 2008); Eva Norvrup Redvall, *Writing and Producing the Television Drama in Denmark* (Basingstoke, UK: Palgrave Macmillan, 2013); Petr Szczepanik and Patrick Vonderau, eds., *Behind the Screen: Inside European Production Cultures* (Basingstoke, UK: Palgrave Macmillan, 2013); Bridget Conor, *Screenwriting: Creative Labor and Professional Practice* (New York: Routledge, 2014).
19. Gaut, *A Philosophy of Cinematic Art*, 108–14.
20. This is not to say that Perkins offers the most nuanced or sustained versions of these strategies. In the pages cited above, Gaut does not discuss Paisley Livingston's subtler sufficient control analysis of film authorship, although he does so later in the same chapter. I do not find Gaut's objections to Livingston's account threatening for reasons to be explained presently. See Gaut, *A Philosophy of Cinematic Art*, 118–24.
21. V. F. Perkins, *Film as Film: Understanding and Judging Movies* (Harmondsworth, UK: Penguin, 1972), 184.
22. Mittell, *Complex TV*, 88.
23. Ibid. As Mittell correctly notes and Gaut's brief indicates, sufficient control and restriction strategies for characterizing authorship have a more substantial history in film studies. Of course, the best known example here is *la politique des auteurs* promulgated in the pages of the *Cahiers du cinéma* in 1950s France and later appropriated by the American critic Andrew Sarris in the guise of "auteur theory." To my mind, the ambiguous and contested term *auteur* only troubles the conceptual clarification of authorship I seek here; hence, my intentional eschewal of it in the present context. See, in particular, François Truffaut, "A Certain Tendency of the French Cinema," and Andrew Sarris, "Notes on the Auteur Theory in 1962," in *Auteurs and Authorship: A Film Reader*, ed. Barry Keith Grant (Malden, MA: Blackwell, 2008), 9–18 and 35–45, respectively.

24. Although individual authorship is most commonly discussed with reference to show-runners in the U.S. context, it is often credited to writers in other television industries. This is evident, for example, in Manchester University Press' "The Television Series," which focuses mostly on British writers. Sarah Cardwell's installment of this series offers a particularly conscientious and subtle sufficient control argument. See Sarah Cardwell, *Andrew Davies* (Manchester, UK: Manchester University Press, 2005).
25. Paisley Livingston, *Cinema, Philosophy, Bergman: On Film as Philosophy* (Oxford: Oxford University Press, 2009), 71.
26. On this point, also see Sellors, *Film Authorship*.
27. Gaut, *A Philosophy of Cinematic Art*, 125. In earlier work, Gaut says something more expansive about this: "We have seen the importance of actors to a film, and considerations for the importance of scriptwriters and for those producers who concern themselves with the actual making of the film could easily be advanced as well. So there is no reason to deny the potential artistic contribution, and therefore co-authorship, of any of those mentioned ..." ("Film Authorship and Collaboration," in *Film Theory and Philosophy*, edited by Richard Allen and Murray Smith (Oxford: Oxford University Press, 2009), 149–72). It is not clear to me if Gaut still holds this view or not, so I do not want to saddle him with it, although if he does, then I would regard it as further evidence of the problem I identify in his above argument.
28. Caldwell, *Production Culture: Industrial Reflexivity and Critical Practice in Film and Television* (Durham, NC: Duke University Press, 2008), 201.
29. Livingston, *Cinema, Philosophy, Bergman*, 70.
30. Ibid., 71. Note that this goes for works with expressive content. Livingston allows for artworks without expressive content by referring to agents' "artistic and expressive goals" and artworks' "non-expressive artistic properties" (71).
31. Gaut, *A Philosophy of Cinematic Art*, 121.
32. Ibid., 133.
33. Note, however, that to the extent that Vince Gilligan had the power to overrule Slovis's decision making, the latter's claim to authorship is vitiated. It was, apparently, Gilligan who reassured the studio when questions were raised about Slovis's first batch of dailies.
34. Perkins, *Film as Film*, 184.
35. Livingston, *Cinema, Philosophy, Bergman*, 80.
36. Discussing a disagreement between director Spike Lee and actor Danny Aiello regarding the latter's character, Sal, in *Do the Right Thing*, Gaut claims that Aiello's vision of his character "wins the argument" in so far as *supposedly* it is evident from Aiello's performance that Sal is not a racist—despite Lee's claims to the contrary. But if it is true of the fiction that Sal is not a racist, this is ultimately true because of how Lee situated Aiello's performance in the film's overall organization. For example, surely part of the reason some viewers are inclined to interpret Sal as a man "pushed over the edge" rather than a racist is that, in the film's climax, when Radio Raheem and Buggin' Out enter the pizzeria, Mookie initially takes Sal's side and Buggin' Out hurls the first racist epithet—two important structural choices made by Lee.
37. For a discussion about editing's influence on screen comedy performances, see Jonah Weiner, "The Man Who Makes the World's Funniest People Even Funnier," *New York Times Magazine* (April 19, 2015). http://www.nytimes.com/

2015/04/19/magazine/the-man-who-makes-the-worlds-funniest-people-even-funnier.html?_r=0 (accessed September 21, 2015).
38. Alan Sepinwall, *The Revolution Was Televised From Buffy to Breaking Bad—The People and the Shows That Changed TV Drama Forever*. (Collingwood, Australia: Black Inc., 2013), 364. I am grateful to Elliott Logan for bringing this example to my attention.
39. For example, Caldwell writes that one of the aims of his research on production is "to understand the artistic contributions of crews," ("Authorship Below-the-Line," in *A Companion to Media Authorship* (Malden, MA: Wiley-Blackwell, 2008), edited by Jonathan Gray and Derek Johnson, 350). Incidentally, I think both his research and the artistic contributions of below-the-line crew members are important; I just don't think what Caldwell is investigating is authorship in the same sense I am analyzing it here. Also see Gaut, *A Philosophy of Cinematic Art*, 129–30.
40. Here some readers may wonder what makes the features I list artistic flaws. For the moment, I have to offer a promissory note that I intend to redeem in Chapter 6 on the evaluation of television. However, I take it that all of the features I mention are, at least, prima facie artistic flaws, except perhaps for didacticism, which may not be so straightforward. See Charles Repp, "What's Wrong with Didacticism?," *British Journal of Aesthetics* 52, no. 3 (July 2012): 271–85.
41. For example, see Margaret Lyons, "*The Newsroom* Is Incredibly Hostile toward Women," *Vulture* (July 17, 2012). Accessed February 29, 2016. http://www.vulture.com/2012/07/newsroom-aaron-sorkin-women-hostile-misogyny.html More examples follow below.
42. See, for example, Emily Nussbaum, "Broken News," *The New Yorker* (June 25, 2012), http://www.newyorker.com/magazine/2012/06/25/broken-news (accessed March 8, 2016); Alessandra Stanley, "So Sayeth the Anchorman," *The New York Times*. http://www.nytimes.com/2012/06/22/arts/television/the-newsroom-an-hbo-series-from-aaron-sorkin.html?_r=0 (accessed November 11, 2014); and, in less subtle terms, Daniel D'Addario, "Aaron Sorkin Gets More Sexist Every Year," *Salon.com* (September 10, 2013), http://www.salon.com/2013/09/09/aaron_sorkin_gets_more_sexist_every_year/).
43. Sellors, *Film Authorship*, 115.
44. C. Paul Sellors, "Collective Authorship in Film," *Journal of Aesthetics and Art Criticism* 65, no. 3 (Summer 2007), 266.
45. Livingston, *Cinema, Philosophy, Bergman*, 94.
46. Sellors, *Film Authorship*, 123.
47. Ibid., 124.
48. See, for example, Sondra Bacharach and Debora Tollefsen, "We Did It: From Mere Contributors to Coauthors," *Journal of Aesthetics and Art Criticism* 68, no 1. (Winter 2010).
49. Livingston, *Art and Intention*, 83.
50. Livingston, "On Authorship and Collaboration," 221.
51. Bratman, *Shared Agency*, 7–8.
52. Michael E. Bratman, "Shared Cooperative Activity," in *Faces of Intention Selected Essays on Intention and Agency* (Cambridge, UK: Cambridge University Press, 1999) 7–8.
53. Christopher Kutz, "Acting Together," *Philosophy and Phenomenological Research* 61, no. 1 (July 2000): 14.

54. Livingston, *Art and Intention*, 39.
55. Ibid, 82.
56. Bacharach and Tollefsen, "*We* Did It," 27.
57. Sellors, "Collective Authorship in Film," 267.
58. Newman and Levine, *Legitimating Television*, 38–58. It is also worth pointing out that I think Newman and Levine are absolutely right on this count: "Television shows, like any cultural artifacts, are the products of human agency. In this sense, they are authored by the people who create them …" (38). Newman and Levine and I are all trying to analyze somewhat more technical concepts of authorship—theirs an attributional one, mine a causal one. But it seems we agree on something basic.
59. Baker, *Naturalism*, 186–95.
60. I owe this point to Andrea Sauchelli. In thinking through the ramifications of the point, I have also been aided by Larry May, "Collective Inaction and Shared Responsibility," *Noûs* 24 (1990): 269–78.
61. Whether any members of the production collective, such as caterers and costume designers, should be exonerated is not a straightforward question, however. May's point is that "loosely structured groups" like this one may, indeed, bear shared responsibility for failing to act as a group to prevent harm. May's general claim strikes me as plausible enough, but the difficulty would be in working out the details of individual cases.
62. For an argument that holds Milch and Mann (and others) responsible, see Gary Baum, "What Really Happened on HBO's *Luck*—And Why Nobody Was Held Accountable," *The Hollywood Reporter* (November 25, 2013). Accessed December 16, 2014. http://www.hollywoodreporter.com/feature/what-really-happened-on-hbos-luck-and-why-nobody-was-held-accountable.html.

2 The Medium

Introduction

Because this is a book about appreciating the art of television, there had better be something out in the world identifiable as "television" which is distinctive in a way that demands a particular kind of appreciation. But here is a paradox that might immediately raise an obstacle: On the one hand, it is common to find in popular criticism claims to the effect that we are in the midst of a new Golden Age of television. This is not my claim, but, like mine, its plausibility depends on the existence of something identifiable and appreciable as "television." On the other hand, however, it is common to encounter in academic discourse claims regarding the end of television or, at least, the disappearance of television as it converges with a variety of other media in the digital age. What accounts for the currency of these apparently mutually exclusive claims, and what should we make of the paradox?

The temptation, I suspect, is to accept the truth of one and deny the truth of the other. However, it is important to recognize the possibility that the paradox is merely apparent rather than real. The question is whether both claims involve the same conception of television. I think they do not. Rather, the critics who claim we are in a new Golden Age of television are referring to television as an art, while scholars who speculate on the disappearance of television have in mind television as a medium (on a rather narrow construal of "medium"). The failure to make this distinction between medium and art form, for which I shall argue presently, is what generates the (apparent) paradox and a number of theoretical confusions prevalent in some of the contemporary television studies literature.[1]

Still, if scholars are right about the disappearance or, at least, convergence of the television medium with other media, then the concept of "the art of television" might seem to be similarly threatened. For it seems plausible that, if there is an art of television, it is partly constituted by the television medium. Or, to put it another way, it could seem there cannot be an art of television without the medium of television.

Therefore, my first goal in this chapter, before I argue for a distinction between the medium of television and the art of television, is simply to establish that there is in fact a medium of television distinct from a broader class of, say, moving image media. (As Berys Gaut has argued, media "nest," so the medium of television and the medium of the moving image are not mutually exclusive categories; a work may fall under the latter in virtue of falling under the former.)[2] Only if this initial aim is achieved can I proceed to the questions that sit at the heart of the chapter: Does our appreciation of television as an art in any way depend upon particular features of the television medium? If so, how and what features?

A Medium of Television?

The first order of business is to demonstrate that there is a television medium. Of course, it would be easier to simply stipulate that there is, pointing to the vast quantities of ink spilled on theorizing the nature of the medium in the early days of television studies. However, I think this would be premature for three reasons: First, although I will merely allude to rather than detail the history, early characterizations of the medium in terms of concepts such as "flow," "hot/cold," "the glance," and "liveness" have been roundly critiqued. Second, in the wake of these attempts to characterize the medium, general arguments advancing an anti-essentialist perspective have emerged and demand attention. Third, and relatedly, these theoretical arguments are bolstered by the fact that, at the moment, digital technology seems to be leading to the dispersal of what we call "television" across other media, thus raising the question of whether what used to be the medium of television has now (or will shortly be) converged with other media. So, even if the general, theoretical arguments for anti-essentialism fail, it may still be the case that, as a matter of historical, empirical fact, there is no longer anything unique about the television medium and/or it may no longer exist as a discrete kind, distinct from a broader category like that of the moving image.

Perhaps it will be helpful to begin by recalling that the field of television studies has a history of difficulty pinning down the nature of its object of study. Twenty-five years ago Stephen Heath anticipated the sort of uncertainty about the nature of the medium so prevalent today:

> Hence television is a somewhat difficult object, unstable, all over the place, tending derisively to escape anything we can say about it: given the speed of its changes (in technology, economics, programming), its interminable flow (of images and sounds, their endlessly disappearing present), its quantitative everydayness (the very quality of this medium each and every day), how can we *represent* television?[3]

Interestingly, for Heath, the assumption that features like "flow" and "everydayness" plausibly characterize the nature of television to some degree does not ameliorate the problem; ironically, those concepts seem to be at the root of it, despite the fact that they were theorized at least partly to explain television's nature. Thus, when traditional accounts of the essence of the medium—those centering on "flow" and "everydayness," as well as "liveness" and "the glance"—were extensively criticized in the years that followed, notably by John Thornton Caldwell, television studies' "object problem" became acute.[4]

In his critique, Caldwell notes that a "mythology of 'essential media differences' [between film and television] espoused by McLuhan forms the categorical basis for many future speculations on television, including glance theory."[5] Noël Carroll's subsequent, critical survey of putative differences between film and television elaborates this general point. As Carroll himself puts it, the goal of his brief is to "undermine these alleged distinctions ... [which] are based on too narrow a conception of TV (and sometimes of film)."[6] Moreover, Carroll claims, "Once one takes a broader view of the possibilities of TV ... the philosophical difference between film and TV, construed as a matter of contrasting essential characteristics, disappears."[7] This claim will sound familiar to those who know of Carroll's dogged attacks on medium essentialism in the context of film theory. What might be surprising, though, is the proximity of this view (and the support it lends) to that of contemporary television studies scholars who, like Carroll, are wary of ascribing essential properties to television.

Although not much of importance depends on whether my sociological speculations are right, the current anti-essentialist tendencies in television studies seem to be influenced both by general theoretical considerations and by the television medium's current transformation. Summarizing the field's general perspective on these matters in a recent, level-headed analysis, Alexhander Dhoest and Nele Simons observe, "The sense of an end is looming, both in conferences (e.g., the *Ends of Television Conference,* in Amsterdam, 2009) and in book titles (e.g., *The End of Television?, Television after TV,* and *Beyond the Box*)."[8] As the authors correctly note, this "sense of an end" is largely attributable to technological changes that have ushered in an "era of digitization and convergence,"[9] which, we all know, has substantively changed the way television is transmitted and received.

For some scholars, the radical nature of these changes has both transformed and thrown into question what it means for something to be "television." As Amanda Lotz puts it, "The convergence among technologies uncertainly connected other than by their digital language raises ambiguity about whether something like YouTube is best categorized as 'television,' 'video,' 'computer,' or perhaps even just as a 'screen' technology."[10] In a similar vein, Glen Creeber writes, "where 'television' starts and ends is increasingly difficult to determine in a world where we now watch TV on a number of different media platforms, meaning that any aesthetic characteristics of 'TV' (if we can now even call it that) seem to be as transitory and ephemeral as the ever-changing technology on which it is broadcast."[11] Moreover, for Creeber and like-minded scholars, the shifting boundaries of "television" in the era of media convergence serve to alert us of the perils of medium essentialism.[12]

Thus, in the wake of sustained criticism of traditional, essentialist theories of television and momentous technological change, anti-essentialism now enjoys considerably currency in television studies. John Hartley, for example, holds a particularly bold anti-essentialist view: "What is the 'is' of television? Luckily for those who don't like metaphysical questions, the answer is that it doesn't have one. Television is a product of history and therefore subject to change. Because it doesn't have an essence it is defined by its context."[13] Call Hartley's view *strong anti-essentialism* about the medium of television.

Strong anti-essentialism is motivated by the observation that television is not a natural kind, like water, the identity of which is constituted by an intrinsic essence such as a chemical structure. Rather, as Hartley correctly notes, television is a historical kind and, moreover, a cultural kind. As such, television is not defined by a timeless, unchanging essence in the way that water might be.[14] However, strong anti-essentialism does not follow from these facts. The central problem is that Hartley erroneously assumes that the question, "What is the 'is' of television?," presupposes an answer comprising a set of necessary and sufficient conditions that constitutes the *intrinsic* essence of television. The error here is perhaps clearer if we consider other examples: What is the "is" of being a husband? being European? being an American League team in Major League Baseball? "Husband," "European," and "American League team" are all concepts that lack an intrinsic essence and are, rather, defined *relationally*.

It does not follow, however, that they do not have essences, where "essence" is just the set of properties that are individually necessary and jointly sufficient for being a member of a particular kind. Like television, these are cultural kinds, the identities of which are shaped by history. Plausibly, such cultural kinds have essences that are defined relationally (at least in part) and that change over time. In fact, some philosophers of science have even advanced a neo-essentialist view according to which natural kinds have essences constituted by relational properties. In short, Hartley's view is undermined by the plausible distinction between intrinsic essentialism in particular and essentialism *tout court*. Showing that television has no intrinsic essence does not demonstrate that it has no essence at all.[15]

However, suggesting that television's essence is partly a matter of its relational properties does not entail that its essence is *wholly* relational. It is, for example, hard to imagine a concept of television under which television lacked *any* sort of material basis whatsoever. Here we see an additional way in which Hartley's anti-essentialism needs refinement: his claim that television is defined by history is too strong. For although television is partly defined by history—that is, by the relational properties it possesses as a result of being historically situated—it is not *solely* defined by history. In addition, the television medium is partly defined by certain physical or material properties. On the one hand, this is obvious: it is simply not the case that the television medium, as we currently conceive of it or as we conceived of it in the past, could be constituted by no other physical materials than Silly Putty. On the other hand, it is much harder to say what exactly those physical properties are, not least because it appears they have changed over time.

This tension—between acknowledging that the television medium *is* changing over time and still holding on to the idea that there is something distinctive about television—is prevalent in much contemporary theoretical writing on television. For example, this awkwardly expressed thought by Creeber is indicative: "So, rather than imply that I understand what the *essential* aesthetics of television are ... I hope this book reveals just how varied, multifarious, and historically situated any medium-specific aesthetic style really is ..."[16] The difficulty is this: On the one hand, Creeber wants to deny there is essence of television, which, he appears to think, would be incompatible with what Tom O'Regan identifies as "television's changing aesthetic norms."[17] But on the other hand, Creeber claims that those changing aesthetic norms are nevertheless "medium-specific" in some way he leaves unexplained.

Notwithstanding the historically situated nature of television, it is hard to shrug the intuitive pull of the idea that there is something distinctive about the medium—that its identity is at least partly constituted by certain medium-specific features. And yet as technology continues to develop and convergence proceeds apace, it is increasingly difficult to ascertain what those might be. As Jason Jacobs has eloquently asked, "Can we continue to think about the specificity of a medium that seems so dispersed and unstable as an object of study?"[18] And, if so, how?

Of course, at this point, one option would be to resolve the dilemma by answering "No" to Jacobs's question, yet still deny that strong anti-essentialism follows from this. For it could be the case that series like *Game of Thrones* (HBO 2011–present) are indeed of a medium that is constituted by both relational and intrinsic properties—just not the medium of television. Perhaps Laurent Jullier is correct is his assessment that "in these times of transmediality [...] and relocation [...], the 'audiovisual narrative' object has a greater importance and clarity in daily life than the 'cinema' [or 'television'] object, and whether the story is being told in a TV series or a feature film does not much matter as long as it is a good one."[19] This is, after all, one broader implication of media convergence, which Noël Carroll has articulated in characteristically lucid fashion.

Among numerous articles and books that address questions of medium essentialism and medium specificity, Carroll's essay, "TV and Film: A Philosophical Perspective," constitutes his most sustained engagement with television. I shall quote Carroll at length here, both to present his understanding of television vis-à-vis film and, relatedly, his hypothesis about media convergence bringing into relief a single category of "the moving image":

> Of course, the features of TV that are often cited as its essential features, especially in contrast to film, have some basis in fact ... Observing

these features, where they obtain, is informative, especially for critical purposes. It is just not informative in the way that many theorists often suppose. That is, they are not necessary or fully comprehensive features of all TV, but only contingent features of groups of historically specific TV productions. It is useful to note such contingent regularities. The problem only arises when the theorist tries to extrapolate these local regularities into the essence of TV ...

This is not to deny that some TV differs from some films in the way the theorist says ... But these differences, though often critically significant, do not add up to a categorical distinction between TV and film.

In truth, my own suspicion is that as time and technology advance, TV and film will continue to converge. Perhaps they will become amalgamated and combined with digital computers to the point that we no longer talk of TV or film, but more generically of moving images. From that point in the future, we will look back to the history of film and the history of TV and think of them as parts or phases in the history of the moving image, a trans-media form of expression and communication ... that has sometimes been implemented by film, sometimes by TV, sometimes by digital computers, sometimes by some combination of all of these, and sometimes by that we cannot yet imagine.[20]

It is also worth noting that elsewhere Carroll proposes an essentialist definition of the moving image—that is, a definition of the concept in terms of necessary and sufficient conditions—despite the fact that he was reluctant to do so in his earlier work.[21]

Carroll's view has undeniable intuitive appeal. It strikes a balance between the strong essentialism of theories of "flow," "the glance," and "liveness" on the one hand and Hartley's strong anti-essentialism on the other. It recognizes the relevance of "contingent regularities ... of historically specific TV productions" to our critical practices. And it is empirically accurate in its assessment of the convergence of what I want to call the *vehicular media* of film, television, and computers. Nevertheless, we might wonder if Carroll has actually shown that TV and film are not distinct media.

In fact, I think Carroll's essay only gives the appearance of having shown that TV and film are not distinct media—an appearance that arises because of a particular ambiguity that surrounds his use of the terms "categorical distinction" and "moving image." When Carroll claims that the "contingent features of groups of historically specific TV productions ... do not add up to a categorical distinction between TV and film," what exactly does he mean? What category does he have in mind? Suppose, for the sake of argument, Carroll is right that there is no ontological difference between TV and film. Then, that is one sort of categorical difference he is justified in denying. But from this it does not follow that TV and film are not different media unless one is committed to a strong form of medium essentialism. That is, if we reject strong medium essentialism, according to which media are individuated by their essential, timeless natures, it is perfectly coherent to maintain that TV and film are different media in the absence of further argumentation to the contrary. The debate about whether they are of a single medium or not then rests on the question of how media are individuated.

Carroll evidently thinks that media are individuated by their physical properties, which appears to lend support to his hypothesis regarding the convergence of film and television, as well as his own definition of the moving image. However, there are reasons to wonder if such a conception of media is adequate.

Before beginning this line of inquiry, though, it is worth pointing out that Carroll's "medium materialism" creates problems for his own account of the moving image.[22] Carroll often speaks ambiguously of the category of the moving image. In the "TV and Film" essay, he refers to it as "a mode of communication and expression that can be implemented cinematically, videographically, digitally, and/or in ways of which we have still to conceive" and as "a trans-media form of expression and communication ... that has sometimes been implemented by film, sometimes by TV ..."[23] The question is what exactly he means here by "mode of communication and expression" and "trans-media form of expression and communication." It seems clear enough here that he does not conceive of the category of the moving image as a medium, because he refers to it as a "trans-media form." It is strange that shortly after this, Carroll claims this "form" "has sometimes been implemented by film, sometimes by TV," thus raising the question of what constitutes those categories, given that he denies both that they are distinct media and distinct art forms.

On the contrary, across the evolution of Carroll's attempts to theorize the nature of the moving image, there is ample evidence to suggest he conceives of it as an art form. In his 1996 essay, "Defining the Moving Image," he writes, "The moving image is not a medium-specific notion for the simple reason that the artform that concerns us, though born in film, has already undergone and will continue to undergo transformation as new media are invented and integrated into its history."[24] In his 2003 essay, "Forget the Medium!," he claims, "if we put the two preceding criticisms together—that each artform is a multiplicity of (sometimes overlapping) media, and that the relevant media are open to physical reinvention—then we arrive at the conclusion that film is not one medium, but many media ..."[25] And, most recently, in *The Philosophy of Motion Pictures,* Carroll mentions "at least one limitation in calling the relevant artform *moving pictures* ... Thus, rather than speaking of moving pictures, it may be more advisable to talk of *moving images.*"[26] So, despite a general ambiguity around the category that term "moving image" picks out, the best candidate is a particular art form.

However, if the moving image is an art form, Carroll's account faces two serious problems. The first is that the account cannot make the intuitive distinction between art and non-art made in the same medium. For example, according to the standard distinction, an instructional film screened for factory employees and *Chimes at Midnight* (1965) are both instances of the medium of film, but only the latter is an instance of the art form of film. Prima facie, this is a necessary distinction that does important analytic work. But according to Carroll's account, no such distinction is possible. Rather, it seems he must allow that based on his account the instructional film is an instance of the art form of the moving image—a conclusion we should resist.

The second major difficulty for Carroll's conception of the moving image as an art form is that it collapses categories that are important to our critical practices. A number of prominent film and television theorists, such as V. F. Perkins and Jason Jacobs, and philosophers including Kendall Walton and Carroll himself, have persuasively argued that the proper appreciation of a given artwork necessarily involves correctly identifying it as a member of a particular category.[27] In the context of film, for example, Perkins claims, "we can evolve useful criteria only for specific types of film, not for the cinema. Our standards of judgment will have to follow from definitions of types in terms of both their possibilities and their limitations."[28] More specifically, Perkins writes, "the claims we make for a comedy by Howard Hawks will not yield ammunition for use against an Ingmar Bergman allegory because they belong to types almost as distinct as cartoon and documentary."[29] Similarly, according to Carroll's own proposal for film evaluation, "the pluralistic-category approach": "Movies are evaluated in terms of whether they succeed or fail in realizing their purposes. Generally, these purposes are rooted in the categories the motion pictures under evaluation inhabit—which categories include genres, subgenres, cycles, styles, movements, and so forth."[30]

If this general thesis is correct—and categories of the sort Carroll enumerates are relevant to our proper appreciation of works of film and other arts—the problem with subsuming film and television under the single art form of the moving image is this: *Qua* arts, television and film have developed somewhat different general purposes and, importantly, this is plausibly a result of the distinct capacities of the respective media. True, a film like *Neighbors* (2014) and a television show like *Saturday Night Live* (NBC 1975–present) are both comedies and, to this extent, can be evaluated *qua* comedies. However, a comparative evaluation of these works would also need to take into account the fact that part of the humor of *Neighbors* stems from foul language and raunchiness that is not available to *SNL* as a program on network television. Furthermore, whereas scenes of *Neighbors* could be reshot when an actor flubbed a joke, *SNL* has no comparable luxury; the comedy of the latter, which is shot live, necessarily depends on the ability of actors to perform "in the moment"—to execute their jokes, to not break character, and, sometimes, to improvise new material as a result of unforeseen developments. For these reasons, the more salient categories of evaluation here are "film comedy" and "live television comedy."

In general, then, the problem with the putative art form of the moving image is that it denies us the ability to make categorical distinctions between television and film that are necessary for the proper appreciation of works in those distinct categories. As Jacobs puts it, "It is hard to 'forget the medium' of television precisely because its various instantiations can insist on our taking its value and achievements as a medium into account."[31] Here, Carroll may reply that the art form of the moving image does not foreclose upon the possibility of drawing categorical distinctions because the relevant categories are neither film/television medium nor film/television art, but rather some *other* set of categories that I have not canvassed as possibilities. However, in the absence of an argument to this effect, it is hard to see what those categories would be. This difficulty is related to my earlier uncertainty regarding what Carroll means when he claims that, historically, the art of the moving image has been instantiated by film and television. We can now see the relevant question more precisely: what kinds of things are film and television when Carroll conceives of them this way? Under what broader category do they fall? And what are the other members of that category?

At the same time, Carroll's conception of an art form of the moving image leaves us guessing as to what sorts of categories film and television are—assuming he is persuaded that this distinction is essential to our critical practices. We also have good prima facie reasons to think that in fact we typically use the terms "film" and "television" to categorize works according to their medium *given a correct understanding of the concept*. Moreover, as David Davies argues, there is evidence to support the intuition that "these groupings ... are most naturally thought of as the basic *categories* of art that bear more fundamentally than ... other principles of grounding ... upon our understanding of things as artworks."[32] In contrast to Carroll, then, I want to argue that we need to hold on to the standard dyads—the medium of television versus the medium of film and the art of television versus the art of film—in order to properly appreciate different kinds of works that are all, undeniably, part of a broader category of moving images. In order to do so, I now need to show what is wrong with Carroll's "medium materialism" and offer an alternative characterization of a medium.

Rethinking Media

As a point of reference, here is how Carroll characterizes his conception of a medium, against which I shall now argue. Writing on the topic of medium specificity in *The Philosophy of Motion Pictures*, he says, "With respect to the debates to be canvassed [here], the notion of media is to be understood primarily in terms of *physical* media. Media, on this construal, are (1) the materials (the stuff) out of which works are made and/or (2) the physical instruments employed to shape or to otherwise fashion those materials."[33] Of course, Carroll is not unaware that some philosophers prefer to draw a distinction, for which I shall advocate presently, between a physical or, more precisely, vehicular medium and an artistic medium. However, he thinks the notion of artistic medium is not what is involved in medium specificity claims and, in any case, the term is too ambiguous to be of much analytic use. Here is how he puts the latter claim:

> Obviously what is meant by the phrase "artistic medium" is very vague, referring sometimes to the physical materials out of which artworks are constructed, sometimes to the implements that are used to do the constructing, and sometimes to formal elements of design that are available to artists in a given practice. This ambiguity alone might discourage us from relying on the notion of the medium as a theoretically useful concept. In fact, I think that we might fruitfully dispense with it completely, at least in terms of the ways in which it is standardly deployed by aestheticians.[34]

To be fair to Carroll, the concept of an artistic medium, as well as the reasons for insisting upon a distinction between this and a physical or vehicular medium, has been greatly clarified since he wrote this passage in 2003, thanks to work by David Davies, Berys Gaut, and Dominic Lopes.[35] Still, drawing on the work of these philosophers in particular, I want to argue for retaining the distinction.

First, though, what is wrong with the view that a medium is simply the physical stuff out of which works are made and/or the physical implements for shaping that material? One initial problem is that some artworks, such as literary works, are not constituted by physical materials. Carroll seems willing to bite the bullet here and accept the view that literary works therefore have no medium: "Literature, for instance, does not appear to have a medium at all. This may sound strange to you. You may be tempted to regard words as the distinctive medium of literature. And yet, are words the right sort of thing to constitute a medium? Aren't media, in the most clear-cut sense, physical, and are words physical in any aesthetically interesting way?"[36] However, this is simply begging the question. Furthermore, despite the fact that our *access* to tokens of many multiple-instance works of the literary, cinematic, televisual, and musical variety depends upon the existence of a physical template (e.g., a book, a film strip, a videotape, a CD), the works themselves all seem to lack physical properties in Carroll's sense—otherwise, they could not be multiply instantiated. The sheer number of works in this category, which would be media-less according to Carroll's account, ought to make us hesitate in assenting to his view.

A related problem is that it seems implausible that the above-mentioned class of works could possess the representational and semantic properties we commonly ascribe to them if they did not have a medium. It seems implausible that, say, a fictional character named Mrs. Crawley (Penelope Wilton) could be represented at all or that *Downton Abbey* (ITV 2010–2015) could be about class tensions in the absence of any medium whatsoever. How, exactly, would such representations and meanings be transmitted? In a reply to a critical essay by film theorist Murray Smith, Carroll attempts to soften his position: "But don't we have to access literature through some medium? Of course. Yet we need to draw a distinction between cases where it is claimed that the physical media associated with an artform have an artistically significant impact on the nature of what is created in that artform, versus the case where the media in question are merely delivery systems."[37] Even if we suppose this is true, neither does it follow that a medium need be constituted by physical materials, nor that arts like literature lack a medium in *any* substantive sense.

On the contrary, it seems more plausible to say that artworks are standardly embodied in a *vehicular medium*—roughly, the structure that gives us access to the work, which comprises materials that are either physical (e.g., bronze in the case of sculpture) or symbolic (e.g., lexical signs in the case of literature). As Paisley Livingston has painstakingly documented, a work/vehicle distinction along these lines can be found in philosophical investigations of art as far back as the late nineteenth century. According to Livingston, Hermann Siebek and Eduard von Hartmann "both used the term *Vehikel* to refer to the material or perceptible bases of aesthetic objects and works of art."[38] As this use of the term suggests, the general idea motivating a distinction between an artwork and its vehicle is that the two do not necessarily share the exact same properties.

The necessity for such a distinction is perhaps most clearly seen in the case of the "multiple-instance" arts, including literature and music. In rare cases of literature, such as George Herbert's "Easter Wings," the way in which the work is concretely instantiated is essential to its identity; if you don't see the poem printed on the page, you miss one of its more important artistic properties. Typically, however, the poem *qua* work of art is not to be identified with a physical text because, among other reasons, one can apprehend the same artistically relevant properties of the work through hearing the poem read aloud.[39]

That said, a further motivation for the work/vehicle distinction is the thought that, in Livingston's words, "reference to the vehicle or artistic structure alone does not suffice to identify the object of critical evaluation, or what artistic and aesthetic appreciation is really about."[40] Why not? The literature on this topic is extensive, but work within the last thirty years or so has emphasized the ways in which artistically relevant properties adhere to certain artworks (e.g., Marcel Duchamp's snow shovel, Andy Warhol's Brill boxes, Tracy Emin's messy bed) that do not adhere to their quotidian counterpart objects. The puzzle is that the artworks and their ordinary object counterparts are perceptually indiscernible: In these sorts of cases, perhaps counter-intuitively at first, an encounter with the structure in which the work is embodied isn't enough to apprehend all of its artistically relevant properties. One also needs to see the structure as located within a particular socio-historical context. The proposed solution to the puzzle, then,

62 *The Medium*

is to distinguish between the object of appreciation, the artwork properly so-called, and its vehicle.[41]

Here, Carroll could reply that reconceiving his notion of a physical medium as a vehicular medium leaves his central points unharmed. Establishing that even artworks without a physical medium have a vehicular medium shows neither that the vehicular medium is "artistically significant," more than "merely [a] delivery system," nor that there is a need for the additional category of the artistic medium. Let's take each issue in turn.

First, Carroll's characterization of the physical (or, as I prefer, vehicular) medium as a "delivery system" lacking an "artistically significant impact" on the works created in a given art form strikes me as very odd. The vehicular medium is artistically relevant precisely because of the ways in which it enables or impedes the realization of certain artistic properties and/or effects. As Berys Gaut argues, "Artworks are by definition works, not natural products: they are the products of action. And appreciating them involves in part appreciating them as an *achievement*. That involves understanding what the artist was aiming at, and what difficulties she had to reach to overcome her goal."[42] Along with Gaut, I would emphasize that some of the opportunities and challenges artists face, which are thus relevant to our appreciation of their achievements, depend on the vehicular media in which they work.

Here are some examples in support of these claims: I often screen the Stan Brakhage short film *Black Ice* (1994) in my introduction to film courses. The undergraduate students in these courses, many of whom have never encountered celluloid film, tend to be unimpressed at first. Then I tell them that, assuming a frame rate of twenty-four fps (frames per minute) and a run time of about ninety seconds, Brakhage painted by hand in the ballpark of 2,160 frames of 16mm film—that is, 2,160 rectangular pieces of celluloid about 10mm wide by 7.5mm high—in order to create the images they saw. In some of my lectures, a collective gasp is audible at this point. For the magnitude of Brakhage's achievement is not fully appreciable until one understands what challenges he faced in manipulating the vehicular medium in order to create the work. Here is another example: Imagine two indiscernible images next to one another in a gallery. Both seem to be rather mundane photographic portraits of a woman wearing a woven sweater. The artistic achievement they represent is minimal. However, it turns out that only one of the images is a photograph. The other is a photorealist painting that has been painstakingly completed. Everything else being equal, surely the painting is a greater artistic accomplishment than the photograph by virtue of the capacities and constraints of the respective vehicular media. Finally, recall the earlier comparison of *Neighbors* and *Saturday Night Live*. The live shooting of the latter renders it a different kind of artistic achievement. A proper appreciation of *Saturday Night Live* ought to take into account what the show achieves relative to the challenges presented by a live broadcast—challenges that are not faced by film comedies like *Neighbors*. I will have more to say about the artistic relevance of the medium presently, when I turn my attention to the ways in which the medium bears upon our appreciation of televisual art. But now I need to address the outstanding matters of advancing an alternative account of what a medium is and, more specifically, saying something about the distinctive features of the television medium.

I claimed that one motivation for the idea of the vehicular medium is that a work's being constituted of particular materials or in a certain vehicular medium is insufficient for its having certain sorts of artistically relevant properties—say, representational, expressive, or semantic properties. A piece of canvass covered in drops and splotches of paint from a fallen palette does not represent, express, or mean anything. For something to be a work, properly so-called, and have representational, expressive, or semantic properties, something more is needed. So, how is it that vehicular media are able to transmit content, broadly conceived? We need a conception of a medium that, as David Davies puts it, "mediates between what the artist does, naively construed, and what the work 'says,' in a broad sense, in virtue of what the artist does."[43]

For this reason, we need a more robust concept of "medium" that has an inescapable element of agency built into it. Before I said that it was hard to imagine how we could have a representation of Mrs. Crawley in the absence of a medium. Neither, though, does a mere audiovisual display that depicts the actress, Penelope Wilton, constitute a representation of Mrs. Crawley. It is also necessary that such an audiovisual display be intended to be perceived in certain ways, against the backdrop of somewhat stable (if historically contingent and variable) creative practices. That is, television shows and other artworks possess representational, expressive, and semantic properties, because they are the products of relatively coherent, stable practices of working with/in vehicular media. And, as I argued in the first chapter, such practices are only conceivable with reference to intentional agency. Note that I do not characterize such practices as "art practices" or "art-making practices" because I think it is imperative that we retain the distinction between art and non-art within a single medium. For my purposes, the relevant practices could be described as production practices, creative practices, artisanal practices, and so forth.

So, while I do not presume to be offering a full analysis of the concept, a rough and ready characterization of "medium" (in the broad sense close but not equivalent to "artistic medium") that will serve the present purpose is this: A medium is something like a cluster of relatively, stable, coherent practices of making things in a particular vehicular medium. I acknowledge this account needs further development. In particular, there are difficult questions to be asked about just how stable and coherent such practices need to be to constitute a numerically distinct medium. Furthermore, to what extent can one distinct medium change qualitatively before it becomes a numerically distinct medium? And how are vehicular media, which partly constitute media in the broader sense, to be individuated? Yet while further elaboration is clearly needed, it may also be the case that some such questions admit of no determinate answers. There may be no answers to such questions beyond what is implicit in our practices—an idea to which I shall return in the next chapter.

Nevertheless, with this rough-and-ready characterization in hand, we are in a position to defend and explain a distinction between the film medium and the television medium. Historically, the distinction has been understood as being constituted by materials. So, at one point what seemed unique to the television medium was the technology that permitted live transmission of a relatively impoverished square image, and so forth. And what seemed to distinguish television from film was the fact that the latter medium lacked those materials and was constituted by materials that television lacked. However, it is now evident that materials alone are insufficient for distinguishing the two media (although in truth materials alone were *never* sufficient for this purpose). Increasingly, the materials of the two mediums are indistinct: many television series and feature films are shot on HD video, after which they are subject to the same CGI manipulations. Then, works in both mediums are digitally encoded so that they may be electronically transmitted and screened (whether at home or in a cinema) or purchased on DVD or Blu-Ray. In terms of materials or vehicular medium, it could easily turn out to be the case that arkworks like *Game of Thrones* and *The Hunger Games* (2012) do not differ in any substantive way. And this is precisely Carroll's point. But although Carroll and others are right to deny that materials alone are sufficient to distinguish the specificity of television, it does not follow that there is no television medium at all. For the medium is constituted not by those materials alone, but also by a cluster of shared practices making things with those materials. This is why, even in the era of convergence, it is possible and important to distinguish between the medium of television and the medium of film, which may be partly constituted by the same vehicular medium and some of the same practices of working in it, but are also partly constituted by distinct practices.[44]

There is, I think, at least one central way the mediums of television and film differ in virtue of possessing different practices of working with what may be the same vehicular medium. Television and film differ in virtue of having quite distinct sets of practices for individuating their works temporally, establishing the temporal duration of those works, and affording viewers temporal access to those works. This is all rather abstract, but the central idea here is this: The two mediums comprise divergent practices of shaping the temporality of works therein; they also comprise distinct understandings, shared by both creators and viewers, of how the temporality of those works affects the ways in which viewers are to approach them. In other words, the film and television mediums are partly distinguished by distinct creative and appreciative practices.[45]

On the one hand, the film medium is partly characterized by (1) the understanding of both non-art and art objects created in it as instances of the stand-alone or one-off film, with duration in the vicinity of a few minutes to a few hours, that is to be accessed in its entirety on a single occasion, and (2) a diverse and complex set of practices for making films along these lines. Somewhat more concretely, we can say that, despite the diversity in practices comprising the medium of film, a general link or similarity is constituted by the fact that the ultimate aim of all these practices is the creation of a single film, intended to be watched in a sitting. Intertwined with this understanding of the medium are practices like writing in three-act structure, casting just one actor for each character, creating formal or structure closure at the end of the work.[46]

On the other hand, the television medium is partly characterized by (1) the understanding of "the work" as being temporally subdivided in various ways: series, season, episode, format, and so forth, and as thus potentially having different sets of temporal boundaries, some of which are malleable in a way the temporal boundaries of films are not, and (2) a diverse and complex set of practices for making these temporally diverse and malleable kinds of works. In the context of television, works are regularly created with no sense of when or how they might end, and are temporally prolonged, bit by bit, for years on end. In such cases, the temporal boundaries of works change after they have come into existence and, somewhat oddly, this happens through the creation of shorter distinct works that together constitute the longer ones. Relatedly, viewers' access to works in the television medium, whether narrative dramas, sitcoms, news magazines, or documentary miniseries, is at once typically a one-off affair *and* piecemeal and processional.

Correspondingly, rather different sets of practices are interwoven with the understanding of the temporality of works in the television medium as more diverse, more variable, more diffuse than of those in the film medium. Here, we might think of writing for narrative television in terms of A plots, B plots, C plots, D plots, and E plots; of shaping narrative structure around commercial breaks; of using the extended passage of real time between access to constituent parts of the work to construct the passage of diegetic time; of casting different actors to portray a single character; of creating "cliffhangers"; of writing for a documentary series in more depth and detail than would be possible in a feature-length documentary film; and more. Because these various ways in which television's temporal boundaries may be diffuse and expansive collectively constitute a single differential feature of the television medium, it will be helpful to refer to them with a single term. My preference is for "temporal prolongation," which, from its use in music theory, carries with it connotations of a temporally unfolding, yet organically unified structure.[47]

An interlocutor inspired by Carroll's work might object here that the preceding remarks just replace one wrong-headed assumption about a medium's essence with another. That is, it may look as though I am still "essentializing" the medium—only now I am positing, as the essence of the medium, a specific cluster of practices for working with particular materials, (that is, a vehicular medium) rather than just materials themselves. However, while a real advocate of medium essentialism might be under the illusion that materials constitute the timeless, intrinsic essence of the medium, my own claim is significantly more moderate. My emphasis on the ways in which shared practices partly constitute a medium necessarily allows that media themselves change as practices change. Thus, my claim—that part of what distinguishes the television medium from the film medium are different practices of working with temporality—should be understood as identifying a contingent fact about the state of the medium as it is currently constituted rather than as advancing a modal claim about the only possible nature of the medium. As Gaut notes, only the latter view is rightly identified with the sort of medium essentialism that Carroll has criticized.[48]

Moreover, as a claim regarding a contingent truth, my thesis about the distinction between the film and television media can also appeal to at least one difference in materials. For although liveness may not be the essence of television, I think the possibility of live broadcasting is something that partly distinguishes it from film.[49] In this sense, television studies' sense of the importance of liveness has always been on the right track.[50] But the claim needs to be stated with care to give it plausibility. In particular, it should not be understood as asserting that liveness is a *unique* or *defining* property of television. It is evident that liveness is a feature of the radio medium and is thus not sufficient for something to be television; it is also clear that liveness is not necessary for something to be television because little television is actually live. However, following Gaut's argumentation, we may avail ourselves of the concept of a "differential feature," to argue that liveness partly distinguishes television from film and furthermore to explain the relevance of liveness to the television medium.[51] For although liveness is not unique to television and, indeed, less television is live than is not, this feature can nevertheless play an important role in explaining and evaluating works in the medium in a way it does not in the context of the film medium—an idea that I have flagged already and that I will pursue further in Chapter 6.

More generally, the thesis underlying this claim is, in Gaut's words, that "medium-specific features should be construed not in absolute terms [i.e., as *unique* to the medium], but rather as being relative to other media, as differential features, that is, as features that differ between one group of media and another specified group."[52] This is part of the reason for insisting upon a conception of a medium partly in terms of creative practices—that is, in terms of relational properties. Such an understanding of a medium furnishes a more moderate, plausible version of medium specificity—one that avoids Carroll's criticisms precisely because it does not presuppose that media are individuated in virtue of possessing unique, intrinsic essences. Thus, our interest is not in the set of properties putatively shared by only and all instances of television; rather, because we want to understand the relationship between television and film, our interest is in those properties possessed by (at least some) instances of television ("the target class") that are not possessed by films ("the contrast class").

Gaut notes a potential objection here—"the triviality worry"—according to which shifting focus from unique or even essential properties to differential properties dilutes medium-specificity claims to such an extent that they simply become trivial. This challenge is, of course, relevant to my present purpose. I have claimed that the television medium is distinct from the film medium in at least two ways: (1) creative practices for temporally individuating works; and (2) the possibility of liveness in television. But because these are claims about contingent features, rather than necessary and sufficient conditions, one may wonder if they carry any real explanatory power. My next goal is to show that they do, both in terms of establishing film and television as distinct art forms and in terms of facilitating our appreciation of individual works in those art forms. For the present purpose, though, I will focus only on television's temporal prolongation, leaving the matter of liveness for a later discussion of the medium's relevance to our evaluation of televisual works.

The Art of Television

Drawing on my claims regarding the differential features of media, I want to now establish that film and television are not only two distinct media but two distinct art forms. It seems plausible for two distinct mediums to be instantiated in a single art form and, despite his medium skepticism, Carroll seems to have something like this in mind when he suggests that the art of the moving image has been "implemented" by both television and film. To build the case that the film medium and television medium do in fact constitute two distinct art forms, we can felicitously make use of this plausible thesis advanced by Berys Gaut: "For a medium to constitute an art form it must instantiate artistic properties that are distinct from those that are instantiated by other media."[53]

First, though, as Angela Curran notes in remarks on Gaut's book, we need to be clear about what's meant by "artistic properties."[54] Following a widely, albeit not universally accepted distinction in philosophical aesthetics, I take artistic properties, broadly construed, to comprise both aesthetic properties and non-aesthetic properties. In turn, I understand aesthetic properties to be (roughly) objective, perceptible features of an object that often (but not always) have an evaluative valence. (Although this characterization will hardly be met with widespread assent, I should stress that it is not *meant* to be controversial, because I have no desire to wade into debates regarding the nature of aesthetic properties here.) Properties characteristically regarded as "aesthetic" include, for example, beautiful, unified, balanced, trite, garish, lifeless, serene, and dynamic. In contrast, non-aesthetic artistic properties are, I take it, those properties that are not directly perceptible—that is, not appreciable merely through an experiential encounter with an object—but are, nevertheless, artistically relevant. By being artistically relevant, I mean that such properties matter to our appreciation of the works in which they are instantiated—to our understanding, interpretation, and evaluation of those works. Here we might think of properties such as being original, being derivative, being symbolic of x, being a reference or allusion to y, being in the style of z, and so forth.

However, Gaut's Medium Specificity of Forms (MSF) thesis seems to involve a somewhat narrower construal of the notion of artistic properties. Clarifying matters in his reply to Curran, Gaut says, "What I mean by 'artistic properties' in this context is artistic evaluative properties, and properties, such as narrative structure, that can figure in the grounds of artistic evaluations. So [MSF] is true if either there are distinctive artistic values or distinctive devices (or effects) in cinema."[55] Later in the book I shall explore the questions of *how* such devices and effects "figure in the grounds of artistic evaluations" and whether television instantiates particular artistic values. For now, though, I want to focus on the understanding of "artistic properties" in MSF as devices and effects in order to argue for a distinct art form of television.

My general claim, then, is that television is an art form (distinct from related moving-image art forms, like film) because it achieves distinct artistic effects in virtue of the medium's differential features. Moreover, a *full* appreciation of the artistic achievement of a particular instance of television necessarily involves correctly classifying that work as *in* the television medium, the nature and differential features of which one must have at least a tacit conception. Of these differential features, it seems to me that temporal prolongation is the most salient—an intuition that will ground the focus of an extended argument in support of three related theses. (1) In a variety of fictional series, including daytime soap operas and prime-time serial dramas such as *One Life to Live* (ABC 1968–2012) and *The Good Wife* (CBS 2009–2016), as well as long-running sitcoms and other more episodically based programs, such as *M*A*S*H* (CBS 1972–1983) and *Friends* (NBC 1994–2004), temporal prolongation fosters a particular, intense kind of engagement with characters. (2) In suspense dramas, such as *Breaking Bad* (AMC 2008–2013) and *Homeland* (Showtime 2011–present), temporal prolongation sustains narrative suspense over longer periods of time and with more intensity than film. (3) In comedies, such as *Curb Your Enthusiasm* (HBO 1999–present) and *Arrested Development* (Fox 2003–2006; Netflix 2013), temporal prolongation affords the possibility of long-running, recurring gags, which furnish a particular sort of cognitive pleasure unachievable in film (at least, as film is presently constituted).

A few disclaimers and qualifications are in order before I begin. First, most of my examples are from U.S. television simply because it is popular, accessible, and the television I know best. However, the features to which I attend are not at all specific to U.S. television; on the contrary, they are easily identified in different examples from around the globe. Second, this is not intended to be anything like an exhaustive enumeration of either the television medium's differential features or the art form's distinctive properties and effects. There is much more to be said about both. In addition, in the remaining portion of this chapter I will not say very much about how the artistic properties and effects I identify relate to axiological matters; for the time being, I will assume it noncontroversial that effects like intensely felt character engagement, sustained suspense, humor, and cognitive pleasure are all prima facie artistic values. But because my main focus in this chapter is to simply establish warrant for talking of a medium of television and an art of television, and to clarify the relationship between the two, I will not say anything here about how or why such properties and effects constitute artistic values. Nor will I say anything here more generally about the role of the medium in our evaluation of television artworks. However, I will return to all of these questions later in the book.

Temporal Prolongation and Character Engagement

My thinking about the distinct artistic effects generated by television's temporal prolongation is generally influenced by some pioneering work in television studies.[56] More specifically, I will try to build upon two recent, interdisciplinary contributions—one by Robert Blanchet and Margrethe Bruun Vaage and the other by Henry John Pratt. In a recent article, Blanchet and Vaage argue that the long-term engagement with characters afforded by television series engenders a depth of feeling for those characters that is infrequently matched by feature films. Marshaling both empirical research in experimental psychology and theoretical work in film studies, Blanchet and Vaage claim that "it is pleasurable to engage with characters in television series partly because, after a season or two, we have become so used to them and know them so well."[57] In contrast, they contend, while feature films certainly engender emotional engagement with characters (and through many of the same mechanisms), the stricter temporal boundaries of feature films limit their capacity to foster the same level of "familiarity" with characters.

Blanchet and Vaage support this thesis with a number of more specific claims. First, following the philosophical literature emphasizing "shared history" as a crucial element of friendship, they argue: "television series are better equipped to allow spectators to develop a bond with fictional characters than feature films. This is because television series more effectively invoke the impression that we share a history with their characters: first, because of the series' longer screen duration, and second because our own lives progress as the series goes on."[58] For example, I can hardly conjure up a mental image of Tony Soprano (James Gandolfini) without thinking about both my first encounter with him in an undergraduate dorm room and debating, with my future wife, whether he had been shot after the infamous cut to black in the final episode of the series. Thus, Blanchet and Vaage claim, "engagement in long-term [television] narratives activates some of the same mental mechanisms as friendship does in real life."[59]

Second, they hypothesize that our ongoing interest in television characters can be partly explained by social psychologist Caryl Rusbult's "investment model," according to which the prior investment of resources like time and energy ("sunk costs") in personal relationships tend to keep us committed to those relationships, lest we face the loss of investment that ending them would necessitate. Thus, for example, despite my increasing dissatisfaction with *Damages* (FX 2007–2010; Audience Network 2011–2012) in Season 2, I had a hard time weaning myself off the series because of the time and energy I had already invested in anticipating Ellen Parsons (Rose Byrne) exacting revenge upon Patty Hewes (Glenn Close). As Blanchet and Vaage put it, "The basic idea is that narrative engagement not only contains the forward-looking desire for pay-off and closure, but also a backward-looking concern over what has already been put into the project."[60]

The third and fourth features identified by Blanchet and Vaage, "instant intensity" and "surprise," relate not only to television's ability to foster a particularly deep kind of character engagement but also to its ability to sustain suspense, which I shall discuss presently. In their words, engaging a fictional world and characters with which one is already familiar from watching multiple episodes—perhaps multiple seasons of a television series—is "cognitively less demanding" than acquainting oneself with a new world and new characters portrayed by a feature film; indeed, they, claim, "tuning into [sic] a new episode of a well-known series is cognitively and emotionally attractive to the spectator, partly because she returns to a fictional world and characters with which she is already familiar."[61] Moreover, most viewers are not merely "familiar" with such characters; rather, for reasons already canvassed by Blanchet and Vaage and advanced by cognitive film theorists like Murray Smith, viewers *like* many of those characters or, perhaps, feel even stronger emotional attachments to them. In any case, the familiarity with characters that is furnished by prior episodes is sustained and built upon through the incorporation of gestures, moments, and events that are imbued with emotional weight based on information parceled out previously. Returning to the above example of *The Sopranos*, it seems fair to say that part of what kept viewers hooked during the darker and less narratively interesting fourth and fifth seasons was simply the pleasure afforded by "being with" Tony—pleasure afforded not by his actions, but by the ease with which we were able to infer his mental states from a mere furrowing of his brow or a flashing of his toothy grin.

The link between character engagement and temporal prolongation can be elucidated here by considering a particular episode like Season Six's "Remember When," much of the pleasure of which depends upon our ability to infer the mental states of Tony and Paulie (Tony Sirico) from a combination of their facial expressions and our knowledge of their personalities and shared history. In a wonderful example of what Blanchet and Vaage identify as "instant intensity"; informed viewers are, from nearly the start of the episode, able to draw on this knowledge to read from Tony's face years of suspicion and irritation with Paulie and, from Paulie's face, years of envy and fear of Tony. This intensity reaches a climax when, after only about forty-five minutes of screen time, Tony suggests to Paulie that they go on a deep-sea fishing trip. This invitation is imbued with suspense by years of shared history between the two characters (and viewers)—including, most importantly, their collaboration in murdering Big Pussy (Vincent Pastore) on Tony's fishing boat in the second season. The weight of this knowledge infuses the scene with a degree of narrative suspense and emotional intensity that cannot be perceived simply by attending to the formal means (camera angle and movement, performance, sound) by which we are cued to wonder if Paulie might be in trouble. Shortly after, when Paulie and Tony are on the boat, we get a flashback, from Paulie's perspective, of Big Pussy's murder. Importantly, this affords new viewers the knowledge necessary to make sense of the scene, but the flashback alone cannot provide new viewers with the same degree of suspense or emotional intensity more generally, for such effects are partly the result of our long-term engagement and investment in the characters.

It might be a bit more precise, then, to say that the combination of long-form television's affordance of familiarity with characters and temporal prolongation means that, after a certain point, episodes come to us "pre-packaged" with the tools to quickly foster intense levels of narrative suspense and emotional weight. To continue the metaphor, feature films, by contrast, need to start from scratch in building a structure of interrelated characters and situations before they can secure suspense and emotional engagement at the same pitch as television episodes. "Intensity," then, understood as either heightened narrative suspense or emotional weight, tends not to be exactly instantaneous, but it can be achieved much more quickly in television series. Of course, there are exceptions in which "instant intensity" is exactly the right term—cases in which feature films and television episodes seem to begin in fifth gear. But again, because of the combination of familiarity with characters and temporal prolongation, the intensity with which *Breaking Bad*'s "Ozymandias" begins seems of a different kind than that of, say, *Psycho* (1960) or *Jaws* (1975).

Finally, Blanchet and Vaage claim that serial television affords a particular kind of surprise. As with "instant intensity," this is a quality that television instantiates in a substantively different way than feature films because of the way familiarity with characters and temporal prolongation interact. Of course, feature films are capable of surprising viewers—a fact exemplified by "twist films" like *The Sixth Sense* (1999) and *The Usual Suspects* (1995). However, Blanchet and Vaage maintain that television's temporal prolongation promotes more deeply entrenched expectations about character behavior, thus engendering a magnified sense of surprise if those expectations are violated. The authors offer Don Draper's emotional breakdown in "The Suitcase" after two and a half seasons of stoicism as an example. To this, we might add the moments when the apparently pragmatic Frank

Underwood (Kevin Spacey) unexpectedly shoves Zoe Barnes (Kate Mara) in front of a subway in season 2 of *House of Cards* (Netflix 2013–present); when, after five seasons of surviving "the game," Omar Little lets his guard down just long enough to be shot by a child in *The Wire* (HBO 2002–2008); and when Walter White, whom we have been cued to think is good at heart if not without his fair share of character flaws, allows Jesse Pinkman's (Aaron Paul) girlfriend, Jane (Krysten Ritter), to choke to death on her own vomit. In such cases, it seems, we are dealing with the same sort of surprise that is instantiated by feature films, but of a pitch that appears to depend on the differential features of the television medium. Indeed, it is hard to resist the speculation that this explains the current fascination in popular culture with viewers' reactions to surprising moments in long-form television.

Blanchet and Vaage's discussion of surprise seems like an aim to conceptualize an effect that is similar—or at least related to—the "sustained suspense" that Henry John Pratt identifies as a particular quality of serial television and serial art more broadly. Before turning to Pratt's work, however, it is worth emphasizing two points. First, although Blanchet and Vaage's study focuses on American serial drama, using *Mad Men* as a case study, the central point regarding the ways in which temporal prolongation fosters a particular kind of character engagement is applicable to other television formats produced in American and other socio-cultural contexts. For example, some of television studies' pioneering research on the reception of soap operas and telenovelas meshes nicely with Blanchet and Vaage's hypotheses, and it seems plausible that some of the findings of those earlier studies are partly explicable in terms of the latter.[62] Moreover, it seems plausible that the effects Blanchet and Vaage describe can be fostered by long-running, episodic television series to which audiences are committed in large part because of their familiarity with and investment in characters—both episodic dramas such as *Columbo* (NBC 1968–1978; ABC 1989–2003) and *Star Trek: The Next Generation* (CBS 1987–1994), as well as sitcoms such as the previously mentioned *M*A*S*H* and *Friends*. So, to be clear, I think that the way temporal prolongation fosters engagement with television characters is a general, differential feature of the medium rather than specific to any single form of television or socio-cultural context of television viewing.

Secondly, it bears emphasizing that although I find plausible Blanchet and Vaage's hypotheses regarding the psychological mechanisms underlying the various effects related to our sense of familiarity with television characters, the accuracy of those specific, psychological hypotheses does not actually matter for my present purpose. Rather, what matters are the effects that Blanchet and Vaage identify and the artistic devices that give rise to them. So, for example, one might be suspicious of the "familiarity principle" and unconvinced that it functions to endear characters to viewers as Blanchet and Vaage suggest.[63] However, this would not undermine my argument as long as one still accepts the existence of the phenomenon the authors enlist the familiarity principle to explain—namely, the particular depth of character engagement engendered by television's potential for temporal prolongation. Indeed, it seems plausible that, in specific cases, such engagement is fostered by a complex interaction of factors including the audio-visual and narrative features of the program, the psychological mechanisms detailed by Blanchet and Vaage, *and* the socio-cultural considerations identified in the television studies literature.

Temporal Prolongation and Suspense

Pratt, who, like me, takes a philosophical perspective on these matters, is similarly more concerned with describing the artistic effects created by serialization. Of his observations on the "advantages" and "pitfalls" serialization presents artists, I want to focus and elaborate upon just one—serial narratives' ability to sustain suspense. For our purposes here, we can rely on media psychologist Dolf Zillmann's plausible characterization of "drama-evoked" suspense as "a noxious affective reaction that characteristically derives from the respondents' acute, fearful apprehension being mediated by high by not complete subjective certainty about the occurrence of the anticipated deplorable events."[64] Furthermore, Zillmann describes "suspenseful drama" as a dramatic work that "features sympathetic, liked protagonists in apparent peril, frequently so and in a major way, thus having the capacity to instigate sustained experiences of [drama-evoked] suspense."[65]

Pratt touches only briefly and suggestively on suspense, which I want to think about further here as one of several closely related effects achieved in the context of television through temporal prolongation. Here is the nub of Pratt's argument: One-off narratives—including feature films and single episodes of strictly episodic television series like *The Simpsons* (Fox 1989–present)—can, of course, create suspense *within* or *internal to* the work. But that suspense ends when the narrative ends; in the case of most feature films and episodes of strictly episodic series, this is when the closing credits role. In contrast, the gaps in between installments of a serial *interrupt* rather than conclude all of the salient narrative threads, thus allowing the serial to sustain suspense more or less indefinitely until the concluding installment.[66] Pratt's point applies to serial narratives *tout court;* my emphasis is on the fact that television's temporal prolongation abets the sustainment of suspense in a manner that distinguishes it from the film medium.

One potential objection to this claim needs to be addressed right away: Serialized film is of course a logical possibility, not to mention an empirical fact. In film, the sustainment of suspense is most commonly instantiated by spreading a narrative across several films, all but the final installments of which end with some sort of cliffhanger. For example, the first *Back to the Future* (1985) movie ends with Doc Brown (Christopher Lloyd) warning Marty (Michael J. Fox) and Jennifer (Claudia Wells) that something terrible happens to their children in the future before ushering them into his time machine and blasting off. And although franchises like *Back to the Future*

(1985–1990) and *Star* Wars (1977–present) exhibit a rather weak or loose form of serialization (because all but a few of the narrative threads of individual installments are concluded), films exhibiting the sort of strong serialization I am claiming for television were prevalent and popular in both the silent and early-sound eras of film. (Some notable examples include Louis Feuillade's *Fantômas* (1913–1914), *Les Vampires* (1915–1916), and *Judex* (1918), as well as superhero serials like *Flash Gordon* (1936), *The Green Hornet* (1940), and *The Adventures of Captain Marvel* (1941).)

This objection may be devastating to the medium essentialist, who, as we noted earlier can be understood as making a modal claim not only about what the medium is like as a matter of fact, but also about what the medium possibly could or could not be like in virtue of its essential nature. However, the moderate version of medium specificity I have suggested we adopt insulates my view from the real force of the complaint. For we can and should admit that serialization is not unique to television, while plausibly maintaining that, as a matter of contingent fact, the creative practices that partly constitute the television medium centrally involve serialization. On the other hand, serialization is on the periphery of those practices that partly constitute the film medium. For contemporary practitioners, critics, and viewers, strong serialization is, thus, tacitly (and rightly) understood as a quality that differentiates television from film. If television had existed 150 years ago, this might not have been the case. But it is today, as long as we conceive of media as historically situated cultural kinds, the boundaries and properties of which shift along with changes in practices.

How, then, does serial television drama sustain suspense in a way that differentiates it from film? To start, there is no real film equivalent of a television series comprising multiple episodes and, usually, multiple seasons of episodes. This quality of television allows creators to conclude individual episodes in relatively open-ended fashion, as the narrative thread will be continued in the following week or, perhaps, a few weeks later, after other narrative threads have been progressed. Although suspense is generated by a narrative question raised within a particular episode—just as suspense is generated by a narrative question raised within a particular film—the interludes between episodes sustain and, in some cases, amplify suspense. On the other hand, filmmakers tend not to leave many questions unresolved, instead striving for narrative closure.

There are, of course, exceptions. For example, some filmmakers like Michelangelo Antonioni and Luis Buñuel deliberately eschew narrative closure. But the films of Antonioni and Buñuel cannot be said to generate much suspense in the first place, because it quickly becomes clear that narrative is not the overriding concern in their work, and the viewer is cued to engage their films in different ways. Furthermore, even if one thinks that a film like *L'Avventura* (1960) does indeed generate suspense, it certainly does not sustain it in the same way a television series does. Once the credits of the film roll, whatever suspense viewers might have felt is transformed into some other emotion—frustration, irritation, bemusement, and so forth—because the narrative is complete; without any forthcoming story information, suspense is not possible.

Movie franchises constitute another exception to narrative film's general tendency towards narrative closure and, as I noted earlier with reference to *Back to the Future*, there are undeniably some movie franchises that sustain suspense across installments. However, I think the suspense involved in these cases differs in substantive ways from the way suspense is sustained in television series. First, for a variety of reasons, including the length of feature films and the cost of both producing and attending them, installments of movie franchises have to reckon with what we might call a commercial imperative of closure. In other words, neither film producers nor viewers will happily accept a feature-length installment of, say, *Harry Potter* (2001–2011) or *X-Men* (2000–2014) that concludes on a major note of narrative uncertainty. Rather, the restricted or diluted suspense that such installments generate tends to be created by a new narrative question, raised towards the end of the film after most of the central narrative threads have been concluded, in which the audience thus has very little emotional stake. We do not, for example, leave the cinema and toss and turn at night wondering what problem will beset Marty and Jennifer's children in 2015. If the film ended just before the lightning storm that provided the 1.21 gigawatts of electricity needed to power the time machine for its trip back to the future (that is, back to 1985 from 1955) and we were uncertain if Marty would make it home, perhaps we would toss and turn at night. But it is precisely this sort of strong open-endedness narrative filmmakers have a commercial imperative to avoid. And, even if they didn't, our felt suspense would quickly wane with the knowledge that the promise of narrative closure would be out of reach for at least another year when the next film was released.

That is, perhaps paradoxically, narrative suspense seems to partly depend upon the anticipation we feel in the real time that elapses between narrative installments. In the four years that pass between *Back to the Future* and *Back to the Future II* (1989), our suspense dissipates. At some point, the question of whether Marty and Jennifer will be able to rewrite history to fix whatever has gone wrong with their children probably fades from our mind altogether. Not so, however, in the week that elapses before we get an answer to the question raised by "To'hajiilee," the thirteenth episode of the fifth season of *Breaking Bad*, which I describe in detail below. In this case, the relatively short time that passes between narrative installments sustains our suspense to a degree that seems unattainable by weakly serialized movie franchises.

In contrast to film, television has several different resources that may be deployed to foster a more intense form of suspense. First, unlike installments of a weakly serialized film franchise, television episodes in serials can and do end on strong cliffhangers. Perhaps the most striking example of this is the episode just mentioned, "To'hajiilee." After nearly five full seasons (about a year of diegetic time) of evading capture, Walter White (Bryan Cranston) has finally been apprehended by his brother-in-law Hank (Dean Norris), who works for the Drug Enforcement Agency. Walt has been in cahoots with a very dangerous group of neo-Nazi drug runners, whom he had called for help after being cornered by his pursuers on the To'hajiilee reservation. After realizing that it is Hank who is on his tail, Walt tells the neo-Nazi leader, Jack (Michael Bowen), not to bother coming. But this request is not heeded, and when the neo-Nazis arrive, a shootout ensues between them and Hank (and his partner Steven Gomez (Steven Michael Quezada)). Walt is trapped in the middle, handcuffed in the back of a locked SUV. As the rattle of automatic weapon fire and shattering of glass rings out, Walter closes his eyes, clenches his teeth, and lowers his body as far down as he can. The screen cuts to black. Uncertain as to whether Walt will live and, if so, whether he will be arrested by Hank or saved (or something else?!) by the neo-Nazis, we are left in a state of suspense extraordinary even for serial television and nearly impossible for film.

Homeland is another drama that makes considerable use of television's ability to sustain suspense. Consider the conclusion of "The Vest," the penultimate episode in Season 1. CIA agent Carrie Matheson (Claire Danes) anticipates an imminent terrorist attack by an Iraq War veteran who was turned by the terrorist Abu Nazir (Navid Negahban). However, she is unsure exactly by whom, how, and when the attack will be carried out, and she is engaging in increasingly paranoid and erratic behavior because of her untreated bipolar disorder. Viewers know that returned Marine Sergeant Nicholas Brody (Damian Lewis), whom Carrie originally suspected but has trusted since their affair, has recently acquired a suicide vest, with which he is supposed to carry out the attack. When Carrie calls Brody for his help in getting a lead on the terrorist, Brody senses she is too close, and he tips off the CIA director to their relationship, knowing that this will discredit her. The episode ends with the director apprehending Carrie in her home after finding her in a manic state, surrounded by a chart made of classified documents. Carrie was the only one close to cracking the case; there are no other obstacles in the way of Brody's attack. Suspense is generated from the uncertainty about whether Carrie will be able to extricate herself from the clutches of her inept superiors in time to stop Brody.

It is important to note here that, unlike the cliffhangers of the installments of movie franchises, the cliffhangers I have described above do not necessarily involve completely new narrative threads, but rather interrupt narrative threads that we have followed and become invested in over an extended period of time. This is important for two reasons: one is that suspense is not just sustained across the gap between two episodes, but oftentimes across multiple episodes, a full season, or even longer; the other reason is that the intensity of the suspense we feel seems correlated to the amount of time it is sustained. Again, the best example here is probably *Breaking Bad*.

Undoubtedly, one of the principal pleasures of the series stems from the way that, for four and a half seasons, it sustains and, indeed, builds suspense around a single question: Will Hank realize that Walt is a drug dealer? As time passes in the diegesis, the stakes of this question increase: Walt rapidly transforms from an amateur meth cook into Heisenberg, a drug kingpin whose product is the source of a major DEA investigation. Walt's criminal activity indirectly leads to Hank being shot and nearly paralyzed. After Hank's investigation leads him to conclude that Gus Fring's (Giancarlo Esposito) deceased employee, Gale (David Costabile), was Heisenberg, Walt's pride spurs him to convince Hank to revisit the case, looking for someone much smarter than Gale. So, the narrative events afforded by the passage of extended periods of diegetic time—which are, in turn, made possible by the prolongation of the series in our, real time—not only sustain suspense, but gradually build it.

The passage of real time also contributes to suspense by securing and fostering our investment in the characters of Walt and Hank in the way characterized by Blanchet and Vaage. It is in this way that the intensity of the suspense we feel seems to increase proportionally with the amount of real time it is sustained. The more time we spend with *Breaking Bad* and other serialized television series, the more "familiar" we become with the characters that inhabit the story world and the more invested we become in their fates. For this reason, the suspense fostered by the question of whether Hank will discover that Walt's criminal activity is of an entirely different pitch in two "near-misses" that occur at different points in the series. In "Grilled," the ninth overall episode of the series, Hank shows up at the home of Hector Salamanca (Mark Margolis), where the drug lord Tucco (Raymond Cruz) is holding Walt and Jesse captive. The suspense here is substantial: Will Hank see Walt? Or will Tucco tell Hank that Walt is Heisenberg?

But if the suspense here makes this one of the more pleasurable early episodes of the series, the suspense generated in "Bullet Points," the thirty-seventh overall episode, makes one squirm. In this episode, Hank reveals to Walt that he has obtained Gale's notebook, which has all the information about the cooks who are working in the underground meth lab. What's more, on the first page of the notebook there is a dedication to "W. W." "Wonder who that is," Hank asks Walt. "Woodrow Wilson? Willy Wonka? Walter White?" Until we cut back to a shot of Hank that reveals he does not think this is really a possibility, we're on the edge of our seats. Since we viewed "Grilled" some thirty more episodes earlier, we have become increasingly invested in these characters, and our emotional engagement with them—and the suspense we feel in this scene—is significantly more intense.

Temporal Prolongation and Running Gags

As I indicated above, television's temporal prolongation furnishes comedy series with a particular pairing of artistic device and artistic effect—the running gag and the humor it elicits. More specifically, temporal prolongation provides television series with the ability to foreshadow gags far in advance, sometimes on multiple occasions, to keep gags running over extended periods of time, and to interweave running gags.

As with my discussion of suspense, I need to head off an immediate objection. Of course it is not the case that running gags are unique to television comedy. One classical example from film, mentioned in Steve Neale and Frank Krutnik's *Popular Film and Television Comedy*, involves Groucho and Harpo Marx on the motorbike and sidecar in *Duck Soup* (1933). In the first two iterations of the gag, Groucho is sitting in the sidecar and Harpo speeds away on the motorcycle. The third time, Harpo gestures Groucho toward the sidecar, but the latter protests: "Oh, no you don't. I'm not taking any more chances." Harpo hops into the sidecar and Groucho mounts the motorcycle. But after he revs the engine, it is the sidecar that accelerates, leaving Groucho behind once again. Neale and Krutnik also accurately note that in many Buster Keaton pictures, including *The General* (1926) and *College* (1927), part of the humor derives from the fact that "gags and situations are systematically repeated, but second time round they are symmetrically inverted or reversed so as to result in triumphant success."[67] And one could enumerate many more examples.

Once again, my response is that while this objection might have force against a medium essentialist who claimed that running gags were unique to television, it does not imperil my more moderate thesis that the differential feature of temporal prolongation allows television to instantiate running gags that appear to be structurally different from running gags in film. Here one might wonder what this putative structural difference amounts to in terms of artistic effects. Although I did claim that the strong serialization possible in television engenders more intense suspense than the weak serialization prevalent in film, it would be specious, I think, to similarly suggest that the structural difference makes running gags in television funnier than running gags in film *tout court*. However, I think the structural difference of running gags in television generates at least one more modest distinctive artistic effect: such gags afford cognitive pleasure of a different order from that provided by running gags in film.

The cognitive pleasure afforded by running gags in television is *not*, to be sure, entirely dissimilar to the simple set-up/pay-off structure that is ubiquitous in film comedy. The cognitive pleasure furnished by the ending of *Caddyshack* (1980), for example, stems from the fact that the golf course is blown up (thus inching a short putt forward just enough to win the game for our heroes) as a result of the Bill Murray character's increasingly intemperate attempts to rid the grounds of gophers, which we have watched since early on in the film. Nor is it dissimilar to the cognitive pleasure we experience at the end of a Buster Keaton film like *The General*, in which "the symmetrical structure of the plot" creates parallels between gags in the first half of the film (which result in pratfalls) and gags towards the end of the film (which, incongruously, allow Johnnie to demonstrate his competence).[68]

However, in contrast to these film comedy structures, television's temporal prolongation allows for both set-up and pay-off to be distributed over more time and repeated on multiple occasions. In part, this is because television series are created progressively such that the writing staff can devise new ways to work old gags into additional episodes and, more interestingly, can concoct gags with set-ups that are only established post hoc—that is, that initially served as set-ups for *other* gags or that were not initially conceived as set-ups at all. All of this has consequences for our appreciation of television comedy. My contention is that identifying a gag as set up by a series of events that occur on several different occasions over an extended period of time richens the cognitive pleasure it affords. So, too, I think, does the fact that the pay-off comes not once—at a more or less expected point in the narrative, namely the ending—but over and over again at unexpected moments and in unexpected ways.

To start with a structurally simple example, consider, one of the better known gags from *Curb Your Enthusiasm*—Larry's stare down of people he (erroneously) believes have lied to him. As a helpful chart by Sean Petranovich demonstrates, the stare down originated in Season 2, as a stand-alone gag, when Larry deployed it against his acupuncturist in an attempt to discern whether orchids are a traditional Japanese gift from a man.[69] However, in the ninth episode of Season 3, the gag is revisited and amplified: accompanied by a non-diegetic musical motif, Larry stares down not one but three people—not coincidentally, all of whom are in low-wage service jobs: a waiter, his landscaper, and his housekeeper. Thereafter, the gag appears at least once in every season and, in all but one case, in multiple episodes in each season. Part of the cognitive pleasure of the gag, then, derives from its longevity, but also from the various ways in which it is able to be instantiated thanks to the temporal prolongation of television. In "The Larry David Sandwich," from the fifth season, Larry's stare down of his own father is funny in its own right, but a special cognitive pleasure is available to viewers who recall that, characteristically, Larry deploys the stare down against people towards whom he imagines himself superior. In season seven, the gag is inverted such that Larry *receives* the stare down from Mr. Takahashi in one episode and Jerry Seinfeld in another. Again, the gag here is funny in its own right, but a special cognitive pleasure is furnished by the way in which it is inverted after we have seen it run for such a long period of time.

Turning to *Arrested Development* will allow us to see how television's temporal prolongation can be used to devise running gags of more structural complexity, which again engenders cognitive pleasures not available from film comedy. Let's start with the running gag of Buster's (Tony Hale) back rubs, which is established in the pilot episode. Arguably, there's nothing particularly funny about this gag, which is first repeated in the third episode, beyond Buster's general social awkwardness—even around his family members. Starting in the fourth episode, the gag is amplified with a catchphrase involving Buster's tendency to refer to people by their relationships to him rather than by their names (for example, "Hey, brother!").

Perhaps surprisingly, this is enough to make things very interesting after some additional narrative development afforded by temporal prolongation. Apparently unrelatedly, we are introduced to J. Walter Weatherman (Steve Ryan) in the tenth episode and Oscar Bluth (Jeffrey Tambor) in the twentieth episode. Weatherman, who only has one arm, has been enlisted by George Bluth (Jeffrey Tambor) to teach his children various "important" lessons by pretending to lose his arm as a result of their various oversights such as "forgetting to leave a note." This becomes important later on. So too does the Episode 20 introduction of Oscar Bluth, the twin brother of George Bluth and the (apparent) uncle of the Bluth children—Michael (Justin Bateman), G.O.B. (Will Arnett), Lindsay (Portia de Rossi), and Buster. In this episode, Buster's backrub and catchphrase gags are repeated and, in a sense, amplified by Oscar greeting Michael with "Hey, nephew!" and a backrub. But the pay-off comes later, when we discover that Oscar is Buster's biological father (hence the similarity of behavior), which, as one can imagine, becomes its own running gag from this point forward. However, once *all* of these gags have been established, a further pay-off for the initial backrub gag is achieved one brilliant moment in the second season episode "Hand to God." After having his hand bitten off by a seal, Buster is fitted with a hook. Attempting to give Oscar a backrub, Buster accidentally impales him with the hook. "I'm a monster!" he screams later.

The point here is that part of cognitive pleasure afforded by television comedies like *Arrested Development* is only possible due to the differential feature of temporal prolongation. The cognitive pleasure we get from gags like the ones described above stems from the ways in which the temporal expansion of a series allows television comedies to devise pay-offs for running gags on multiple occasions and in multiple ways. In particular, after the initial pay-off of a running gag, the gag may be interwoven with others to realize an additional, amplified pay-off down the line. There is a particular cognitive pleasure in perceiving how such gags are interwoven, in catching moments where the set up seems to be established, in anticipating how the pay-off will be implemented, and, once the pay-off has been realized, in reflecting back on the structural choices made to set it up.[70]

Conclusion

I began this chapter by attempting merely to establish that there is, in fact, a medium of television distinct from a broader class of moving images. I argued that this is plausible if a medium is conceived not as a set of materials with a timeless, intrinsic essence, but rather as cluster of socio-historically contingent practices for creating things in a vehicular medium. I proceeded to argue that the television medium possesses certain qualities, including the capacities for temporal prolongation and liveness, that differentiate it from the film medium, despite the fact that those features are not unique to television. However, I also urged that we keep the television medium distinct from the art of television. To support the case for an art of television, therefore, I appealed to Gaut's MSF thesis: "For a medium to constitute an art form it must instantiate artistic properties that are distinct from those that are instantiated by other media."[71] With reference to character engagement, suspense, and running gags, I attempted to show that temporal prolongation has allowed television to instantiate artistic devices and effects distinct from those achieved in the medium of film. Thus, I claim, television should be recognized as an art form distinct from the art form of film.

I believe I have provided sufficient evidence to support this claim, but it is worth emphasizing that I have not provided anything like an exhaustive account of the artistic effects afforded by temporal prolongation. I focused on the engendering of character engagement, sustainment of suspense, and fostering of cognitive pleasure in the context of comedy largely because these are topics on which some work has already begun and because these topics are of interest to me. However, there is surely something to be said about the importance of temporality to television documentary mini-series like Ken Burns's *The War* (PBS 2007) and to at least some reality television shows such as *Top Chef* (Bravo 2006–present). Furthermore, of television's various differential features, I have only focused here on temporal prolongation, because it seems to me the most important and most philosophically interesting, but that is not to deny that television has other such features, of which liveness is the only other that occurs to me in the absence of extensive research along these lines. I hope that my work here will lead to further research on the art of television, exploring the ways in which television's differential features, and the devices and effects to which they give rise, are manifested in specific cases.

To be clear, I am *not* claiming there is a direct, causal link between temporal prolongation, or any other differential feature, and artistic value. For the purposes of making my job fun, I have discussed examples of television that I think are good and that I like. But it needs to be said that there is no necessary connection between temporal prolongation and artistic achievement. Plainly, some television shows do not make much use of temporal prolongation and are excellent. And, as well, some television shows do make use of this differential feature but are not very good at all. In this sense, I have absolutely no quarrel with Carroll's criticisms of medium essentialist claims that putatively predict the artistic failure or success of a work in terms of the extent to which it makes use of the supposedly unique qualities of the medium. Indeed, here as in many other areas of the philosophy of the arts, Carroll's work is invaluable. We should follow his lead in taking care to avoid this sort of conceptual error, instead of proceeding piecemeal in our evaluative criticism.

However, Carroll's exhortations are not at odds with the main argument of this chapter—that the television medium, understood as a group of shared practices for working with a vehicular medium, figures essentially in the full and proper appreciation of particular television artworks. Perhaps Carroll would respond here with the triviality objection; he might, for example, reiterate that the differential features of temporal prolongation, liveness, and so forth are not "fully comprehensive features of all TV, but only contingent features of groups of historically specific TV productions."[72] My reply is that we should reject, as a false dilemma, the idea that claims about the medium must either be medium-uniqueness claims or be trivial. The claims I have made for the temporal prolongation are only trivial relative to the project of defining the essence of television in terms of necessary and sufficient conditions– a project which, I agree, seems neither promising nor particularly worthwhile.

In contrast, my aim is to think through what is special—not necessarily unique, but different from film—about the creation and appreciation of the art of television, as it is currently constituted, and why. From this perspective, there is nothing trivial about the temporal prolongation of, say, soap operas and the particular appreciative practices such temporal prolongation affords. Carroll might agree yet respond that the features and practices I have in mind simply don't have anything to do with the medium *per se*. If that were the case, then I would be satisfied that Carroll and I were merely having a terminological dispute.

Yet I stand by the argument developed in the first part of this chapter that it is indeed the medium that is relevant to our creative and appreciative practices. As Timothy Binkley puts it, "By being told which medium a work is in, we are given the parameters within which to search for and experience its aesthetic qualities ... The medium tells you what to experience in order to know the aesthetic artwork."[73] Our understanding of what a group of people have achieved *in* a particular television artwork depends essentially on a prior understanding of the work *as* a work in the medium of television, the differential features of which we must also have at least some background conception. Only with this much established can we proceed to investigate further questions about the relationship between the television medium, the particular artistic properties and effects it affords, and the relationship between those artistic properties and effects to the artistic value of television artworks.

But before we can explore this connection, we need to clarify the nature of the object we are to evaluate. That is, we need a better sense of what "the work" is in the context of our appreciation of television. It is to this matter I turn in the next chapter.

Notes

1. For a refreshingly lucid and cogent discussion of the concepts of medium and art form in the context of television, see Sarah Cardwell, "Television amongst Friends: Medium, Art, Media," *Critical Studies in Television* 9, no. 3 (Autumn 2014): 6–21.

2. Berys Gaut, *A Philosophy of Cinematic Art* (Cambridge, UK: Cambridge University Press, 2010), 19; 290.
3. Stephen Heath, "Representing Television," in *Logics of Television: Essays in Cultural Criticism*, ed. Patricia Mellencamp (Bloomington: Indiana University Press, 1990), 267.
4. John Thornton Caldwell, *Televisuality: Style, Crisis, and Authority in American Television* (New Brunswick, NJ: Rutgers University Press, 1995), 25–31, especially. For a subsequent critique of medium essentialist theories of television, see Noël Carroll, "TV and Film: A Philosophical Perspective," in *Engaging the Moving Image* (New Haven, CT: Yale University Press, 2003), 265–280. I borrow the term "object problem," from a discussion of a similar issue in screenwriting studies in Steven Maras, *Screenwriting: History, Theory and Practice* (London: Wallflower, 2009). On television's object problem, see, for example, Kevin Dowler, "Television and Objecthood: The 'Place' of Television in Television Studies," *Topia: Canadian Journal of Cultural Studies* 8 (Fall 2002): 43–60.
5. Caldwell, *Televisuality: Style, Crisis*, 25.
6. Carroll, "TV and Film," 266.
7. Ibid.
8. Alexander Dhoest and Nele Simons, "Still TV: On the Resilience of an Old Medium," *European Journal of Media Studies* 2, no. 1 (2013): 19.
9. Ibid.
10. Amanda Lotz, *The Television Will Be Revolutionized* (New York: New York University Press, 2007), 80.
11. Glen Creeber, *Small Screen Aesthetics: From Television to the Internet* (London: BFI, 2013), 3.
12. For example, Creeber writes, "it is always easy to fall into the problem of essentialism when trying to define the nature of a medium as complex as television." (Creeber, *Small Screen Aesthetics*, 1).
13. John Hartley, *Television Truths: Forms of Knowledge in Popular Culture* (Malden, MA: Blackwell, 2008), 221.
14. However, even this claim is open to various challenges. See, for example, Paul Bloom, "Water as an Artifact Kind," in *Creations of the Mind: Theories of Artifacts and Their Representation*, ed. Eric Margolis and Stephen Laurence (Oxford: Oxford University Press, 2007), 150–56.
15. Paisley Livingston helpfully pointed out to me that it is worth noting how hard it is to pin down the notion of intrinsicality in the first place. Indeed, I think this difficulty relates to the fact that objections to ontological and axiological views that purport to identify an entity's essence or value in purely intrinsic terms are often directed at straw men. I return to difficulties around the concept of intrinsicality in the final chapter on evaluation, Chapter 6.
16. Creeber, *Small Screen Aesthetics*, 3.
17. Tom O'Regan, "Transient and Intrinsically Valuable in Their Impermanence: Television's Changing Aesthetic Norms," *LOLA* 3 (December 2012). Accessed March 8, 2016. http://www.lolajournal.com/3/tv.html. I hasten to add that I don't think O'Regan means to use the term "intrinsically" in the completely pure, autonomous sense I have just suggested is hard to conceive of.
18. Jason Jacobs, "Television, Interrupted: Pollution or Aesthetic?," in *Television as Digital Media*, ed. James Bennett and Nicki Strange (Durham, NC: Duke University Press, 2011), 257.

84 The Medium

19. Laurent Jullier, "Specificity, Medium II," in *The Routledge Encyclopedia of Film Theory*, ed. Edward Branigan and Warren Buckland (New York: Routledge, 2014), 442.
20. Carroll, "TV and Film," 278–79.
21. An essentialist definition of the moving image is advanced in Noël Carroll, *The Philosophy of Motion Pictures* (Malden, MA: Blackwell, 2008), 53–79; a characterization of the moving image in terms of necessary but *not* sufficient conditions is offered in Noël Carroll, "Defining the Moving Image," in *Theorizing the Moving Image* (Cambridge, UK: Cambridge University Press, 1996).
22. This description of Carroll's view comes from Dominic McIver Lopes, *Beyond Art* (Oxford: Oxford University Press, 2014), 138.
23. Carroll, "TV and Film," 279.
24. Carroll, "Defining the Moving Image," 72.
25. Noël Carroll, "Forget the Medium!," in *Engaging the Moving Image* (New Haven, CT: Yale University Press, 2003), 8.
26. Carroll, *Philosophy of Motion Pictures*, 63.
27. See references to Perkins and Carroll in the ensuing discussion. Also in the context of film and television, see Jason Jacobs, "Issues of Judgement and Value in Television Studies," *International Journal of Cultural Studies* 4, no. 4 (2001): 427–447. For the general form of this claim, and more sustained argumentation in support of it, see Kendall L. Walton, "Categories of Art," in *Marvelous Images: On Values and the Arts* (Oxford: Oxford University Press, 2008), 195–220, and Noël Carroll, *On Criticism* (New York: Routledge, 2009), 153–96.
28. V. F. Perkins, *Film as Film: Understanding and Judging Movies* (Harmondsworth, UK: Penguin, 1972), 59.
29. Perkins, 62.
30. Carroll, *Philosophy of Motion Pictures*, 213, 221.
31. Jacobs, "Television, Interrupted," 270–71.
32. David Davies, "Categories of Art," in *The Routledge Companion to Aesthetics*, 3rd ed., ed. Berys Gaut and Dominic McIver Lopes (New York: Routledge, 2013), 225.
33. Carroll, *Philosophy of Motion Pictures*, 35.
34. Carroll, "Forget the Medium!," 6.
35. On the long history of the related distinction between artwork and vehicular medium, see Paisley Livingston, "History of the Ontology of Art," *Stanford Encyclopedia of Philosophy*, ed. Edward N. Zalta (Summer 2013 edition). Accessed July 24, 2014. http://plato.stanford.edu/entries/art-ontology-history/.
36. Carroll, "Forget the Medium!," 3.
37. Noël Carroll, "Engaging Critics," *Film Studies: An International Review* 8 (Summer 2006): 162.
38. Livingston, "History of the Ontology of Art."
39. See, for example, C. I. Lewis, *An Analysis of Knowledge and Valuation* (LaSalle, IL: Open Court, 1962 [1946]), 472–76.
40. Livingston, "History of the Ontology of Art."
41. See, for example, Walton, "Categories of Art"; Arthur C. Danto, *The Transfiguration of the Commonplace* (Cambridge, MA: Harvard University Press, 1981).
42. Gaut, *Philosophy of Cinematic Art*, 293.
43. David Davies, *Art as Performance* (Malden, MA: Blackwell, 2004), 59.

44. One caveat here: Given the protean nature of our creative practices, media have an ineluctable temporal dimension. (On this point, also see Cardwell, "Television amongst Friends.") So, I admit that, in principle, the practices that partly constitute the media of film and television respectively, could shift so as to end up being identical. Film and television's convergence into a single medium is, therefore, an open possibility in my view; I just don't think it has happened. For further discussion, see Ted Nannicelli and Malcolm Turvey, "Against 'Post-Cinema,'" *Cinéma & Cie* (forthcoming).
45. For a slightly different take on this point, see Cardwell, "Television amongst Friends."
46. There are, of course, exceptions to all of these features. I am not suggesting, though, that these are anything like necessary conditions or essential features for membership in the medium of film. The point also applies to my characterization of television below. I shall respond in detail to one potential objection regarding serialization as a differential feature of television presently.
47. Perhaps needless to say, this is putting things very simplistically—which I am happy to do because I am wary of stretching the analogy too far. For some background, however, see Isabel Cecilia Martinez, "The Cognitive Reality of Prolongational Structures in Tonal Music," Ph.D. diss. (Roehampton Univeristy, 2007). Accessed March 11, 2016. http://roehampton.openrepository.com/roehampton/bitstream/10142/107557/1/Isabel%2520Martinez%2520PHD%2520Thesis.pdf.
48. Gaut, *Philosophy of Cinematic Art*, 290–91.
49. Although I believe he puts his claim a bit too strongly, I am sympathetic to Stanley Cavell's effort to "characterize the material basis of television as *a current of simultaneous event reception*" (italics in original). It is important to see here that this characterization refers to *the material basis* of the medium rather than the medium *tout court*. See Stanley Cavell, "The Fact of Television," *Daedalus* 111, no. 4 (Fall 1982): 75–96.
50. See, for seminal discussions, John Ellis, *Visible Fictions* (London: Routledge, 1982); and Jane Feuer, "The Concept of Live Television: Ontology as Ideology," in *Regarding Television: Critical Approaches*, ed. E. Ann Kaplan (Los Angeles, CA: American Film Institute, 1983), 12–22. For more recent discussions see, Jérôme Bourdon, "Live Television Is Still Alive: On Television as an Unfulfilled Promise," *Media, Culture & Society* 22, no. 5 (2000): 531–56; Stephanie Marriott, *Live Television: Time, Space and the Broadcast Event* (London: Sage, 2007); and Paddy Scannell, *Television and the Meaning of "Live": An Enquiry into the Human Situation* (London: Polity, 2014). For a particularly cogent and incisive description of liveness and its importance to practitioners' conceptualizations of early British television drama, see Jason Jacobs, *The Intimate Screen: Early British Television Drama* (Oxford: Oxford University Press, 2000).
51. Gaut, *Philosophy of Cinematic Art*, 224, 291.
52. Gaut, *Philosophy of Cinematic Art*, 224.
53. Gaut, *Philosophy of Cinematic Art*, 287.
54. Angela Curran, "Medium-Involving Explanations and the Philosophy of Film," *British Journal of Aesthetics* 52, no. 2 (April 2012): 194.
55. Berys Gaut, "Replies to Ponech, Curran, and Allen," *British Journal of Aesthetics* 52, no. 2 (April 2012): 206.

The Medium

56. See, in particular, Robert C. Allen, *Speaking of Soap Operas* (Chapel Hill: University of North Carolina Press, 1985); David Buckingham, *Public Secrets: East Enders and its Audiences* (London: BFI, 1987); Jostein Gripsrud, *Dynasty Years: Hollywood Television and Critical Media Studies* (London: Routledge, 1995); Robin Nelson, *TV Drama in Transition: Forms, Values, and Cultural Change* (Basingstoke, UK: Palgrave Macmillan, 1997); John Caughie, *Television Drama: Realism, Modernism, and British Culture* (Oxford: Oxford University Press, 2000); Kristin Thompson, *Storytelling in Film and Television* (Cambridge, MA: Harvard University Press, 2003); Glen Creeber, *Serial Television: Big Drama on the Small Screen* (London: BFI 2005); Jason Mittell, *Complex TV: The Poetics of Contemporary Television Storytelling* (New York: New York University Press, 2015).
57. Robert Blanchet and Margrethe Bruun Vaage, "Don, Peggy, and Other Fictional Friends? Engaging with Characters in Television Series," *Projections: The Journal for Movies and Mind* 6, no. 2 (Winter 2012): 24.
58. Blanchet and Vaage, 28.
59. Ibid., 28.
60. Ibid., 31.
61. Ibid., 32.
62. See, for example, Ien Ang, *Watching Dallas: Soap Opera and the Melodramatic Imagination* trans. Della Coulilng (London: Methuen, 1985), especially 28–34 and 52–53; Christine Geraghty, *Women and Soap Opera: A Study of Prime Time Soaps* (Cambridge, UK: Polity, 1991); C. Lee Harrington and Denise D. Bielby, *Soap Fans: Pursuing Pleasure and Making Meaning in Everyday Life* (Philadelphia, PA: Temple University Press, 1995), especially 125–133; Robert C. Allen, ed. *To Be Continued: Soap Operas Around the World* (London: Routledge, 1995); Jennifer Hayward, *Consuming Pleasures: Active Audiences and Serial Fictions from Dickens to Soap Opera* (Lexington: University of Kentucky Press, 1997), especially 135–196. Portuguese readers interested in the Brazilian telenovela may also be interested in consulting two more recent publications: Maria Immacolata Vassallo de Lopes, Silvia Helena Simões Borelli, and Vera da Rocha Resende, *Vivendo com a telenovela: mediações, recepção, teleficcionalidade* (São Paolo, Brazil: Summus, 2002); and José Roberto Sadek, *Telenovela: Um olhar do cinema* (São Paulo, Brazil: Summus, 2008).
63. It is worth noting that there might a negative thesis compatible with what Blanchet and Vaage propose. That is, it may also be the case that increased familiarity with characters can also foster stronger negative reactions to them. Although I do not have space to explore this possibility in depth, it seems plausible based on anecdotal evidence (consider the irrational negative responses to Skyler White) and the fact that the familiarity eventually plateaus and may even reverse such that increased exposure begins to foster disliking. For a discussion in relationship to screen characters, see Malcolm Turvey, "'Familiarity Breeds Contempt': Why Repeat Exposure Does Not Necessarily Turn TV Characters into Friends," in *Screening Characters*, ed. Johannes Riis and Aaron Taylor (forthcoming).
64. Dolf Zillmann, "The Psychology of Suspense in Dramatic Exposition," in *Suspense: Conceptualizations, Theoretical Analyses, and Empirical Explorations*, ed. Peter Vorderer, Hans J. Wulff, and Mike Friedrichsen (Mahwah, NJ: Lawrence Erlbaum Associates, 1996), 208.

65. Ibid., 209.
66. For a broader reflection on "interruption" in television, see Jacobs, "Television, Interrupted."
67. Steve Neale and Frank Krutnik, *Popular Film and Television Comedy* (London: Routledge, 1990), 59.
68. Noël Carroll, *Comedy Incarnate: Buster Keaton, Physical Humor, and Bodily Coping* (Malden, MA: Blackwell, 2009), 170.
69. Sean Petranovich, "How to Philosophize with a 5 Wood," in *Curb Your Enthusiasm and Philosophy*, ed. Mark Ralkowski (Chicago: Carus Publishing, 2012), 184–85.
70. In the case of particularly long-running and/or self-aware television comedies, this latter process may be extensive indeed: National Public Radio hosts just one of the websites devoted to mapping out the set-ups and call-backs to *Arrested Development*'s diverse array of running gags. In relation to the gags I discussed above, one might note that prior to Buster's loss of his hand, there are a variety of ways in which the incident is foreshadowed even though they are too subtle to constitute part the of set-up. Thus, viewers are afforded additional cognitive pleasure by recalling what appeared to be inconsequential moments from much earlier in the series such as Buster saying, "This party is going to be off the hook," and a camera pan to a shot of Buster during a television news report of a seal attack. See Jeremy Bowers et al., "Previously, On Arrested Development," *NPR.org* (May 18, 2013). Accessed July 24, 2014. http://apps.npr.org/arrested-development/.
71. Gaut, *Philosophy of Cinematic Art*, 287.
72. Carroll, "TV and Film," 278.
73. Timothy Binkley, "Piece: Contra Aesthetics," *Journal of Aesthetics and Art Criticism* 35, no. 3 (Spring 1977): 270.

3 Ontology

Introduction

Any appreciation—understood as involving things like interpretation and evaluation—of a television artwork makes assumptions about a number of prior issues. Minimally, there are two: First, to appreciate *a* television artwork is to make some tacit ontological assumptions inasmuch as the work first needs to be identified and individuated from other works. This much is widely accepted among television scholars and philosophers of varying theoretical commitments—including those who engage in interpretation with aims other than appreciation.[1] Second, and less acknowledged, is that paradigmatic appreciative activities like interpretation and evaluation also make some implicit assumptions about the relationship (or lack thereof) between the work's ontological status and artistic intentions. One usually has some underlying rationale or motivation for taking the work's ontological features to be what one takes them to be, and it usually involves either an acceptance or denial that artistic intentions have a role to play in the determination of those features. As I shall explain in more detail presently, in the former case, the work's ontological features are often regarded as fixed by the successfully realized intentions of its creators. In the latter case, the work's ontological features are usually assumed to be constructed by its audience(s).

For these reasons, philosophical aesthetics' past and current debates about ontology and artistic intentions directly bear upon the work on interpretation and evaluation that is already being done in television studies.[2] That is, theoretical questions regarding the ontology of television works are important because the way we answer *those* questions affects our debates about what a television artwork means or what its artistic merits are. Furthermore, we need to ask about the conditions under which our tacit assumptions about ontology and artistic intention are justified and under what conditions they ought to be overruled by more formal theories—and, if so, which theories. Finally, despite the fact that television studies has been admirably pluralistic in many ways, we need to acknowledge the fact that for the interpretation and evaluation of television artworks to be coherent and meaningful, we need at least a rough consensus about some of the ontological questions. The possibility of appreciating a work of television depends upon our ability to identify and individuate it such that our appreciation is of *the* work and not some other work(s). Without such a consensus, our interpretations and evaluations will not be of the same works, and we will be talking past one another.

I should emphasize that this stress on "a rough consensus" entails neither a fully developed account of the ontology of television or artworks more broadly nor agreement about *all* of the individual theses that might jointly constitute such an account. For example, it seems to make little difference to our appreciative practices whether television programs are, ontologically speaking, real entities or useful fictions that have no place in a fundamental metaphysical picture of the world.[3] Rather, the thought motivating this admonishment is that meaningful critical discourse requires agreement about the object of criticism and, thus, its identifying and individuating properties. Behind this claim lies the idea that agreement or disagreement about what a work's identifying and individuating properties are will depend on *how* one thinks they are established.

Therefore, my primary goal in this chapter is to clarify how television artworks are identified and individuated. I argue it is the successfully realized intentions of television creators that establish the temporal boundaries and other identifying and individuating properties of television works. I use "creators" here in a way that is intended to be consistent with the arguments in Chapter 1. When a television work has authors, in the sense previously analyzed, then those are the relevant creators in this context. When it does not, then the relevant creators are those agents who successfully realize executive-level intentions with regard to the identifying and individuating features of the work. This is meant to be somewhat vague to accommodate the idea that the particular individuals who establish the identifying and individuating features of a work of television will vary on a case-by-case basis. Again, we should defer to production studies scholarship when we are interested in the details of a particular case.

Yet generally speaking, the art of television, in its current manifestation, is partly constituted by some relatively stable, conventional practices for creating works. In particular, it is evident that some whole works constitute parts of larger works. That is, television works are frequently distinguished by terms like "episode," "season," and "series." These observations may seem almost too obvious to be worth discussing in depth. But on the descriptive approach to metaphysics I embrace here, the ingrained, conventional creative practices that make these concepts and distinctions obvious are just what need analysis. For it is these practices that actually establish the facts about the ontology of television artworks.

The chapter proceeds as follows: First, I review some common claims about the putative critical problems raised by television's ontological complexity and some of the tacit ontological conceptions of television. I argue that, in both cases, progress has been impeded by the use of an imprecise theoretical vocabulary and, in particular, a term that has long been part of the basic lexicon of television studies—"text." "Text," of course, has been used as a way of trying to account for television's ontological complexity; it has, in part, become an umbrella term that encompasses episodes, seasons, series, and so forth. But I will argue that the term has become so ambiguous that it now muddies rather than clarifies our understanding of the ontology of television. One may wonder if this really has any practical import—if there is any reason to think that use of the term "text" is at all problematic *beyond* concerns with the ontology of television, which, after all, is not a major preoccupation of the field. I do not want to deny that the term "text" has facilitated some important scholarship. But as I indicated above, our ontological conceptions of television have important implications for how we understand television's meaning and value, and these *are* among the field's central concerns. Therefore, I argue it is imperative to clarify ontological matters, which, in turn, necessitates moving beyond the term "text."

The second part of the chapter goes on to claim that part of the theoretical confusion has arisen as a result of the way some of the literature in the field has collapsed an important distinction between work and "text." After retrieving this distinction from the early work of John Fiske, I turn to the neo-pragmatist movement in philosophical aesthetics to find the strongest case for the claim that audiences construct—that is, impute the identifying and individuating properties of—television works. I raise several objections to this idea before offering my own account of the identifying and individuating properties of television works, which, I claim, are established by the successfully realized intentions of the creators of television.

The Television "Text": Contemporary Views

A brief canvass of recent work in television studies reveals strikingly disparate conceptions of television's identifying and individuating features. Some views so widely diverge that the possibility of agreeing upon the object(s) of criticism seems fundamentally threatened.[4] In particular, we seem to lack widespread agreement about two related questions: First, when is a television work finished? Second, when is a television work a distinct whole rather than a constitutive part of some other work? As I indicated in the previous chapter, with reference to the "object" problem noted by Stephen Heath, both of these questions have dogged television studies for some time. At present, they appear particularly vexing because of two relatively recent developments—the increased convergence of media and the increased serialization of television drama. With regard to the first point, Glen Creeber claims, "Knowing where a 'text' starts and ends seems increasingly difficult to ascertain, a problem clearly heightened in the multi-media age."[5] Tracing the roots of television studies' retreat from close analysis, Creeber writes, "Extra-textual material, such as product merchandising, DVD extras, fanzines, and Internet sites, made textual analysis frustratingly unsure of its object of study."[6] In addition to the complications raised by "extra-textual," multimedia material, the recent shift towards greater serialization in television drama may also seem to trouble our understanding of the boundaries of television works. As Jason Jacobs puts it, "Any attempt to account for excellence in television must tackle the issue of its messy textuality, and in the dramatic serial this means deciding what exactly is the object of critical attention."[7] How, then, do differing accounts of work-identity handle these problems?

Let us briefly put the issue of seriality aside to focus upon work completion. Roughly speaking, there are, on one hand, tacit conceptions of most television works as finished once their creators make them accessible to viewers. If we want to unpack implicit assumptions underlying this idea, we would do well to turn to the work of Paisley Livingston, who posits that a necessary condition for the completion of an artwork involves both a first-order, uncoerced decision on the part of its creators to intentionally stop work *and* a second-order decision (also uncoerced) that the artwork is indeed complete. Livingston stresses that these decisions "need not be reached consciously by the artist or result from lucid process of explicit deliberation."[8] In the context of television, we might think of such decisions being manifest in the transmission of the work to a viewing public—even if, as Livingston argues, this sort of "publication" does not constitute a sufficient condition for a work's completion.

In any case, this view implicitly construes the notion of a television work quite narrowly: Things like episodes and series are the works; merchandizing, DVD extras, fanzines, Internet sites—in short, any material pertaining to a series but not intended to be part of the series by its creators—are ontologically distinct from the television works themselves. In other words, on this account, such "extra-textual" or "para-textual" material does not affect work-identity, which is determined by the creators of a television work.[9] Note that this is just an ontological view: It makes no judgment about the value of para-textual material. Rather, it simply holds (usually implicitly) that paratexts and associated activity are ontologically distinct from the object(s) of appreciative focus—episodes, series, and so forth—the identifying and individuating features of which are established by their creators. Greg M. Smith's *Beautiful TV: The Art and Argument of Ally McBeal*, which limits itself to the program itself, is an instance of scholarship that implicitly accepts such a view. This position is widely held outside of academia; it is evident in the contexts of press reviews, award shows, and the legal system.

There is also a view, prevalent in some of the television studies literature, which construes the idea of a television "text" much more broadly. This view is implicit in Creeber's remarks, and it is explicit in oft-heard claims like John Caldwell's: "The most effective websites for TV succeed by keeping viewer-users engaged long after a series episode has aired, *and this requires greatly expanding the notion of what a TV text is*."[10] Moreover, as I shall explain presently, the general tendency towards an expansive view of "the television text" has been in circulating in television studies for a long time, if in slightly different forms. Before positing that "para-textual" material like websites demanded an expansive conception of the text, some television scholars claimed that it was required by "'incrustations': the fan magazines, the ads, the product tie-ins, the books, the myriad publicity articles, the fashions ..." And before claims that serialization necessitated an expansive conception of the "text" became prevalent, some television scholars supposed that such a conception might be needed if the "text" "includes all those 'interruptions' of the diegesis in the form of commercials, promos, [and] newsbreaks."[11] For some scholars, like Caldwell, this conception of an expansive television "text" does not entail an ontological claim. Rather, "text" here is a catch-all term to simply refer to the social circulation of television. If the point that Caldwell and like-minded scholars want to make is that tracking the contemporary social circulation of television requires us to further expand our view to incorporate emerging para-textual material and practices, then I wholeheartedly agree and my only quibble is that the point could be more clearly expressed.

However, there is a version of this expansive view of the "text" that does entail an ontological claim, and it is with *this* position that I sharply disagree. According to this view, which I will call *ontological constructivism*, it is the process of *reception* that establishes the identifying and individuating properties of the "text." Consider, for example, Matt Hills's claims about the power of episode or program guides:

> [T]he position I want to develop here is the notion that cult TV's narratives and very seriality are *actively worked over by secondary texts such as the programme guide* ... [A]pproaches to seriality cannot restrict themselves to formal analysis of "the TV series" as an isolated "text" [...] but must consider the ways in which seriality is produced, managed, and activated, such as the episode guide.[12]

Jonathan Gray pushes this line of thinking somewhat further in a discussion of how fans, "anti-fans," and "non-fans" engage with television, asserting:

> [T]he very nature and physicality of the text changes when watched by the non-fan, becoming an entirely different entity and spelling out serious ramifications for the study of texts ... non-fan engagement with the television text denies us the existence of the solitary, agreed-on text.[13]

Importantly, although ontological constructivism is often advanced in fan studies contexts, a similar view is evident in more general discussions of television as well. Moreover, this is in some part because ontological constructivism names a broader view about the ontology of artworks that is in circulation in literary studies, philosophical aesthetics, and other related fields.

For this reason, I want to spend some time critically analyzing ontological constructivism. Ontological constructivism in television studies seems to gain succor from the ambiguity that envelops the term "text." One of the reasons I believe the term is irredeemable is that the plausibility of claims made about "texts" usually depend upon just how one conceives of the referent of that term, which is exactly what the term itself obscures. So, specific claims about "texts" cannot be evaluated without first disambiguating the way in which "texts" are conceived.

Gray and Hills conceive of the "text" in particular ways that seem to support ontological constructivism, but which, in fact, do no such thing. Gray's comments are helpful in this context, because he explicitly invokes Roland Barthes's distinction between work and "text."[14] Gray explains: "I use Roland Barthes's terminology of the 'work' as the actual, physical object of the presence on the screen, and the 'text' as existing only in the interaction, and as 'practical collaboration' with the reader."[15]

This is a rather curious appeal to authority because in the essay to which Gray refers, "From Work to Text," Barthes explicitly states that he offers no arguments in support of his position: "these are speech-acts, not arguments, 'hints,' approaches which agree to remain metaphorical."[16] Rather, Barthes baldly asserts a number of propositions that seem to need substantial explanation and support: "The Text is a methodological field," "*The Text is experienced only in an activity; in a production*," "The Text is always paradoxical," "The Text ... practices the infinite postponement of the signified," and "it solicits from the reader a practical collaboration."[17] So, the first question to ask is whether, in light of Barthes's oracular tone and lack of supporting argumentation, it seems wise to accept this conception of "the text" and, moreover, use it as a starting point to theorize the nature of *television* reception. I would gently suggest that, in light of the abundance of more cogent, substantiated accounts on offer in television studies, the answer is, clearly, "no."

But suppose we accept Barthes's work/ text distinction and his conception of "the Text"—notwithstanding the lack of argumentation for either. Although this will get Gray's argument off the ground, it comes at significant cost. First, if "texts" are, *by stipulation*, not things, but activities or processes in which the "reader" collaborates, then claims that fans, anti-fans, and non-fans change the nature of television "texts" are true, but only trivially so. The argument is circular; the conclusion that "readers" alter "texts" is assumed from the outset by adopting Barthes's conception of "texts."

A second problem is that if "texts" are perpetually in flux—being produced by "readers" and infinitely postponing the "signified"—then their identities are wholly indeterminate. On this account, asking when a television "text" is finished or what its boundaries or identity conditions are is pointless, because "The Text cannot stop."[18] Such a conception of television "texts" seems deeply implausible, and it can explain neither how it is we seem to successfully individuate at least some television "texts" nor how intersubjective access to the same "text" appears possible. That is, this variety of ontological constructivism is unable to account for our ordinary appreciative practices, which are predicated upon our ability to agree upon an object of analysis.[19] If Gray were right, then such practices would simply be incoherent because there is no "agreed-on text." On the contrary, we seem largely capable of agreeing upon which "texts" we discuss and debate. One wonders why people would employ and read the work of television critics if things were otherwise. If it were the case that no "agreed-on text[s]" existed, why would we continue to discuss and debate what we watch on television?

Gray's position is incoherent and self-defeating. He claims that "non-fan engagement with the television text denies us the existence of the solitary, agreed-on text," but his own argument denies that he can speak of "*the* television text" at all, let alone write a book about *The Simpsons*, which he evidently has done.[20] Perhaps Gray would claim he could block this objection because he maintains that there is an objective work "on the screen." But this is an unpromising line of defense, because if "readers" engage the "work," then his work/"text" distinction dissolves.

Similar problems arise if we accept, with Matt Hills, a conception of the "text" derived from reading formation theory. Hills cites Tony Bennett and Janet Woollacott's *Bond and Beyond: The Political Career of a Popular Hero*, which develops and expands claims made in Bennett's seminal essay, "Texts, Readers, and Reading Formations." In the earlier publication Bennett writes, "It is high time that the text be placed into the melting pot of variability; it is necessary to recognize that the history of reading is not one in which different readers encounter 'the same text.'"[21] Moreover, Bennett seems to understand the untoward consequences of this view: "once the seductive facticity of the 'text itself' is challenged, there seems to be nothing to stop the total dissolution of the text into a potentially infinite series of different readings—in which case there seems to be nothing left for criticism to get hold of or to address."[22] Unlike Barthes, however, Bennett is not "speaking metaphorically."

Hills's account faces the same objections as did Gray's. Claims about audiences actively working on television "texts" are trivially true because Hills's adoption of reading formation theory *ensures* that fans "actively work over" the seriality of television "texts." The argument is circular because Hills does not actually demonstrate his point; his preferred theoretical framework gives it to him at the outset. Nevertheless, *why* Hills would want to accept the core assumptions of reading formation theory is a puzzling question. For as Bennett himself indicates, the truth of this view would render our ordinary appreciative practices nonsensical, yet it offers no explanation of how it is that we do in fact seem to have intersubjective access to and agreement upon the objects of criticism. One wonders, for example, if Hills has received angry letters from people who have bought his books on *Doctor Who*, demanding an explanation as to why he was discussing some other "text" rather than the "text" that *they* encountered.[23]

Gray and Hills want to explain fan practices. Nothing I have said here is meant to suggest that this is not a worthy endeavor, let alone deny the facts about the reception practices of fans (and other viewers). Rather, my point is that embracing ontological constructivism for the purposes of analyzing the reception of television is self-defeating. It is self-defeating because it depends upon a circular argument and it posits an ontological view that, rather than *explaining* reception practices, makes nonsense of them. The study of television reception is too important for us to uncritically accept approaches underpinned by ontological constructivism.

From Work to "Text" in Television Studies

At this point, I think it might be productive to look back at the original motivations underlying television studies' conceptualization of "the text" and embraces of ontological constructivism to see if we can put these ideas in more promising formulations. To be fair to Gray and Hills, it may be the case that one reason they do not offer more sustained argumentation for either treating television as "text" or ontological constructivism is because, in television studies, both views have been in currency and largely unchallenged for quite some time.

However one wishes to date the genesis of television studies, it was only in the 1970s that the "text" became a significant *theoretical* concept in the scholarly study of television, as the influence of semiotics spread throughout the Anglophone academy.[24] Of particular note here are two papers: First, Umberto Eco's 1972 essay, "Towards a Semiotic Inquiry into the Television Message," which posited "television outputs as a system of signs," comprising "a sender and an addressee [and] a code supposed to be common to both."[25] After detailing the supposed "system of codes and subcodes" and "ideological system" constitutive of the "'significance system which the [television] message as a whole connotes," Eco points out, "What the semiotic analysis cannot define is the actual system of every addressee … In the finished message, codes and subcodes interact with the receiver's framework of reference and make the different kinds of meaning reverberate one upon another."[26] Whether or not one wants to accept the semiotic approach advanced here, Eco's main point is separable from his approach and is cogent: The uptake of a television "message" cannot simply be read off the "text" itself, for the "text" may, to some extent and within certain limits, be interpreted in different ways that may vary according to viewers' individual "framework[s] of reference." In short, how viewers actually interpret "television texts" cannot be discovered through analysis of the "texts" themselves; rather, as an empirical matter, "this can only be discovered through field research on the audience."[27]

The second paper of this period to invigorate the "text" as an important theoretical concept in television studies was Stuart Hall's classic "Encoding/Decoding" essay written a year later in 1973, but not formally published until 1980. Not unlike the way in which television studies scholars have sometimes overlooked Barthes's warnings that he was speaking "metaphorically," the field has made the encoding/decoding model a focal point of attention—first to "apply" it, then to criticize it—despite Hall's own conception of it as a "rudimentary paradigm"; its influence, however, is undeniable.[28] According to Hall, "The codes of encoding [by producers] and decoding [by viewers] may not be perfectly symmetrical ... The lack of fit between the codes has a great deal to do with the structural differences of relation and position between broadcasters and audiences, but it also has something to do with the asymmetry between the codes of 'source' and 'receiver' at the moment of transformation into and out of the discursive form."[29] Like Eco, Hall advances his model against the backdrop of semiotics, but his underlying point is separable from this approach and is sound. Sometimes, "Television producers ... find their message 'failing to get across.'" There is no guarantee that receivers will understand the message(s) intended by producers. Moreover, in what Hall terms "negotiated" and "oppositional" "readings," viewers choose to make use of "texts" that are not intended by producers.[30]

The important theoretical points that both Eco and Hall make, then, are that viewers' interpretations and, more broadly, uses of television "texts" may depart from what is intended by television producers ("senders" or "encoders" of "messages"), and the ways in which they do so demand *empirical* investigation. Interestingly, one sees this central idea investigated and expanded upon in subsequent research in two rather distinct paradigms of television studies: empirical, audience reception studies *and* purely theoretical "reception study" influenced by reception theorists in literary studies. The first category includes research such as David Morley's *The "Nationwide" Audience* and Ien Ang's *Watching Dallas*, while the second group includes, most notably, the work of John Fiske.[31] For some time—through to the late 1980s, by my reckoning—there was a significant overlap in how these two distinct traditions of television reception studies conceived of "the text." In most cases, "the text" refers to what I have been calling "the work"—that is the episode, series, program, or whatever is transmitted. Here the value of conceiving the object as a "text" is that it emphasizes the variability of interpretation and use on the part of receivers. This point, as I've indicated, is basically sound and entails no contentious ontological commitments.

For the second group of television reception scholars, at least, this conception of the "text" then undergoes a shift. Motivated, perhaps, by the idea that it is logically possible that any number of individual viewers might all "read" a given "text" in different ways, John Fiske advances a Barthesian work/"text" distinction in the context of television. "A program," Fiske writes, "is a clearly defined and labeled fragment of television's output. It has clear boundaries, both temporal and formal ... Programs are stable,

Ontology   97

fixed entities ..."[32] On the other hand, Fiske claims, "A text is a different matter altogether. Programs are produced, distributed, and defined by the industry; "texts" are the product of their readers. So a program becomes a "text" at the moment of reading, that is, when its interaction with one of its many audiences activates some of the meanings/pleasures that it is capable of provoking."[33] Moreover, according to Fiske, to the extent that television "texts" must be "produced" by viewers, they are akin to Barthesian "writerly" texts, which must be "produced" by readers; thus, Fiske dubs this sort of text "producerly" and says that it "needs to be understood as a category that need not be determined only by the structure of the work, but one that can be entered by the strategy of reading."[34] While there are number of questions we could raise about the cogency of this proposal, note here that the version of ontological constructivism here is a weak one inasmuch as the putatively constructed *object*, the "text" is susceptible to a deflationary re-description as a *process* of constructing meaning out of one's sociocultural background and the program on the screen. We should, I think, resist assenting to this account of how television programs acquire semantic content and are interpreted, but that is beside the point here. The important point is that if the constructive activity Fiske details in *Television Culture* is redescribed as a socio-culturally influenced process of meaning-making rather than the creation of a nebulous abstract object, then there need not be anything ontologically contentious about his proposal.

Just two years, later, however, Fiske advances a significantly more extreme version of ontological constructivism.[35] Note, in this passage, first the conflation of the two entities he keeps separate in *Television Culture*, program and "text," and, second, the subsequent conflation of "text" and audience:

> [T]he television text, or program, is no unified whole delivering the same message in the same way to all its "audience." The old literary idea of the organic, self-contained text has been exploded so comprehensively that there is no need for me here to contribute further to its demolition. But we still need the term, or something like it, to refer to television's meaning-making potential, though we might do better to make it less concrete, less comfortable to handle, and to use the word "textuality," whose abstraction signals its potentiality rather than its concrete existence.[36]

In sum, Fiske claims, "There is no text, there is no audience, there are only the processes of viewing—that variety of cultural activities that take place in front of the screen which constitute the object of study that I am proposing.[37]

Given the complexity of even this oversimplified historical sketch, it is not surprising that cultural studies and television studies perennially pause to note the vast amount of chaos and confusion around the nature of television and other cultural "texts."[38] Furthermore, the problem is compounded by the fact that "text" is a deeply ambiguous word to begin with. For example, whether or not it is true, as Caldwell claims, that "extra-textual" elements like websites "require greatly expanding the notion of what a TV text is" depends entirely on how one defines a television "text" in the first place. In short, it is hard to get a grip on the various claims of "textualists" *tout court* and ontological constructivists more specifically. Therefore, in what follows, I will critically address a few distinct ideas individually, starting with Fiske's ontological constructivism and finishing with some comments on the received wisdom of referring to television "texts" even in the absence of any significant theoretical commitments.

Ontological Constructivism and Pragmatism

To give Fiske and his intellectual descendants the best possible case for ontological constructivism, it will be helpful to bolster his claims with arguments that have been advanced by theorists who take a pragmatist approach in philosophical aesthetics.[39] As the object of inquiry here is television, rather than texts properly so-called, I will not directly engage with the work of the major pragmatist contributions to literary studies by scholars such as Richard Rorty and Stanley Fish. However, I don't think much important depends on this and I sincerely hope that television studies folks who are sympathetic to Rorty and Fish will find the general pragmatist approach well represented in what follows. One prefatory note: Pragmatism—especially that of Fish—is often associated not just with ontological constructivism, but also with interpretive constructivism, or, constructivism about meaning. Note, however, that ontological constructivism and meaning constructivism are logically distinct theses; in principle, one could reject ontological constructivism and endorse meaning constructivism. In this chapter, I limit my discussion to ontological constructivism. I wait to turn to interpretive issues in the next two chapters, although I will briefly flag some of the ways the discussion here bears upon what comes later.

The pragmatist philosophers I have in mind are John Dewey, one of the key figures of the original pragmatist movement, Stephen C. Pepper, who was immediately influenced by him, and contemporary pragmatists (sometimes called "neo-pragmatists"), including Michael Krausz, Joseph Margolis, and Richard Shusterman.[40] However, a comment from another founding figure of pragmatism, William James, clearly and pithily expresses the central idea upon which the ontological constructivist might wish to build: "In our cognitive as well as our active life we are creative. We *add*, both to the subject and to the predicate part of reality. The world stands really malleable, waiting to receive its final touches at our hands ... *for pragmatism* [reality] is still in the making, and awaits part of its complexion from the future."[41]

To start, recall from the previous chapter the distinction between a work's vehicular medium and its artistic medium. It is common among philosophers of art to embrace a related distinction between the vehicle of an artwork and the work itself, where the latter is the proper object of criticism, aesthetic appreciation, and so forth.[42] For reasons that will become clear later in the chapter, when I sketch some more constructive ideas about ontological issues, I think the distinction is sound, but nevertheless it leaves open a wide variety of options to account for the ontology of artworks.

One broadly pragmatist thought here, which might be harnessed in support of ontological constructivism, is this: Owing to the temporal nature of perception, the apprehension of the work must be built up from a successive series of perceptions of the vehicle. As Stephen Pepper puts it with reference to some of the ideas of Dewey, the object of criticism … "is the full potentiality of aesthetic perception available to the aesthetic vehicle. But what connects the two and actualizes both for aesthetic appreciation is the sequence of perceptual immediacies stimulated by the vehicle."[43] Pepper acknowledges that his claim, "The object of criticism is some sort of assemblage of perceptions," appears to entail a relativist view, but he regards this as an untoward outcome and resists the conclusion, saying instead: "It is this fact that gives an illusory support to the view that there are as many works of art as there are perceptions of it, and that one perception is as good as another, and that there is no verifiable significance in saying that one perception is less adequate aesthetically than another."[44]

Hopefully the sort of view Pepper wants to resist sounds familiar to some television scholars, because it clearly parallels debates about interpretation and aesthetic judgment, which is one of the reasons I want to examine here in the context of ontology.[45] In television studies, a common perspective, which I shall discuss in Chapter 6, is that aesthetic or artistic judgments of television are basically viewers' *projections* of aesthetic or artistic properties and values, which seems to entail that aesthetic or artistic properties and values are relative to the tastes or sensibilities of individual viewers. So, the argument goes, judgments of artistic or aesthetic value are *expressions* of taste and, as such, also relative. Television scholars might wish to also take this sort of line with regard to the properties of "texts" *tout court*—that is, with regard to all perceptual properties and, more broadly, individuating properties of a "text" rather than just their aesthetic or artistic properties. Such a broad ontological view would, seemingly, make the route to projectivism and relativism about aesthetic or artistic value easier; if all the properties of a "text" are constructed (via projection or other means), then this includes aesthetic or artistic properties. I will try to show, however, that this is a difficult line to tow. Nevertheless, one can coherently deny ontological constructivism and accept a projectivist or expressivist account of aesthetic or artistic value. So, even if ontological constructivism fails, the common expressivist view about aesthetic or artistic value in television will need to be addressed on its own merits in due course. (The same points apply, *mutatis mutandis*, for questions about meaning, as I discuss in Chapters 4 and 5.)

So, the ontological constructivist might seem to be on firmer ground by borrowing the idea that the object of criticism encountered by any viewer must be constructed by successive perceptions—ground that is, to some extent, shared with E. H. Gombrich in art history and David Bordwell in film studies. Although neither ultimately embrace the sort of ontological constructivism at issue here, both accept broadly constructivist theories of perception, emphasizing the top-down cognitive processing that is constitutive of "the beholder's share" in the perceptual experience of artworks.[46] Although I do not want to saddle Bordwell with a view he merely hinted at thirty years ago, one passage is too apt to pass by here, for it summarizes, roughly, the argument I am suggesting is open to the ontological constructivist:

> Seeing is thus not a passive absorption of stimuli. It is a constructive activity, involving very fast computations, stored concepts, and various purposes, expectations, and hypotheses. A comparable account can be provided for auditory perception. No one has yet delineated a Constructivist theory of aesthetic activity, but its outlines look clear enough. The artwork is necessarily incomplete, needing to be unified and fleshed out by the active participation of the perceiver.[47]

That is, the ontological constructivist might further argue that his or her view finds support in constructivist accounts of perceptual psychology.[48]

However, the development of an ontological constructivist position along these lines faces significant empirical and conceptual challenges. I will skip over the empirical challenges here, but suffice it to say that, given the debate in the scientific literature, Pepper's claim regarding our limited perceptual capacities is subject to scientific dispute, as is the general, constructivist account of perception.[49] The conceptual challenges are significant in their own right: First, the constructivist idea that perception is partly constituted by or essentially involves inferences arguably depends upon an ambiguous conception of "inference" that, when disambiguated in any number of ways, makes the claim significantly less compelling.[50] Second, Bordwell's suggestion that the artwork is incomplete and needs to be "fleshed out" by the constructive activity of the perceiver simply conflates the putatively "impoverished stimulus" that generates perceptual content (however one wants to conceive of those things) with the objects of perception themselves. One would need to tell a distinct, idealist, metaphysical story to support the claim that the objects of perception were also constructions.[51] So, in fact, the ontological constructivist thesis gets no traction from the constructivist account of perception anyway.

Furthermore, Pepper's metaphysical account, which, incidentally, does tend toward idealism, faces its own problems.[52] How exactly could the object of criticism be an assemblage of perceptions? There are significant ontological and axiological puzzles here. Presumably, the assemblage of perceptions is built up from a series of perceptions, but how does this process get going at first, when there is no assemblage to be perceived? And how does one make sense of the idea of perceiving a perception, let alone perceiving an assemblage of perceptions?[53] If Pepper or the ontological constructivist could answer these questions, they would still owe a compelling answer to the question posed by one of Pepper's original critics: "In construing 'object of critical evaluation' as a construct or a collection, is there not a danger of misunderstanding *what* it is that a particular critic is likely to be criticizing?"[54] Furthermore, like Gray and Hills, advocates of Pepper's view would also owe an explanation of how critics can have intersubjective access to the same object of criticism and engage in rational debate about its various properties.

Here the ontological constructivist can call in the cavalry: the neo-pragmatists. Joseph Margolis and Michael Krausz, in particular, have advanced a doctrine the latter calls "imputationalism," which attempts to explain away the sorts of objections that can be leveled at constructivist ontological accounts of artworks. "According to the imputationalist view," writes Krauz, "an interpretation may constitute or impute features of its object-of-interpretation ... Imputational interpretation involves imputing properties which, in being imputed, actually become intrinsically part of the work."[55] Interestingly, Krausz's first move to motivate this view is to draw upon a putatively non controversial distinction between describing and interpreting a work advanced by Joseph Margolis. Description, he claims, "implies a stable, public, relatively well-defined object available for inspection."[56] Interpretation, however, is a very different matter, according to Margolis, who I will quote at length here because, to my mind, quite a bit hangs on how one conceives of "interpretation":

> [It] ... suggests a touch of virtuosity, an element of performance, a shift from a stable object whose properties are enumerable (however complex they may be) to an object whose properties pose something of a puzzle or challenge—with emphasis on the solution of the puzzle, on some inventive use of the materials present, on the added contribution of the interpreter, and on a certain openness toward possible alternative interpretations. In description, the emphasis is upon an object independent of any particular effort of description, an object that *has* or *has not* the properties attributed to it ... In interpretation, the emphasis is upon the critic's performance, on what is added beyond the mere materials provided.[57]

For television scholars who are unfamiliar with this literature, I hope at least the parallels between Margolis and Krausz's account of the objects of interpretation and Fiske's "textual" constructivism are apparent. If these neo-pragmatists are right, their arguments would provide the best support for Fiske's ontological constructivism. But are they?

I think they are not and wish to raise several objections. This version of constructivism, by which interpreters supposedly impute properties to the objects of interpretation, depends on a tendentious account of interpretation.

Because I will explore interpretation at length in the next two chapters, I will not elaborate upon the point here; note, though, that while it is plausible that Margolis describes *some* interpretive practices, it seems very unlikely that his account is comprehensive. For even if some interpretive practices, which we can think of as individuated by their particular *aims*, are constructive in the way Margolis claims, it is still the case that some fairly standard practices of interpretation aim to offer an account of what a given work means *independent* of the critic's own "contribution."[58] In other words, it seems implausible that the boundary between description and interpretation is as hard as Margolis implies; some interpretive practices involve just the sort of activity Margolis describes as "describing" and, thus, in no way construct the objections of interpretation.

Furthermore, if we respect Margolis's distinction between describing and interpreting, it is not entirely clear how the imputationalist view can get off the ground unless it posits a rather odd and implausible view of interpretation and its objects. For the acknowledgment of a practice of "describing," which involves "a stable, public, relatively well-defined object available for inspection," implies that works themselves are not constructed or imputed with any properties in the activities of reception. If things were otherwise, "describing" wouldn't be possible. So, the imputationalist view depends upon accepting the idea that what is "constructed" is *not* the work itself, but rather some *other* object—that is, the work + interpretation. Here again there are parallels with Fiske's constructivist view of the television "text," and these two accounts also share the same problems.[59] Although Krausz claims otherwise, it is hard to see how the advocates of this view could avoid an extreme multiplication of objects of interpretation, as it looks like every interpretation constructs a distinct object.[60] This comes at significant cost: again there is no explanation of how intersubjective access to the same object of interpretation is possible and thus no foundation for the rationality of our ordinary critical practices. Further, it is entirely unclear why people should be sufficiently interested in "texts" to discuss them with others the first place, as the view seems to result in a kind of solipsism. And, rather than being theoretically interesting, the view is tautological: Given a sufficiently expansive ontology, it is trivially true that every time one experiences a work a slightly distinct entity (i.e., a particular experience of the work) is created.[61]

Now despite Krausz's dependence upon Margolis's distinction between describing and interpreting, he tries to deny all of this. He claims that "the imputationalist view holds that cultural entities are the class of their interpretations and that there is no object-of-interpretation as such ... What is interpreted is not constituted independently of interpretation; interpretation constitutes objects-of-interpretation."[62] But the imputationalist lacks a satisfactory account of how this actually happens. There is no compelling argument to support the claim that we impute, in any substantive sense, properties to the things we interpret; this just seems to conflate interpretations with their objects. How, exactly, does interpretation get off the ground if there is no object-of-interpretation as such? Pressed to explain the apparent circularity here, Krausz (and advocates of similar views) inevitably point to a "constraint" that supposedly *partially* constitutes the object-of-interpretation, but this is of course nothing other than a *work* (for television scholars, it is the program on the screen), which obviates the need for an inflationary concept of the "object-of-interpretation." When it is the work as presented to us, whether on a television screen or other means, that we are interested in studying, there is simply no need to posit that it is incomplete or just one part of some "object-of-interpretation" or "text"—concepts which simply beg the question in favor of constructivists.[63]

I have spent some time rebutting ontological constructivism because, it seems to me, it has so much currency in television studies, and yet it is deeply misguided. Nevertheless, I do not think that it is necessary to accept such contentious ontological commitments to establish some of the key points ontological constructivism seems deployed to support in television studies; in fact, I will touch on some them in greater length in the next chapter. For example, I am happy to accept the claim that interpretations and, indeed, even perceptions of a given television show diverge among viewers of differing backgrounds and/or with differing interpretive aims. Perhaps, for example, it is the case that I think *M*A*S*H* is *really* about the Vietnam War, whereas my students think it is just about what it appears to be about—the Korean War. Or perhaps in a classroom tutorial, I encourage my students to interpret the show as being about the Vietnam War because this has the effect of making it a more interesting and better show, rather than because I am intent that they are persuaded that my interpretation is correct. Diversity in our perception of television works and interpretive aims is undoubtedly part of what makes the study of television so interesting. But neither does it follow that there is no objective work that exists prior to reception, nor that we need an ontologically inflationary conception of the "text" to account for such diversity.

In this sense, I am advocating for retaining the insights that reception studies of television have produced, but abandoning the concept of the "text" for the sake of theoretical parsimony and conceptual clarity. I recognize that part of the original impetus to "textualize" television was, laudably, to make a claim for its worthiness as an object of study, as well as to reject the stereotype of television viewers as passive dopes.[64] Thanks to the work our field has done, these claims no longer require defense. Furthermore, the cogent points regarding the variability of reception, made by theorists from Hall to Fiske and empirical researchers from Ang to Skeggs and Wood, can all be secured without appeal to the "text." Therefore, it is hard to see the advantage of retaining the term given its imbrication with ontological constructivism and, furthermore, its coarseness as a theoretical concept. With regard to this latter point, I have two specific thoughts. First, television studies' ongoing disavowal of the fact that its object of inquiry is actually

104 *Ontology*

audio-visual rather than textual has impeded the field from developing the sorts of apposite and precise critical approaches common in contemporary film studies.[65] Surely if we as television scholars are interested in the reception of television, we ought to be thinking of television as something that engages us visually, aurally, haptically, cognitively, and emotionally rather than as "text" to be "decoded."[66]

"Texts," properly so-called, are composed of words, which bear conventional relationships to their meanings. However, pictorial and photographic representations (not to mention sound recordings) are not arbitrary signs akin to words; pictures (photographic and otherwise) instead involve a non-arbitrary relationship to the things they depict.[67] Shots of kangaroos do not represent kangaroos as a matter of convention in the same way that the word "kangaroo" refers to kangaroos. A shot depicts what it is a shot *of*, and a well-taken shot of a kangaroo cannot be a representation of a whale in the way that the word "kangaroo" could, in principle, be used to refer to not kangaroos but to whales. Apprehending works of film and television is in no small part a matter of recognizing what shots are *of* (and this is to say nothing of our perception of sound) and is in *no* part a matter of "decoding" texts (unless there is literal text, like subtitles, on the screen).[68]

I am aware that television studies is not oblivious to the view I advocate. Quite the contrary, it was challenged at the very emergence of the field, most notably in Hall's seminal "Encoding/Decoding" essay. Indeed, this may be part of the problem: Television studies has, from the start and inveterately, conceived of its object of inquiry as textual; Hall even says, "[Television] is itself constituted by the combination of two types of *discourse*, visual and aural."[69] In support of this discursive or textual view of television, Hall claims, "Simple visual signs appear to have achieved a 'near-universality' [...] though evidence remains that even apparently 'natural' visual codes are culture-specific. However, this does not mean that no codes have intervened; rather, that the codes have been profoundly naturalized."[70] This bit of received wisdom, which has since tacitly undergirded television studies' conception of its object of inquiry as "textual," is manifestly false and has not been subject to nearly enough scrutiny in the field. Defending this claim at length is beyond my purview here, but support for it in film studies, philosophical aesthetics, and the psychological sciences is substantial.[71]

My second thought about the coarseness and inappropriateness of the "text" as a theoretical concept is that the ambiguity of the term leads to conceptual confusion. When a term like "text" is used ambiguously, the ontology of television "texts" will certainly appear nebulous—not because the individuating and identity conditions of television works are themselves fuzzy, but rather because the reference of the term is indeterminate.[72] Moreover, we already have a more precise lexicon at our disposal, which includes terms like "episode," "season," and "series"—all of which, in my view, name distinct sorts of television artworks. A more specific term, like "episode," picks out a concept that has clearer ontological boundaries. In short, what may seem to be vexing ontological questions about television "texts" are, in at least many cases, actually problems of reference unrecognized as such. Therefore, a preliminary step in determining the identity and individuating conditions of television works is simply to abandon the term "text" in favor of more precise terms.

My argument here has appealed to the premise that background ideas about the ontology of works are actually built into our television lexicon.[73] That is, our use of terms like "episode," "season," and "series," involves tacit conceptions of the ontology of these things to which these terms refer.[74] However, this idea needs further explanation and defense. Furthermore, even if this claim is true, one may still want a more precise explanation of what determines these tacit ontological conceptions and, additionally, what determines television work-identity.

From "Text" to Work in Television Studies

Although I hinted at this in my critical remarks, I want to now explicitly argue that our ontological theorizing must be constrained in important ways by our appreciative practices. This insistence upon what P. F. Strawson called "descriptive metaphysics" is not new but has recently attracted an increasing number of advocates in philosophical aesthetics.[75] In Strawson's words, "Descriptive metaphysics is content to describe the actual structure of our thought about our world, [and] revisionary metaphysics is concerned to produce a better structure."[76] Arguably, this view of metaphysics has particular traction in philosophical aesthetics because the object of inquiry is often (but not exclusively) artworks, which seem non-controversially described as human-kinds rather than natural kinds. For example, writing about the ontology of musical works, Jerrold Levinson argues that works of music must be individuated such that they can "bear the aesthetic and artistic attributes we importantly ascribe to them. We have to conceive of them so that they are what such attributions are *of*."[77] As another philosopher of art, David Davies, points out, this argument applies, *mutatis mutandis*, to how we conceive the ontology of art more generally: "the work of art, as a subject of inquiry in the philosophy of art, is the unit of criticism and appreciation—the entity of which we predicate the properties we ascribe in criticism and appreciation—and the individuation of works must reflect this fact."[78] In short, what I am advocating here is, to use Davies's term, a "pragmatic constraint" on our theorizing about the ontology of television.[79]

This proposal is open to two immediate worries. First, one may want to know why ontological assumptions embedded in our appreciative practices cannot simply be misguided. Consider the critical consensus that, with its series finale, "Everyone's Waiting," *Six Feet Under* (HBO 2001–2005) ended on a note of unity and resolution.[80] But what ensures that the ontology of *Six Feet Under* is what the critical consensus takes it to be, and that the series ends where and when critics and viewers assume it ends? Why can't it be the case that such assumptions are sometimes (or usually) just wrong? This sort of idea is implicit in the arguments put forth by Gray and Hills. Second, one may object that our appreciative practices do not have the uniformity that the proposal seems to assume. Further, one may want to know precisely which or whose practices of criticism the proposal invokes. I want to address these objections with a counterargument grounded in Amie L. Thomasson's proposal for even stronger constraints on theorization than those suggested by Davies.[81] However, I will continue to use Davies's term, "pragmatic constraint," as a shorthand and, hopefully, a transparent way of referring to the sort of limits we ought to place upon our ontological theorizing.

The idea that our collective, common-sense views of the ontology of art could be wrong presupposes that there are certain mind-independent facts about the nature of artworks. In other words, for our collective, common-sense intuitions about the ontological boundaries of a television series to be erroneous, there must be some mind-independent, empirically discoverable truth about the nature of television series of which most of us are ignorant—for example, that viewers, in Hills's terms, "work over" a program's serial narrative. (Of course, if the claim is not that our common-sense views of things like television series are wrong vis-à-vis some real truth about their nature, but rather that we should treat television series differently—for example, *as if* they were perpetually revisable "texts"—then the objection loses its force). Consider a natural kind like water. Children may insist that ice is not really water, but we can explain why they are wrong by appealing to mind-independent facts about ice and water—specifically, that both are essentially H_2O. There are important differences in these two situations, as I explain below, but in each case, if our collective, common-sense beliefs can be overruled, it is because there are, putatively, mind-independent facts about the *real* nature of these things.

This general view is arguably plausible when it comes to natural kinds. The view is supported by direct reference theories, according to which natural kind terms acquire reference based upon a causal relationship to a set of objects that are individuated by their underlying essence. On this kind of theory of reference, a natural kind term like "water" just refers to whatever things have the underlying structure—irrespective of what we believe the nature of water to be.[82] For example, we could successfully refer to ice even if we had erroneous beliefs about its nature—say, that it had the same chemical structure as liquid nitrogen. And this belief does not bear upon what its nature actually is; a collective intuition that what we all call "ice" has the nature of liquid nitrogen does not make it so.

However, as Thomasson argues, there are serious problems with this view if we try to employ it to understand the ontology of human-kinds like artifacts and artworks. The reference of an art-kind term cannot be established in virtue of a causal connection to a mind-independent essence like a chemical structure. To establish the reference of an art-kind term, we need some other way for the term to pick out a specific sort of object. Suppose I point to a DVD box, and I recommend that you check out that "television series." My reference will remain ambiguous unless I have some way of distinguishing the sort of thing I have in mind from the other things to which I could be referring: a box, a disc, special features included on the disc, and so on. What disambiguates the reference of my term—what identifies what I actually mean by "television series" from all the other things to which I could be referring—is a tacit ontological conception of what a television series is. The general argument, as Thomasson makes it, is this:

> In order to unambiguously ground the reference of a general term to name a kind of work of art, the grounder must not only have the idea that the reference of his or her term will be an art-kind, but must also have a background conception of what *ontological* sort of art-kind he or she means the term to refer to, establishing existence conditions and identity conditions for works of that kind. Such an ontological conception then disambiguates potential reference by determining the ontological kind referred to by the art-kind term.[83]

If the term "television series" refers to anything, it refers to the sort of ontological thing competent speakers collectively have in mind when they use it.

The implication of this argument is that competent speakers cannot, collectively, be radically mistaken about the ontology of art kinds like television works. "Instead," Thomasson argues, "the background ontological conception of grounders *determines* the ontological status of the members of the art-kind referred to by the term (if the term refers at all)."[84] This, then, is the reply to the objection that common-sense assumptions about the ontology of television works embedded in our standard appreciative practices might be false. The counterargument is that such assumptions cannot, collectively, be wrong, because they actually determine the ontological features of the kinds picked out by terms used by competent speakers. This also means that revisionist theories that would overturn our common-sense ontological assumptions about television artworks cannot be correct.

Thomasson's argument should not be taken to imply, however, that the grounders of art-kind terms—people who use the terms in their everyday speech and deal with the kinds to which they refer—have well-developed ontological theories at their disposal. Rather, their tacit ontological conceptions of art kinds are grounded in our creative and appreciative practices—practices that are, as Thomasson notes, "already in place and co-evolve with the use of the art-kind term[s]."[85] On the most basic level, folks that gather around the water cooler and want to use the term *Charmed* to talk about a television series (WB 1998–2006), must have some idea of what kind of thing they want to name and some tacit conception of what the nature of that thing is. For example, although *Charmed* has not been on television since 2006, it has not ceased to exist; one can still access the work by using a DVD in the right sort of way; to properly access the work one must watch certain images on a screen and listen to certain sound waves; the work was complete in 2006 and its constitutive properties have not changed since then.

The reply to the second objection, regarding the lack of uniformity regarding appreciative practices, is that there *is* relative uniformity with regard to competent speakers' use of art-kind terms. This is not to say that it is impossible for an individual to misuse or misappropriate a given term. However, there is sufficient uniformity among competent speakers' use of terms that we are largely able to successfully communicate various thoughts and feelings about things on television because our terms refer to the same things. Unless we are, in our everyday language, talking past one another and using terms like "episode," "season," and "series" to refer to different things, the second objection fails.

Here, I hope, the urgency of using a more precise vocabulary becomes fully apparent. Used loosely and ambiguously, as we have seen it sometimes is in television studies (as well as literary studies), the reference of the term "text" is indeterminate. Thus, "text" can refer to any sort of ontological thing a critic wants it to, or, if used imprecisely enough, can simply fail to secure a reference at all. This has serious implications: If theorizing the ontology of television "texts" is an anything-goes game, so too will be interpreting them and evaluating them. Perhaps this is an obvious point, given that literary criticism's general turn "from work to text" was deeply intertwined with political aspirations; indeed, part of the point was to democratize criticism. But although this is a laudable goal, attempting to achieve it by relativizing work-identity is a flawed strategy because it makes criticism incoherent. If we are to have coherent, meaningful debates about the meaning and value of television works, then we need to largely agree about the ontological features of the television works we analyze and what determines those features.

If this general argument is right, then our ontological theorizing of television needs to proceed by unpacking and clarifying the ontological assumptions embedded in our background creative and appreciative practices. I want to conclude this chapter by briefly discussing one such assumption that I believe has not received enough attention in television studies: how artistic intentions play an important part in determining the identifying and individuating conditions of artworks. Reference to artistic intentions, I will argue, can clarify the problems raised by the increased serialization of television drama.

Categorical Intentions and Work-Identity

With the hope that my remarks at the beginning of Chapter 1 forestalled a number of immediate and general objections to the invocation of intentionality with regard to the creation of television and other arts, I will proceed without any further general disclaimers. I would simply remind skeptical readers that talk of artistic intentionality is logically separable from some of the more contentious ideas with which it is commonly associated—for example, the idea that the creation of art necessarily occurs in isolation, the notion that the artist is fully rational and conscious regarding intentions, the "myth" of the genius who successfully realizes all of intentions, and the claim that artworks mean whatever their artists intended.

None of these assumptions are to be found in the more subtle and careful explorations of artistic intentions, the best exemplars of which are Paisley Livingston's recent books.[86] Following his lead, I have been treating the creation of television artworks as an essentially intentional activity, where intentions are, roughly, "attitudes we take towards ends and means to those ends."[87] Such intentions may, of course, not always be successfully realized, but it is at least evident that no work of television is created entirely in the absence of intentionality. In most cases, of course, we can plausibly say a program is collaboratively produced and that either coordinated individual intentions or collective intentions are successfully realized in decisions about everything from costumes, set design, lighting, camera work and editing, to when to *end* a story arc or when *not* to make any more episodes. This is not to deny that sometimes works, including television programs, acquire properties (e.g., a boom in the shot) by accident, but to nevertheless insist that most of a work's central constitutive properties result from the successful realization of intended actions on the part of its creators. The creators' successfully realized decisions and the intentions behind them, thus, also establish work-identity.

Decisions that determine the identifying and individuating properties of works—such as when to end an episode, a story arc, a season, or a series—arise from a particular kind of intention that can plausibly be bracketed off from intentions about what a work is supposed to mean. This is roughly the distinction Jerrold Levinson makes between categorical intentions and semantic intentions. Levinson argues that semantic intentions are logically distinct from intentions artists have about what kind of thing to create and how that thing is to be approached. In his words:

> Categorical intentions involve the maker's framing and position of his product vis-à-vis his projected audience; they involve the maker's conception of what he has produced and what it is for, on a rather basic level; they govern not what a work is to mean but how it is to be fundamentally conceived or approached.[88]

Levinson makes these remarks in a discussion about literature, so the pronoun "he" refers to the singular author of a work. However, his distinction is relevant to the analysis of television inasmuch as works of television are the results of collaborative activity in which the intentions of individual agents are coordinated to some degree or another. In the present context,

110   *Ontology*

focusing on temporal boundaries allows us, I think, to invoke only categorical intentions and to avoid being distracted by the perennial debate about the relationship between semantic intentions and interpretation (although I will argue for a position in that debate in the next chapter).[89]

In the nascent literature on television aesthetics, there has already been some implicit discussion of categorical intentions, but I believe that their importance has not been fully recognized. For example, Jason Jacobs points out that for our critical judgments to be meaningful, "It is necessary to think about the different aspirations of different kinds of television, which ultimately requires thinking less about 'television' and more about particular genres and programmes."[90] He notes that, because they are programs in different genres, *Who Wants to Be a Millionaire* and *E.R.* have different aims, and ought to be evaluated accordingly. I agree and believe that this is an important point, but we ought to recognize that Jacobs is actually talking about categorical intentions. Programs do not have aims; their creators do.[91]

If we acknowledge the weight we place on categorical intentions in our common appreciative practices, we can see that there is a plausible way of answering the question Jacobs asks later in the same essay: "How do we *know* when to halt our judgement, since the boundaries of the episode take us beyond and before it?"[92] We can appeal to the very same categorical intentions Jacobs persuasively argues we should accept in a slightly different context. What guides our critical judgments of serial television works *qua* episodes, story arcs, seasons, or series—what determines the boundaries of the objects of criticism—seem to be the categorical intentions of their creators.[93] This does not mean that we usually appeal to statements creators make in order to figure out what they intend the boundaries of their works to be. Rather, we assume that these sorts of intentions are manifested in their works' artistic properties, and we attempt to uncover the relevant intentions by analyzing the works themselves.

Let me conclude this chapter by offering a few examples to show that our appreciative practices embody tacit ontological conceptions of the boundaries of television works as determined by categorical intentions. First, consider a television series that is not typically serial in nature, *South Park* (Comedy Central 1997–present). The lack of seriality in this case should make it uncontroversial to say that normally the object of our appreciative focus is the individual episode. (As I argued in Chapter 2, however, the proper appreciation of some episodes of even non-serial television involves attention to the series as a whole.) In 2009, for example, the episode "Margaritaville" won the Emmy Award for Outstanding Animated Program Less Than One Hour. However, in 2008, *South Park* won the Emmy Award for Outstanding Animated Program for One Hour or More. The explanation for this apparent paradox is that the 2008 award was given for the three "Imagination Land" episodes, which formed a complete story arc. In this case, the voters recognized that although the three episodes were manifestly individual works in their own right, they were intended to form a triptych—a distinct work whose boundaries were defined by a discrete narrative arc.

Arguably, we also evaluate shows that are typically serial by similar criteria. We usually assess individual episodes as individual works because they are intended as such—even if they are also intended to be parts of a larger work. Perhaps this is most evident in the case of pilots, which often need to be able both to stand alone and to begin a multiple-episode story arc. However, even mid-season episodes are often intended to be regarded as individual works, possessing a certain amount of narrative closure and unity of theme and style.

Consider, for example, "The Cost," an episode from the first season of *The Wire* (HBO 2002–2008). Clearly, this episode is an essential part of at least two larger works—the first season as a whole and the series as a whole. However, there is also good reason to believe the creators of *The Wire* intended this episode—and others—to stand alone as distinct works in their own right. The title, "The Cost," is a rather transparent reference to a clear, unifying theme. The episode centers on the various "costs" of structural inequality and institutional dysfunction in urban America. Most explicitly, the title is a reference to Detective Kima Greggs's near-fatal shooting during a failed undercover drug buy at the end of the episode, but it also refers to "corner boy" Wallace's descent into drug abuse and Bubbles's imminent relapse.

Moreover, the episode's unifying theme is intertwined with its narrative arc. Although it interweaves many different narrative threads that remain unresolved, several of those threads build towards the botched drug buy—including what initially appears to be a purely expository scene in which we learn about Kima's initial drive to become a police officer and her partner's reservations about this line of work. Significantly, however, Kima's shooting is not just a "cost" in its own right; because she has agreed to give Bubbles financial support to help him stay sober, he is another victim of the shooting (and, of course, deeper structural inequalities). The first scene of the episode shows Bubbles sitting in the morning sunshine, enjoying his newfound sobriety. However, he is also clearly struggling with his addiction, and this opening scene poses the question of whether he will be able to remain sober. The episode ends with a frenzied blur of police lights and sirens in the aftermath of Kima's shooting, offering an answer to the initial narrative question. This gives the episode a significant degree of narrative closure even while the cliff-hanger ending emphasizes that the season, a larger work in which the episode nests, is unfinished. Thus, the familiar activity of critically assessing individual episodes seems justified even when those episodes are constituent parts of larger works. Properties like thematic unity and narrative closure offer good evidence to believe that series creators intend us to regard individual episodes as distinct works as well as constitutive parts of other works.

112 *Ontology*

It is also worth briefly mentioning here an issue that I shall take up in more detail in the final chapter—namely, that critical evaluations of a series as a whole appeal to categorical intentions (or lack thereof) about when the series is supposed to begin and end. First, consider *Deadwood* (HBO 2004–2006). It seems to me that we are willing to make certain allowances in our criticism of the series as a whole because the creators did not intend it to end, as it did, with numerous unresolved plotlines. In other words, we would consider *Deadwood*'s lack of narrative closure a greater aesthetic flaw if its creators had actually intended to give the show closure and failed to do so. In any case, it seems that any sort of critical judgment about *Deadwood* that makes reference to the lack of closure in the final episode tacitly conceives of the series as a single work—intended to be so by its creators.

My last example draws upon *Firefly* (Fox 2002). Oddly, Fox aired the episode that *Firefly*'s creators intended to be the premiere, "Serenity," as the eleventh episode, aired other episodes out of their intended order, and did not air the final three episodes at all. Fans and critics have almost universally agreed it is not Fox's broadcast of *Firefly* that establishes when a series begins or ends, but rather the categorical intentions (finally realized with the release of the series on DVD) of the series creators.[94]

At this point, one may wonder if there is anything more to be said about what makes categorical intentions determinative in the case of *Firefly* and similar situations. First, I would acknowledge categorical intentions are contingently, rather than logically or necessarily, constitutive of a work's identifying and individuating properties. Indeed, I think that human and, more locally, cultural interests are at the heart of the explanation here. Broadly speaking, television programs are just one instance of a wide range of human artifacts whose identifying and individuating properties we standardly take to be determined by the successfully realized intentions of their makers.[95] More specifically, though, most television programs have an expressive or communicative function in a very broad sense, which is clearly intertwined with intentions of their creators. The preservation of the intended temporal order of a work's constitutive parts, whether that work is a piece of music, a poem, or a television program, is clearly essential to the work fulfilling its broadly expressive or communicative function. Concretely speaking, the temporal order of *Firefly* is as necessary to the fulfillment of its expressive or communicative function, as is the temporal order of, say, The Beatles' "A Day in the Life," James Baldwin's "Sonny's Blues," or Alexandre Dumas's *The Count of Monte Cristo*: the artist's categorical intentions about the temporal order of the works are decisive not only because we take it that the artists enjoy a certain privilege with regard to the ontology (if not the meaning) of their creations but also because rearrangement of the temporal order would thwart the expressive or communicative function of the works. One standard, which is not to say necessary or exclusive, interest we have in artworks is apprehending what an artist or group of artists intended to express or communicate (again—in a very broad sense, which is inclusive of things like mood as well as semantic content) in the work. It is partly in light of this interest that we take creators' categorical intentions about identifying and individuating properties such as temporal order to be decisive of the way the work actually is.

Moreover, fans and critics have also argued that proper critical evaluation of the series must take categorical intentions into account. Properly apprehended, *Firefly* is not as confusing and disorganized as it appeared to be when it was incorrectly broadcast on Fox. On the contrary, the work's actual structure would seem to merit more positive artistic evaluations in several regards. This example nicely puts a point on the need for us to agree about work-identity and what determines it before critical work in television aesthetics can proceed. In the case of *Firefly*, if we do not agree that successfully realized categorical intentions establish work-identity, then we will just be talking past one another, offering critical evaluations of (at least) two different works with significantly different artistic properties.[96]

In sum, if we trust the coherence of our appreciative practices—as I have argued we must—then we need to reject constructivist accounts of work-identity. We must agree upon the object of appreciation, recognizing that embedded in our appreciative practices is a tacit assumption that the successfully realized categorical intentions of the creators of television works determine work-identity. The centrality of categorical intentions to our appreciative practices suggests that in appreciation of an artwork—whether it is a painting, a symphony, a television episode, or a television series—we are, at bottom, interested in a kind of achievement on the part of an individual or a group of individuals.

Furthermore, though, it looks as if our interests partly involve what the creators of the work have intended to express or communicate. Thus, in many cases, particularly when our appreciative project is interpretation, we are also interested in creators' successfully realized semantic intentions—or so I argue in the next two chapters.

Notes

1. Consider, for example, this instructive comment from the philosopher Joseph Margolis, whose accounts of the ontology and interpretation of art significantly diverge from my own: "It is clear that one's account of the nature of criticism and the nature of an artwork is conceptually linked in the most intimate way. What we indicate we are talking about and what we may justifiably say of it depend on what it is; and what it is will, in turn, be conceded by considering how it may be fixed and identified and what may be said of it." See his *Art and Philosophy* (Atlantic Highlands, NJ: Humanities Press, 1980), 27. For a sample of general agreement, from diverse theoretical perspectives, on the idea that theorizing (or stipulating) the ontology of the television "text" is intimately connected to interpretive or other appreciative activities, see Jane Feuer, "Reading *Dynasty*: Television and Reception Theory," in *Classical Hollywood Narrative: The Paradigm Wars*, ed. Jane Gaines (Durham, NC: Duke University Press, 1992),

275–93; John Fiske, *Television Culture* (New York: Routledge, 1987); Jonathan Gray, *Show Sold Separately: Promos, Spoilers, and Other Media Paratexts* (New York: New York University Press, 2010); Jostein Gripsrud, *The Dynasty Years: Hollywood Television and Critical Media Studies* (London: Routledge, 1995); Jason Jacobs, "Issues of Judgement and Value in Television Studies," *International Journal of Cultural Studies* 4, no. 4 (2001): 432–433; Sonia Livingstone, *Making Sense of Television: The Psychology of Audience Interpretation*, 2nd ed. (London: Routledge, 1998); Cornel Sandvoss, "The Death of the Reader? Literary Theory and the Study of Texts in Popular Culture," in *Fandom: Identities and Communities in a Mediated World*, ed. Jonathan Gray, Cornel Sandvoss, and C. Lee Harrington (New York: New York University Press, 2007), 19–32; Jason Mittell, *Complex TV: The Poetics of Contemporary Television Storytelling* (New York: New York University Press, 2015). For a sample of such general agreement in broader debates about the interpretation of art and other cultural objects, see Margolis, *Art and Philosophy*, as well as Nick Couldry, *Inside Culture: Re-imagining the Method of Cultural Studies* (London: Sage, 2000); Robert Stecker, *Interpretation and Construction: Art, Speech, and the Law* (Malden, MA: Blackwell, 2003); Paisley Livingston, *Art and Intention: A Philosophical Study* (Oxford: Oxford University Press, 2005); Noël Carroll, *On Criticism* (New York: Routledge, 2009); Peter Lamarque, *Work and Object: Explorations in the Metaphysics of Art* (Oxford: Oxford University Press, 2010).

2. For a general introduction to the debates on ontology in the philosophy of art, see Stephen Davies, "Ontology of Art," in *The Oxford Handbook of Aesthetics*, ed. Jerrold Levinson (Oxford: Oxford University Press, 2005), 155–180. For a historical overview of the debates, see Paisley Livingston, "History of the Ontology of Art," *Stanford Encyclopedia of Philosophy* (Summer 2013 edition), ed. Edward N. Zalta, Accessed July 24, 2014. http://plato.stanford.edu/archives/sum2013/entries/art-ontology-history/ For a discussion of debates about the ontology of photographic and moving image artworks specifically, see David Davies, "Ontology," in *The Routledge Companion to Philosophy and Film*, ed. Paisley Livingston and Carl Plantinga (New York: Routledge, 2009), 217–26.

3. Very roughly, the "fictionalist" or "eliminativist" view to which I refer is motivated by the idea that, unlike apparently "single-instance" artworks such as paintings and sculptures, "multiple-instance" or "repeatable" artworks such as musical works, literary works, and moving-image works, seem to be ontologically mysterious abstract objects, which *prima facie* cannot be created or destroyed. So, the argument runs, there are no such works, ontologically speaking. Some so-called eliminativists nevertheless hold that this metaphysical thesis need not impede our ordinary appreciate practices or critical discourse. See, for a relatively early statement of this view, Richard Rudner, "The Ontological Status of the Esthetic Object," *Philosophy and Phenomenological Research* 10, no. 3 (March 1950): 380–88. For a more recent statement, see Anders Pettersson, "P. F. Strawson and Stephen Davies on the Ontology of Art: A Critical Discussion," *Organon F: International Journal of Analytic Philosophy* 16, no. 4 (2009): 615–31.

4. In the context of philosophical aesthetics, consider, for example, a recent debate In David Davies, "Against Enlightened Empiricism," in *Contemporary Debates in the Aesthetics and Philosophy of Art*, ed. Matthew Kieran (Malden,

MA: Blackwell, 2006), 6–36, Davies challenges "the common-sense idea that ready-mades, as works, are properly identified with the mass-produced objects exhibited in galleries" (34) in the context of a debate with Gordan Graham.
5. Glen Creeber, "The Joy of Text? Television and Textual Analysis," *Critical Studies in Television* 1, no. 1 (2006): 82.
6. Ibid., 82–83.
7. Jacobs, "Issues of Judgement," 432–433.
8. Livingston, *Art and Intention*, 57. Compare Livingston's account with Darren Hudson Hick's proposal of a sufficient condition for work completion in "When Is a Work of Art Finished?" *The Journal of Aesthetics and Art Criticism* 66, no. 1 (2008): 67–76. Also see Paisley Livingston, "When a Work Is Finished: A Response to Darren Hudson Hick" and Darren Hudson Hick, "A Reply to Paisley Livingston," in *The Journal of Aesthetics and Art Criticism* 66, no. 4 (2008): 393–98.
9. I take "extra-textual" and "para-textual" to be more or less synonymous and will not worry about subtle differences here. In deference to Jonathan Gray's recent publications, I will restrict my use of terms to the latter. See Gray, *Show Sold Separately*.
10. John Thornton Caldwell, "Convergence Television: Aggregating Form and Repurposing Content in the Culture of Conglomeration," in *Television After TV: Essays on a Medium in Transition*, ed. Lynn Spigel and Jan Olsson (Durham, NC: Duke University Press, 2004), 51. Emphasis in the original.
11. Feuer, "Reading *Dynasty*," 277.
12. Matt Hills, "Cult TV, Quality and the Role of the Episode/Programme Guide," in *The Contemporary Television Series*, ed. Michael Hammond and Lucy Mazdon (Edinburgh: Edinburgh University Press, 2005), 192. Emphasis in original.
13. Jonathan Gray, "New Audiences, New Textualities: Anti-Fans and Non-Fans," *International Journal of Cultural Studies* 6, no. 1 (2003): 75.
14. For a related view, see Sandvoss, "The Death of the Reader?"
15. Gray, "New Audiences, New Textualities," 79, n5.
16. Roland Barthes, "From Work to Text,' in *The Rustle of Language*, trans. Richard Howard (Berkeley: University of California Press, 1989), 57.
17. "The Text is a methodological field," (57); "*The Text is experienced only in an activity; in a production*," (58, emphasis in original); "The Text is always *paradoxical*," (58, emphasis in original); "The Text ... practices the infinite postponement of the signified," (59) and "it solicits from the reader a practical collaboration." (63)
18. Barthes, quoted in Gray, "New Audiences," 76.
19. For criticism of Barthes's notion of the "text," see Peter Lamarque, "The Death of the Author: An Analytical Autopsy," *British Journal of Aesthetics* 30, no. 4 (1990); Paisley Livingston, "From Text to Work," in *After Post-structuralism: Interdisciplinarity and Literary Theory*, ed. Nancy Easterlin and Barbara Riebling (Evanston, IL: Northwestern University Press, 1993); and Margit Sutrop, "The Death of the Literary Work," *Philosophy and Literature* 18 (1994).
20. Jonathan Gray, *Watching with The Simpsons: Television, Parody, and Intertextuality* (New York: Routledge, 2006).
21. Tony Bennett, "Texts, Readers, Reading Formations," *Bulletin of the Midwest Modern Language Association* vol. 16, no. 1 (1983), 15.
22. Ibid., 14.

23. See Matt Hills, *Triumph of a Time Lord: Regenerating Doctor Who in the Twenty-First Century* (London: I. B. Tauris, 2010); and Matt Hills, *Doctor Who: The Unfolding Event—Marketing, Merchandising, and Mediatizing a Brand Anniversary* (Basingstoke, UK: Palgrave Macmillan, 2015).
24. In addition to the papers discussed here, the most important work in this tradition is John Fiske and John Hartley, *Reading Television* (London: Methuen, 1978).
25. Umberto Eco, "Towards a Semiotic Inquiry into the Television Message," reprinted in *Television: Critical Concepts in Media and Cultural Studies*, vol. 2, ed. Toby Miller (New York: Routledge, 2003), 4.
26. Ibid., 14.
27. Ibid.
28. Stuart Hall, "Encoding/Decoding," reprinted in *Television: Critical Concepts in Media and Cultural Studies*, vol. 4, ed. Toby Miller (New York: Routledge, 2003), 46. For his own retrospective commentary, see Stuart Hall, "Reflections upon the Encoding/Decoding Model: An Interview with Stuart Hall," in *Viewing, Reading, Listening*, ed. Jon Cruz and Justin Lewis (Boulder, CO: Westview Press, 1994), 253–74.
29. Hall, "Encoding/Decoding," 45–46.
30. Ibid., 50; 52–53.
31. David Morley, *The "Nationwide" Audience* (London: BFI, 1980), especially Chapter 7; and Ien Ang, *Watching Dallas: Soap Opera and the Melodramatic Imagination*, trans. Della Couling (New York: Routledge, 1989), 24–28; Fiske and Hartley, *Reading Television*. I refer here to Fiske's earlier work for reasons that shall soon become apparent. For another good example in this "textualist" tradition of reception with reference to a specific program, see David Buckingham, *Public Secrets: East Enders and its Audience* (London: BFI, 1987), especially Chapter 2 and the Conclusion.
32. Fiske, *Television Culture*, 14.
33. Ibid.
34. Ibid., 96.
35. Several commentators have lamented the hostility with which Fiske's ideas were subsequently treated in the field. For example, John Hartley writes, "Criticising John Fiske for bad theory was always going to be poor sport. It was like kicking the dog for not being a cat. It was a simple category error that didn't address what he was undoubtedly good at [i.e., teaching.]" I agree with Hartley that the ad hominem attacks were unfortunate, but this passage sells Fiske's work short and drastically underestimates its lasting influence in the field. See John Hartley, *A Short History of Cultural Studies* (London: Sage, 2003), 166.
36. John Fiske, "Moments of Television: Neither the Text Nor the Audience," in *Remote Control: Television, Audiences, and Cultural Power*, ed. Ellen Seiter et al. (New York: Routledge, 1989), 56.
37. Ibid., 57. For another representative of this sort of view, see Feuer, "Reading Dynasty."
38. See, for example, Richard Johnson, "What Is Cultural Studies, Anyway?" *Social Text* 16 (1986–1987); Charlotte Brunsdon, "Text and Audience," in *Remote Control*, 116–129; Couldry, *Inside Culture*, 67–90.
39. The ontological constructivism endorsed by Fiske and Feuer has been criticized from within television/media studies. William R. Seaman, for example, writes in

response to Fiske, "it is simply false to suggest that the viewer's individual interpretation constitutes 'interaction' with the television text. The text, in its concrete manifestation as an audiovisual signal, is not altered by the viewer" (306). See "Active Audience Theory: Pointless Populism," *Media, Culture, Society* 14 (1992): 301–11. See also Jostein Gripsrud, *The Dynasty Years: Hollywood Television and Critical Media Studies* (New York: Routledge, 1995), where Gripsrud writes, "More or less common-sensically, it seems quite obvious that a study of the 'processes of viewing' presupposes the factual existence and methodological acknowledgement of audiences and texts as distinct categories" (126–27). I think both of these criticisms are sound, but, as indicated above, I appreciate later commentators' complaints that they dispatch ontological constructivism too quickly and dismissively. See, for example, Gray and Lotz, *Television Studies* (London: Polity, 2012), 69–71.
40. I will cite Pepper and the "neo-pragmatists" specifically in what follows. But for a broad view, see John Dewey, *Art as Experience* (New York: Penguin, 2005 [1934]); and Richard Shusterman, "Pragmatism," in *The Routledge Companion to Aesthetics* 3rd ed., ed. Berys Gaut and Dominic McIver Lopes (New York: Routledge, 2013), 96–105.
41. William James, *Pragmatism* (New York: Longmans, Green, and Co., 1907), 256–57. Emphasis in original.
42. Paisley Livingston has traced this distinction back to at least the late nineteenth century. A relatively recent and often-cited argument for it is given by Arthur Danto with reference to artworks such as those of Marcel Duchamp and Andy Warhol that are indiscernible from ordinary objects. Livingston, "History of the Ontology of Art"; and Arthur Danto, *The Transfiguration of the Commonplace* (Cambridge, MA: Harvard University Press, 1981).
43. Stephen C. Pepper, *The Work of Art* (Bloomington: Indiana University Press, 1955), 31. Nothing of importance hinges on how one wants to disambiguate the sense of the "aesthetic" in this passage.
44. Ibid., 36; 31.
45. See Andy Egan, "Projectivism without Error," in *Perceiving the World*, ed. Bence Nanay (Oxford: Oxford University Press, 2010), 68–96. Egan writes, "One way to motivate the projectivist thought [about the nature of perception] is to look at cases where we find what looks like interpersonal variability in the content of perception—in which different people seem to perceptually represent the same object in incompatible ways—but where we do not want to attribute asymmetric error (because, e.g., we have no good, question-begging grounds for saying one party is in a better position to track objective facts in the relevant domain than the other)" (70). Of course, the point that would be need to be convincingly shown by television studies folks who took this line.
46. Here is Gombrich, for example: "The importance for art of mobilizing the beholder's projective activities in order to compensate for the limitations of the medium can be demonstrated in a variety of fields. The indeterminate outlines of Impressionist pictures which suggest light and movement are a case in point." *The Image and the Eye: Further Studies in the Psychology of Pictorial Representation* (London: Phaidon, 1982), 100. Also see E. H. Gombrich, *Art and Illusion: A Study in the Psychology of Pictorial Representation* (New York: Pantheon, 1960).
47. David Bordwell, *Narration in the Fiction Film* (Madison, WI: University of Wisconsin Press, 1985), 32.

118 Ontology

48. See, for example, Ulric Neisser, *Cognitive Psychology* (New York: Appelton-Century-Crofts, 1967); Irvin Rock, *The Logic of Perception* (Cambridge, MA: The MIT Press, 1983); R.L. Gregory, *Eye and Brain: The Psychology of Seeing*, 5th ed. (Princeton, NJ: Princeton University Press, 1997).
49. For recent, interesting debates about the relationship between attention, perception, memory, and consciousness, see *The Journal of Consciousness Studies* 9, no. 5–6 (May 2002): 1–202. For recent debates about constructivist versus direct approaches to perception, see Joel Norman's target article, "Two Visual Systems and Two Theories of Perception: An Attempt to Reconcile the Constructivist and Ecological Approaches," and the solicited commentaries in *Behavioral and Brain Sciences* 25 (2002): 73–144.
50. See Robert Schwartz, "The Role of Inference in Vision," in his *Visual Versions* (Cambridge, MA: The MIT Press, 2006), 95–105; Gary Hatfield, "Perception as Unconscious Inference," in his *Perception and Cognition: Essays in the Philosophy of Psychology* (Oxford: Oxford University Press, 2009), 124–152.
51. See Berys Gaut, *A Philosophy of Cinematic Art* (Cambridge: Cambridge University Press, 2010), 170–71.
52. According to Pepper, "for the most part, however, and necessarily so in very complex works, the object of criticism is an objectively defined ideal rather than a particular funded [in Dewey's sense] perception." *The Work of Art*, 39.
53. See, e.g., Nathan Berall, "A Note on Professor Pepper's Aesthetic Object," *The Journal of Philosophy* 48, no. 24 (1951): 750–754; Donald F. Henze, "Is the Work of Art a Construct? A Reply to Professor Pepper," *The Journal of Philosophy* 52, no. 16 (1955): 433–439.
54. James L. Jarrett, "More on Professor Pepper's Theory of the Aesthetic Object," *The Journal of Philosophy* 49, no. 14 (1952): 478.
55. Michael Krausz, *Rightness and Reasons: Interpretation in Cultural Practices* (Ithaca, NY: Cornell University Press, 1993), 67.
56. Margolis, *Art and Philosophy*, 111.
57. Ibid.
58. I expand on this point in the next chapter, but what I have in mind here is Robert Stecker's statement of "critical pluralism"—roughly, the view that people interpret works with different aims, and the evaluation of such interpretations should be relativized to those aims. See Stecker, *Interpretation and Construction*, 55–58.
59. There is also here an echo of Arthur Danto's claim that "each interpretation [of an object] constitutes a new work." Despite my respect for Danto's many contributions to aesthetics, I think this proposal is no more plausible than those I criticize. Even if, on Danto's account, the *object* remains stable, the extreme multiplication of *works* would threaten the coherence of our appreciative practices. We would also need an independent explanation of the convergence of interest in particular "objects" despite divergence in appreciating them as works (that is, as objects under an interpretation). See Arthur C. Danto, *The Transfiguration of the Commonplace* (Cambridge, MA: Harvard University Press, 1981), 125. For critical discussion, see Stecker, *Interpretation and Construction*, 106–110.
60. See Krausz, *Rightness and Reasons*, 94–95. For criticism, see Lamarque, *Work and Object*, 168; and Stecker, *Interpretation and Construction*, esp. 119–126.
61. Krausz agrees that these are problems, but thinks his particular view escapes them. See *Rightness and Reasons*, 96–97.
62. Krausz, *Rightness and Reasons*, 93–94.

63. In my criticisms of the neo-pragmatists, I have drawn upon Stecker, *Interpretation and Construction*; and Lamarque, *Work and Object*, in particular.
64. See, especially, John Fiske and John Hartley, *Reading Television* (London: Methuen, 1978). I am indebted to Tom O'Regan for helpful conversations on this topic.
65. I have in mind here approaches that can roughly be classified as cognitive theory, phenomenological film theory, and affect theory.
66. See, for examples of the sort of work I have in mind, Kristyn Gorton, *Media Audiences: Television, Meaning, and Emotion* (Edinburgh: Edinburgh University Press, 2009); Margrethe Bruun Vaage, *The Antihero in American Television* (New York: Routledge, 2016).
67. Note this is not the same as claiming that pictures involve a non-arbitrary relationship to the things they *represent*, because what a picture depicts and represents may differ. For example, a picture of a lamb depicts a lamb but may also represent Christ. See Christopher Peacocke, "Depiction," *The Philosophical Review* 96, no. 3 (July 1987): 383–410.
68. Two caveats are in order. First, none of what I am saying discounts the puzzling nature of depiction or the vigorous debates about depiction and pictorial recognition in philosophical aesthetics and the psychological sciences. I make no claim to have an adequate account of either, but rather am merely pointing out that "conventionalism," as the view is called in this literature, is deeply implausible. Second, I am not denying that there are cinematic and television conventions, but rather am saying that it would be a mistake to think that conventions like shot/reverse-shot are purely arbitrary or entirely conventional. Rather, they partly depend upon our natural perceptual and cognitive capacities. See David Bordwell, "Convention, Construction, and Cinematic Vision," *Post-Theory: Reconstructing Film Studies*, ed. David Bordwell and Noël Carroll (Madison, WI: University of Wisconsin Press, 1996), 87–107.
69. Hall, "Encoding/Decoding," 47. Emphasis mine.
70. Ibid.
71. The psychologist Julian Hochberg puts this in pithy, forceful terms: "Any theory that holds picture perception to be a culturally acquired skill … can only be considered frivolous" (849). For the evidence and reasoning behind this claim, see "The Perception of Pictorial Representations," *Social Research* 51, no. 4 (Winter 1984): 841–62. For a good summary of related research in the psychological sciences, see James E. Cutting and Manfredo Massironi, "Pictures and Their Special Status in Perceptual and Cognitive Inquiry," in *Perception and Cognition at Century's End*, ed. Julian Hochberg (New York: Academic Press, 1998), 137–168. For objections to "conventionalism" in philosophical aesthetics, see Peacocke, "Depiction"; Richard Wollheim, *Art and Its Objects*, 2nd ed. (Cambridge, UK: Cambridge University Press, 1980); Flint Schier, *Deeper Into Pictures* (Cambridge, UK: Cambridge University Press, 1986); Robert Hopkins, *Picture, Image, and Experience: A Philosophical Inquiry* (Cambridge, UK: Cambridge University Press, 2009); and Michael Newall, *What Is a Picture? Depiction, Realism, Abstraction* (Basingstoke: Palgrave Macmillan, 2011). In the social sciences, see, especially, Paul Messaris, *Visual Literacy: Image, Mind, and Reality* (Boulder, CO: Westview Press, 1994). In film studies, see Stephen Prince, "The Discourse of Pictures: Iconicity and Film Studies," *Film Theory and Criticism*, 6th edition, ed. Leo Braudy and Marshall Cohen (New York: Oxford University Press, 2004), 87–105; Noël Carroll, "Film, Attention, and

120 Ontology

Communication: A Naturalistic Account," in *Engaging the Moving Image* (New Haven, CT: Yale University Press, 2003), 10–58 For a recent, sophisticated defense of conventionalism, see John Kulvicki, *On Images: Their Structure and Content* (Oxford: Oxford University Press, 2006) and *Images* (New York: Routledge, 2014).
72. On this point, see Sutrop, "Death of the Literary Work."
73. Amie L. Thomasson, "The Ontology of Art and Knowledge in Aesthetics," *Journal of Aesthetics and Art Criticism* vol. 63, no. 3 (Summer 2005): 221–229.
74. Sometimes terms vary across language contexts: For example, British viewers might be more likely to use the term "series" than the term "season," and use the term "programme" to refer to what I am calling "series." This does not threaten the point, however, because the *concepts* picked out by the varying terms are the same.
75. P. F. Strawson, *Individuals: An Essay in Descriptive Metaphysics* (London: Methuen, 1959). For a discussion of connections between Strawson and contemporary work in the ontology of art, in particular, excellent work by Stephen Davies, see Anders Pettersson, "P. F. Strawson and Stephen Davies on the Ontology of Art," *Organon F* 16, no. 4 (2009): 615–631. I cite additional contemporary work in this vein below. For an early instance such an approach in philosophical aesthetics, see C. I. Lewis, *An Analysis of Knowledge and Valuation* (LaSalle, IL: Open Court, 1946). For example, Lewis writes: "But esthetics, like physics, is an empirical science; and the positive laws of it require to be elicited by inductive generalization from particular instances of esthetic phenomena. Thus the nature of esthetic value is a question to be answered by analysis and *a priori*, and constitutes a topic for philosophical investigation. But the laws of the positive science of aesthetics are a question which must be left to those who possess sufficiently wide acquaintance with esthetic phenomena and are sufficiently expert to be capable of arriving at trustworthy empirical generalizations in this field" (468–69). I am grateful to Paisley Livingston for pointing me towards Lewis's work. See Livingston, "History of the Ontology of Art."
76. Strawson, *Individuals*, 9.
77. Jerrold Levinson, "What a Musical Work Is, Again," in *Music, Art, and Metaphysics* (Ithaca, NY: Cornell University Press, 1990), 231–247, cited at 241.
78. Davies, *Art as Performance*, 18.
79. Ibid., 16.
80. See the examples of viewer feedback offered in Rhiannon Bury: "Praise You Like I Should: Cyber Fans and *Six Feet Under*," in *It's Not TV: Watching HBO in the Post-Television Era*, ed. Marc Leverette, Brian L. Ott, and Cara Louise Buckley (New York: Routledge, 2008), 190–208.
81. I refer readers who are interested in Davies's defense to *Art as Performance*, 16–24. In these pages, Davies gives a nice gloss on some recent work in philosophical aesthetics that implicitly adopts such a constraint.
82. As philosophers Michael Devitt and Kim Sterelny put it, "Users of a natural kind term need not have true beliefs about the underlying nature of the relevant natural kind nor even have any beliefs sufficient to identify its members" (90). *Language and Reality*, 2nd ed. (Cambridge, MA: MIT Press, 1999).
83. Thomasson, "The Ontology of Art and Knowledge in Aesthetics," 225.
84. Ibid, 226.
85. Ibid, 225.

86. Livingston, *Art and Intention*; and Paisley Livingston, *Cinema, Philosophy, Bergman: On Film as Philosophy* (Oxford: Oxford University Press, 2009).
87. Livingston, *Art and Intention*, 208.
88. Jerrold Levinson, "Intention and Interpretation in Literature," in *The Pleasures of Aesthetics* (Ithaca, NY: Cornell University Press, 1996), 175–213, cited at 188.
89. However, Livingston argues that there seem to be some cases in which the categorical/semantic distinction dissolves. *Art and Intention*, 158–165.
90. Jacobs, "Issues of Judgement," 430.
91. In my view, inanimate objects, including television artworks and cinematic artworks, are not the kinds of things that have the capacity for behaviors like aiming, perceiving, or thinking. Creators' aims or thoughts may be manifest in such works, but inasmuch as the works do not themselves aim or think, they do not, as is sometimes claimed, have aims or thoughts in any ordinary sense. To anthropomorphize the works themselves—as Deleuze and Deleuzian critics sometimes do—is to muddy the conceptual waters.
92. Jacobs, "Issues of Judgement," 444.
93. Jacobs's proposed solution—to think of television along the lines of Romantic fragments—appears somewhat plausible, but does not explicitly acknowledge the extent to which it *depends* on allowing that categorical intentions determine how we approach both television and Romantic fragments. Recognizing that Romantic fragments are finished works that appear unfinished—or, as Livingston puts it, "genetically complete" but not "aesthetically complete"—implicitly grants sovereignty to the artist's categorical intentions. Thus, thinking about Romantic fragments answers Jacobs's worry about how we know where the boundaries of a television work are, but in a way I think he does not see in his article. See Jacobs, "Issues of Judgement," 444–445; and Livingston, *Art and Intention*, 9–61.
94. See, for example, Tasha Robinson, "*Firefly*: The Complete Series," *The A.V. Club* (January 12, 2004). Accessed March 22, 2016. http://www.avclub.com/review/firefly-the-complete-series-11623; Ken Tucker, "*Firefly* Came Back: This Is the Role Nathan Fillion Was Born to Play: A Flawed Leader of Men and Women,"(March 7, 2011), *EW*. Accessed March 22, 2016. http://watching-tv.ew.com/2011/03/07/firefly-nathan-fillion-joss-whedon/.
95. See Risto Hilpinen, "On Artifacts and Works of Art," *Theoria* 58 (1992): 58–82; Risto Hilpinen, "Authors and Artifacts," *Proceedings of the Aristotelian Society* 93 (1993): 155–178; Amie L. Thomasson, "Artifacts and Human Concepts," in *Creations of the Mind: Artifacts and Their Representations*, ed. Eric Margolis and Stephen Laurence (Oxford: Oxford University Press, 2007), 52–73; Jerrold Levinson, "Artworks as Artifacts," in Margolis and Laurence, 74–82.
96. In the case of *Firefly*, I think it would be more accurate to say that we are dealing with a correctly formed instance of the work and an incorrectly formed instance of the work, rather than two altogether distinct works.

4 Interpretation I

Introduction

The previous chapter made a case for conceiving of our object of inquiry, television programming, in a particular way. I suggested that, rather than thinking of television programming as a series of "texts" or as parts of "texts," we approach television episodes, seasons, series, and so forth as *works*, in a predominantly descriptive sense of that term.[1] The locution "work" describes a kind of artifact, or intentionally designed human creation. I argued that, for the purposes of distinguishing works from texts, it is sufficient that the relevant intentions here are categorical intentions—intentions regarding the sort of thing one makes (for example, such as what its function is) and how that thing is to be approached. One can accept this conception of works, I claimed, regardless of one's view on the relevance of semantic intentions—that is, intentions regarding what I referred to as "work meaning"—to the project of television interpretation.

However, this conception of television content will provide some traction in the exploration of interpretation that is now due. In particular, even this minimal conception of television works should prompt us to reconsider widely accepted assumptions regarding the putative proper aim of television interpretation. If television content is merely a collection of texts, the constitutive properties of which are shaped by viewers themselves, then it seems to follow quite naturally that the interpretation of television should be conceived and analyzed as a process through which viewers make meanings. But if, as I have argued, television content comprises *works*, the constitutive properties of which are fixed by their creators, then the interpretation of television has additional proper aims.

The guiding assumption of this chapter and the next is that the proper aims of television interpretation should be understood as relative to our interests in television. I hope to show that if we are interested in appreciating television art—not in an honorific sense, but in a descriptive sense as involving *works*—then the proper aims of interpretation include discerning (rather than constructing) meaning in several different manifestations to be explored, all of which are constrained by the successfully realized intentions of creators. Inasmuch as television works are intentionally shaped artifacts, it is plausible that our interest in them is in why they were made and for what purpose.[2] I claim that, in the context of appreciation, constructivist and relativist claims about the meanings of television works are false.

However, I hasten to point out that this view acknowledges that television interpretation might have additional proper aims relative to different interests. Most notably, television studies' predominant interest in television has been in terms of what it can tell us about various facets of culture. This interest supports the interpretive aim of hypothesizing the significance of a television program for various audiences. In E. D. Hirsch's terms, *significance* "names a relationship between [...] meaning and a person, or a conception, or a situation, or indeed anything imaginable [...] Significance implies a relationship, and one constant, unchanging pole of that relationship is what the [work] means."[3] Nevertheless, if our interest is in television as an art form, then one important proper aim of interpretation is to discern work meaning, which is constrained by makers' successfully realized intentions and is in no way determined by viewers' interpretive activity.

Initially, these two interpretive aims may seem incompatible; indeed, I think many television scholars have tended to see them as such. But I will argue the contrary. If Hirsch's comments about the relational nature of significance are accurate—and I believe they are—then it is hard to see how the "readings" proffered by television scholars can get off the ground without building upon a foundation of intentionally constrained "meanings." This is plausible, at least, if "meaning" is construed broadly enough to include matters such as what is true in a fiction. It seems to me that this fact has been overlooked—and indeed, broader debates about the interpretation of television have been muddied—in large part because we are often insufficiently explicit about what we mean by "meaning." In this chapter and the next, I analyze the interpretation of television as directed at "work meaning," where this refers to propositions, attitudes, themes, and so forth expressed in the work, which are in turn grounded in first-order interpretations of more basic features such the work's mode or genre and fictional content. Part of the reason we ought to reject relativist and constructivist theories of television interpretation is that "readings" of a work are incoherent in the absence of objective facts about the work's mode or genre and what is fictionally true in the work—facts, which I will argue, nevertheless need to be interpreted and, furthermore, partly constitute higher-order meanings. Constructivists and relativists thus face a dilemma: In order to ground their "readings," they may, on the one hand, assent to the idea that television programs contain objective meanings (in the form of mode or genre or fictional truth) that can be correctly or incorrectly interpreted. However, this comes at a high cost—namely, self-refutation of the constructivist's and relativist's central claims. On the other hand, they can deny that there are any objective meanings that can be correctly or incorrectly interpreted, but at the cost of undermining their own proffered "readings."[4]

However, inasmuch as I acknowledge a plurality of interpretive aims, the "moderate intentionalist" account of television interpretation I advocate does not threaten to replace interpretation in television studies as it is standardly practiced but rather underpins it and can further bolster it.[5] On this matter, as with several others in this chapter, my view is indebted to that of Robert Stecker, who holds: "(a) people interpret artworks with different aims; (b) such interpretations need to be evaluated relative to aims; (c) the aim of some interpretations permit, indeed require, them to be evaluated for truth and falsity, while the aim of others do not."[6] Television scholars are correct to think that interpretations of the *significance* of television content are in important senses constructed by viewers, relative to particular viewers, and, thus, neither right nor wrong. In contrast, however, the aim of interpreting work meaning (and its various constitutive parts) is one that *does* allow interpretations to be objectively true or false and, thus, evaluated as correct or incorrect—or so I shall argue.[7]

Constructivism and Relativism: A Close Analysis

To begin, let us examine two interpretive doctrines that, while not specific to television studies, have particular cachet in our field—what I will call interpretive constructivism and interpretive relativism. Both appear in stronger and weaker formulations. Interpretive constructivism, as I understand it, is the view that meanings are constructed by viewers in their apprehension of the work rather than discerned or discovered by viewers in the work. Interpretive relativism is a conceptually distinct doctrine, which is not logically entailed by interpretive constructivism, although in practice the two often appear simultaneously, as we glimpsed in the previous chapter's discussion of ontological constructivism. According interpretive relativism, interpretations are not evaluable for truth or falsity, for correctness or incorrectness. Or, according to some versions of interpretive relativism, interpretations may be true or false, correct or incorrect, but only relative to some specified framework. It is worth stressing the difference between this latter view and Stecker's critical pluralism, which I shall endorse. Roughly speaking, framework relativism holds that no single framework has greater purchase on truth than any other. In contrast, critical pluralism admits that interpretations need to be evaluated relative to their aims but maintains that one interpretive aim is to discern what a work does in fact mean. Such interpretations are evaluable for truth and falsity, not relative to a framework but to how things actually are.[8]

One of the reasons the previous chapter spent so much time rebutting ontological constructivism is that it often underpins arguments for interpretive constructivism and, as a result, interpretive relativism. That is, interpretive constructivism seems to have some plausibility if the object of interpretation is a "text," the constitutive properties of which are partly shaped through a viewer's engagement with a work of television. For if, in the pragmatists' terms, viewers impute features of the objects of interpretation, then it seems plausible that they also construct meaning inasmuch as meaning depends upon the features they impute. And if meanings are constructed by viewers who impute features of the objects of interpretation, then it is hard to see how interpretations could be evaluable for truth or falsity.[9]

As I discussed in the previous chapter, however, there are a number of serious objections to the imputationalist view and ontological constructivism more generally. To summarize: (1) the argument is circular, because there is no satisfactory account of how interpretation gets started when "texts" or "objects-of-interpretation" do not exist prior to interpretation—that is, unless reference is made to a work, the features of which are *not* constituted by interpretation; (2) the argument is tautological, because it assumes a hard distinction between describing and interpreting, according to which what is constructed is not actually a work, but simply the work + interpretation; (3) the argument makes nonsense of common appreciative practices, because it posits an extreme multiplication of "texts" or "objects of interpretation." This proposal leaves us without a satisfactory account of how intersubjective access to one and the same critical object is possible and thus undermines the rationality of debates about the meaning and value of television works, leaving us simply talking past one another in our critical discourse.

If these objections are sound, then interpretive constructivists cannot assume that the construction of meaning is just something that happens as part of the more general process of constructing texts (or imputing features of texts). However, not all theorists of television define the "text" in this way. Some seem to understand the television "text" as something closer with what I am calling television "works"—episodes, seasons, series, and so forth.[10] Thus, as we consider various theses regarding the interpretation of television, it is important to analyze them with an eye to the conception of the television "text" they assume.

One effort that is admirable in its clarity is Alan McKee's *Textual Analysis*, which, strictly speaking, does not offer an account of the interpretation of television but of cultural objects more broadly. In McKee's words, his book investigates "a form of 'textual analysis' whereby we attempt to understand the likely interpretation of texts made by people who consume them."[11] Clearly, the interest of McKee's project—and many others in cultural studies—is not the texts per se, but rather the "meanings" constructed by those who engage with them. "Doing textual analysis," McKee writes, "we're interested in finding out likely interpretations, not in deciding which of them is the most correct one."[12]

Nevertheless, if we unpack McKee's account of textual analysis a bit, we see some tension between its stated aims and the tools at its disposal. First, it seems counterintuitive that the aim of textual analysis is *not* to produce an interpretation but rather to hypothesize the interpretations that others have likely produced. One might wonder whether textual analysis is really the most efficient—or even a good—way to find out about the likely interpretations of a given text, especially when a text is defined loosely as "something we make meaning from." If that's *all* a text is, it is unclear how one could, by investigating the text itself, begin to get a foothold on the project of delineating its likely interpretations. Another problem is that, in his focus on textual analysis, McKee never actually characterizes interpretation itself. The closest we get are references to "meaning-making" and "sense-making," which strongly indicate that McKee is sympathetic to interpretive constructivism. But this puts him on the horns of a dilemma: if it's the case that meaning is constructed by interpretations rather than detected in the text, then no amount of textual analysis is going to offer up an understanding of "the likely interpretations" of a text. On the other hand, if one can hypothesize the likely interpretations of a text merely from textual analysis, this must owe to the fact that the text does, in fact, objectively embody at least one meaning that is likely to be grasped.

Of course, in this latter case, textual analysis no longer involves merely hypothesizing likely interpretations, but is a matter of the activity of interpretation itself. This is a more plausible conception of both the nature of what I'd prefer to call "works" and the aims of close analysis. Moreover, it is a view that McKee has trouble avoiding because, I think, it is the intuitive one. Giving advice to students, McKee writes, "never say 'I'm going to analyse this text,' full stop. That doesn't make any sense. You have to say what you are going to analyse it for. 'I am going to analyse this text in order to see how it represents women'; 'I am going to analyse this text in order to understand what it says about free will in a modern society' or whatever."[13] I agree that this is indeed what many of us tell students and, oftentimes, what we should tell students, because it tacitly embodies a coherent, plausible conception of the aims of close analysis.[14] The problem for McKee is that this hardly sounds like "making an educated guess at some of the most likely interpretations made of a text."[15] Rather, it seems to be a suggestion that students attempt to come to an understanding of attitudes or ideas that the works do, as a matter of fact, convey—that is, work meaning.

Yet skepticism about the idea that television programs may embody one or more work meanings that admit of correct and incorrect interpretation(s) is, for the most part, the common feature uniting various accounts of interpretation in television studies. As neatly summarized by Matt Hills, "Television Studies has frequently taken the audience as its starting point, arguing that meanings of texts are not self-evidently 'just there', but have to be produced by audiences in their social/cultural contexts."[16] This passage nicely encapsulates how interpretive constructivism often seems to gain traction by presenting a false dilemma with an unpalatable alternative, and it clearly reveals how much of this common view depends on how one characterizes "meanings" and "texts."

The previous chapter examined some of the ways in which some television scholars have stipulated contentious, self-serving definitions of "texts"; such definitions *seem* to pay dividends when the matter of interpretation arises. Jonathan Gray and Amanda Lotz's 2012 introductory book is indicative here.[17] Arguing that television "texts" are characterized by polysemy, Gray and Lotz draw on Barthes to offer a typical account of texts; in their view, "a text is always already a product of the work and an audience interacting."[18]

Suppose we accept this definition of texts for the sake of argument. Gray and Lotz then proceed to claim, "Precisely because ... audiences are so unpredictable, texts are similarly unpredictable ... [This] should give all textual analysts cause to be open to other readings." This is all true, but in a trivial sense, because of how Gray and Lotz have stipulated what a text is; the argument is tautological. As Stecker neatly puts it, this sort of view:

> confuse[s] the object being interpreted with the interpretation. It is the latter that tells us how an interpreter conceives of an object, but then it is always open to us to ask, 'Is the conception true or false, plausible or implausible, adequate or inadequate, useful or not useful and so on?' If the object of interpretation is simply an object as conceived in an interpretation, it is not clear how we could sensibly ask these questions. The conception is automatically true of and adequate to the intentional object, since it is defined as having just those properties it is conceived to have.[19]

For Gray and Lotz's argument regarding interpretation to have any traction, then, it needs to involve claims about the interpretation of works rather than mere texts. And Gray and Lotz are only able to achieve this by conflating the two, as they do in passages like this one: "Needless to say, polysemy poses a significant challenge to our examination of programs, since it requires that analysts be aware of the multiple readings that texts might take on."[20] This claim is false. If we accept Gray and Lotz's stipulated definition of texts, the claim that follows is that polysemy poses a significant challenge to our analysis of *texts* –a claim that is, once again, trivially true because of how they define texts. But it does *not* follow that polysemy poses any challenge to the analysis of *programs*, which they have distinguished from texts.

Another dilemma facing Gray and Lotz (and like-minded scholars) becomes fully apparent in a very concrete way when they arrive at the matter of political and ideological criticism. The natural thought, which Gray and Lotz of course want to accommodate, is that television that is politically and/or ideologically pernicious ought to be subject to critique: "Indeed, critical analysis pries under the surface for deeper meanings and connects these meanings to broader social analysis and commentary. Such a process may very well contribute to a scathing critique of a text and its politics."[21] But how could a *text*, as Gray and Lotz have defined texts, be subject to *any* political critique, let alone a scathing one? For the text is supposedly "always already a product of the work and an audience interacting." Thus, there is no set of intrinsic, stable political or ideological attitudes that any text conveys.

According to Gray and Lotz's definition of texts, it would seem to be the case that if a text ever conveys a set of political or ideological attitudes, this necessarily depends upon the ways in which an audience interacts with it. But I doubt this is a coherent idea. It seems implausible that (*All in the Family* [CBS 1971–1979] + audience x) warrants a scathing political critique while (*All in the Family* + audience y) does not. As this example indicates, it's even harder to make sense of Barthesian theories of the "text" once we leave the realm of abstract theory for that of practical application. Rather more plausible is the idea that audiences who appropriate a program for their own politically or ideologically pernicious purposes are subject to criticism, including those socially conservative viewers who were laughing with Archie Bunker rather than at him. There is also another possibility: Rather than saying that (*Family Guy* [Fox 1999–present] + audience *a*) is politically benign and that (*Family Guy* + audience *b*) is politically pernicious, it is more plausible to claim that the work, *Family Guy*, is deserving of political critique because of the attitudes it actually does, as a matter of fact, convey—that is, its work meaning. The problem for Gray and Lotz (and many others) is, of course, that skepticism about work meaning is what motivated the appeal to texts in the first place.

The point can be summarized in terms of a dilemma for textual and interpretive constructivists like Hills and Gray and Lotz.[22] If texts are "always already a product of the work and an audience interacting," then Hills's claim that "meanings of texts are not self-evidently 'just there', but have to be produced by audiences in their social/cultural contexts" is a tautology and, worse, precludes coherent political, ideological, or ethical criticism. But if we substitute "texts" with "works" or "programs," so that such works can be the object of coherent political, ideological, or ethical criticism, then that's because they do in fact convey certain attitudes; they possess work meaning.

If we make the substitution of "works" for "texts," then the truth of both interpretive constructivism and interpretive relativism then depends on how the term "meaning" is disambiguated in Hills's above-cited proposal. There is one sense of "meaning" that, I think, makes the account attractive and, from a pluralist view of the aims of interpretation, is compatible with the "moderate intentionalist" view of interpretation I advocate. If what Hills means by "meanings" here is what Hirsch originally described as "significance," then what I am calling the orthodox view of television interpretation is both coherent and plausible. In more recent work on interpretation, Stecker explains:

> Significance is always significance *for* someone or some group. One finds significance when one relates the meaning or one's understanding of a work to something outside the work that one already feels is important. Significance is essentially a relation between a work, a particular audience of a work, which may be a single individual or a subgroup of the work's total audience across time, and something outside the work that the audience finds important ... [T]he significance relation between a work and a member of its audience is always contingent, and sometimes transient.[23]

This certainly sounds a lot like the ideas advanced by Hills, Gray and Lotz, and the many other television scholars with similar views of interpretation, and I believe it is the most plausible way to interpret their meaning (that is, *grasp* their meaning, which I suspect they would prefer to the prospect of me and other readers *constructing* some unintended meaning from their texts). In fact, a recent introductory work puts it as clearly as I have seen to date: "The goal of such textual analysis is to connect the program to its broader contexts and make an argument about the text's cultural significance."[24] If this statement is an accurate characterization of what the aims of interpretation in television studies have always been and still are, then I have no complaint except with the lack of clarity with which this project is typically described.

My positive point is that the analysis of a television artwork's significance is not only compatible with, but indeed undergirded by, discerning the meaning(s) of television works in senses of "meaning" I shall explain momentarily. For now, though, thinking of "meaning" roughly as what I have been calling "work meaning"—or a set of attitudes conveyed *in* a work—we can see that interpretive aims of understanding significance and discerning work meaning are logically compatible.

One more important point falls out of this discussion: The relativism about interpretation that characterizes television studies is warranted in one sense, but unwarranted in another. Again, by "relativism about interpretation," I mean the commonly held view typically expressed along these lines: "… there is no such 'correct' interpretation, any more than there is a 'correct' way to watch a football game or cartoon."[25] Or, somewhat more strongly, "Remember, critical analyses are, by their nature, subjective. There can therefore be no claims for objective truth …"[26] If one's interpretive focus is on the *significance* of a television work for some persons(s), then this sort of relativism is indeed warranted insofar as people cannot be wrong about the ways in which a work is significant for them.

On the other hand, if one's interpretive focus is what I have been referring to roughly as work meaning, then relativism about interpretation is unwarranted. For, once again, the interpretive aim of discerning work meaning is just the aim of discovering what ideas or attitudes the work itself conveys. As Stecker has cogently argued, one's interpretation simply does not have the causal power to change mind-independent objects. The week I thought my family's mezuzah was a paperweight did not strip the object of its mezuzah-hood. Rather, it was a mezuzah all along and my interpretation of its meaning (broadly construed to include its function or purpose) was simply wrong. Of course, as I have just indicated, what one means by "meaning" in such contexts is important. Although television works are, plausibly, artifacts just as mezuzahs are, it is not so clear that they have an essential function or purpose in the way it seems plausible that ritual objects do. So, while the mezuzah analogy is intended to pump intuitions, it hardly cements my case.

What is needed now, then, is to disambiguate the different senses of meaning that are involved in what I have been calling work meaning. As we proceed, we can plug the various senses of meaning into the standard claims of interpretive constructivism and interpretive relativism to test the coherence and plausibility of these views. In the rest of this chapter, I examine two constituent parts of overall work meaning—the artistic category or categories in which a work is perceived and what is fictionally true in a work. I argue that higher order meanings essentially depend upon these two things. In the subsequent chapter, I turn my attention to higher order meaning per se, looking specifically at ideas that works endorse or criticize based upon the attitudes taken towards what is fictionally true within in them.

Categories of Television Art

In the previous chapter, I drew a sharp distinction between categorical intentions and semantic intentions for the purposes of making the argument that was then at hand. In many cases, I claimed, the two are distinct. But now it is time to admit that in some cases categorical intentions and semantic intentions are deeply intertwined. Sometimes intentions about what sort of work one is making are partly constitutive of a work's semantic content. And sometimes "interpreting" the category to which a work belongs then underpins subsequent interpretations of higher-order meanings.

For the moment, though, let's focus on the category/semantic content distinction in less contentious terms, leaving intention aside. As I indicated in the previous chapter, we can think of a category here as, very roughly, a grouping of works that are to be approached in a particular way. As Kendall Walton points out at the start of the groundbreaking essay in which he coined the term "categories of art," "paintings and sculptures are to be looked at; sonatas and songs are to be heard."[27] In addition to artistic media, categories of art that are relevant to artistic appreciation include genres (e.g., science fiction), modes (e.g., satire), and styles (e.g., German expressionism).

How are categories of art relevant to appreciation? As David Davies nicely summarizes Walton's view, "which appreciable properties we ascribe to a work depends upon the particular category of art under which it is apprehended."[28] Walton argues for this point by first distinguishing three sorts of properties that constitute categories of art: standard, variable, and contra-standard.

> A feature of a work of art is *standard* with respect to a (perceptually distinguishable) category just in case it is among those in virtue of which works in that category belong to that category—that is, just in case the absence of that feature would disqualify, or tend to disqualify, a work from that category. A feature is *variable* with respect to a category just in case it has nothing to do with works' belonging to that category; the possession or lack of the feature is irrelevant to whether a work qualifies for the category. Finally, a *contra-standard* feature with respect to a category is the absence of a standard feature with respect to that category—that is a feature whose presence tends to *disqualify* works as members of the category.[29]

Interpretation I 131

He then proceeds to argue that our perception of a work's aesthetic properties crucially depends upon the category in which we apprehend the work. Although he does not say so explicitly, I think Walton's point applies to our interpretation of a work's semantic content—its themes, expressed emotions, conveyed attitudes, and so forth—which plausibly interacts with its aesthetic properties, as we shall see presently.

In a well-known example, Walton describes an imaginary culture that does not have the category of art "painting" but does have a kind of art called "guernica." "Guernicas," Walton tells us, "are like versions of Picasso's *Guernica* done in various bas-relief dimensions. All of them are surfaces with the colors and shapes of Picasso's *Guernica*, but the surfaces are molded to protrude from the wall like relief maps of different kinds of terrain."[30] Thus, Picasso's painting counts as a "guernica," but the change of category in which the work is apprehended entails a different perception of the work's content: "the flatness, which is standard for us, would be variable for members of the other society, and the figures on the surface, which are variable for us, would be standard for them." As a result, Picasso's *Guernica* "seems violent, dynamic, vital, disturbing to us. But ... it would strike them as cold, stark, lifeless, serene and restful, or perhaps bland, dull, boring—but in any case *not* violent, dynamic, and vital."[31]

The point I want to emphasize here is this: Just as a work's category is partly constitutive of its aesthetic properties, so too a work's category is partly constitutive of its semantic content. That is, sometimes a work's category is partially determinative of what is true in the fiction, of what its narrative events mean within the fiction, and the attitudes the work expresses towards those narrative events. Or, to put it another way, sometimes we are not able to interpret this sort of semantic content unless we have already discerned the work's category. For example, imagine a very slightly different *Gilligan's Island* (CBS 1964–1967), which has no non-diegetic sound—no theme song, no laugh track, and so forth. Call this version *Gilligan's Island**. Taken as a Beckettian work of existentialist drama, *Gilligan's Island** might reasonably be interpreted as expressing an ironic or cynical attitude toward the characters and their foibles and as conveying broader themes of purposelessness or hopelessness. Part of the reason we don't—and shouldn't—interpret *Gilligan's Island* in this way is because it is a television sitcom, which, historically (although contingently rather than necessarily) serves very different functions than existentialist drama.

However, in many actual examples, the work's category is ambiguous, so we need to engage in some first-order interpretive work, which may have significant implications for higher-order interpretations as well as evaluation. *True Detective* (HBO 2014–present) is a recent case in point. As the program's first season progressed over eight weeks, viewers and critics offered extremely divergent interpretations, not only of the show's broader themes and attitudes, but even of what was true in the fiction. Did *True Detective* convey a misogynistic attitude toward its female characters, representing them as "paper-thin ... eye candy," as Emily Nussbaum argued?[32]

132   Interpretation I

Or was the show interrogating and commenting on the ways in which Cohle and Hart, the detective genre, and, perhaps, our patriarchial society abuse and ignore women, as Willa Paskin contended?[33] Was Cohle a mouthpiece for the show's expression of pessimism and nihilism? Was he the killer? Or was he just a broken man, grieving for the loss of his family?

The divergence is most parsimoniously and plausibly explained not in terms of differing reading strategies or community norms as interpretive constructivists and interpretive relativists might have it, but rather as a result of differences in first-order interpretations aimed at determining the work's salient category—an issue upon which critics manifestly disagreed until the series ended.[34] Some claimed it was a metaphysical or cosmic horror story in the style of E. T. A. Hoffman or H. P. Lovecraft. Others claimed it was a more-or-less straightforward detective story. And at least one critic, Jason Jacobs, noted striking similarities to the comedies of remarriage theorized by Stanley Cavell.[35] In short, claims about *True Detective*'s meaning, at various levels, partly depended upon prior interpretations regarding the category or categories into which the show belonged.[36]

Here some theorists might propose that diverging opinions regarding how to categorize *True Detective* is simply indicative of the putative fact that audiences "decode" the "text" in differing ways or, perhaps, that genre categories are inherently contingent and unstable. While I agree that genres are not constituted by timeless, intrinsic essences and the boundaries between them are sometimes fuzzy, it does not follow that there are no boundaries—no identifiable, discrete categories that inform our appreciative practices. So, too, is the idea that genres can be hybridized compatible with the notion that those practices regularly identify and make use of discrete generic categories; indeed, the former idea seems to depend upon the latter. This point is of particular relevance here because my argument does not deny that *True Detective* frequently borrowed from and mixed several different genres. To be sure, this was part of the intrigue and pleasure that the series afforded viewers. Nevertheless, it is still reasonable to ask, as many viewers have, what the correct or, at least, most salient category is for the purposes of interpreting what is fictionally true within the work and, more generally, what it is *about*.[37]

Beyond the overt incorporation of various conventions from multiple genres, I think disagreement about *True Detective*'s genre is simply and plausibly explained by appeal once more to the various ways in which television's temporal prolongation affects our engagement with it. Drawing on the discussion of ontology in Chapter 3, it seems reasonable to say that *True Detective*, the work as a whole, was not complete until the final episode had finished airing, or, perhaps more accurately, had been released to the public in any number of formats, including DVD screeners.[38] For this reason, there was no epistemic warrant for taking *True Detective*'s genre to be a settled matter any earlier precisely because the series had been providing ambiguous cues all along. (In contrast, there is epistemic warrant for taking the genre of *South Park* or *The Simpsons* to be fixed, even though *those* series are not over, because there is no equivalent ambiguity in the salient genre cues.)

More specifically, many viewers, myself included, expected *True Detective*'s final episode to end with some sort of major narrative twist that would have would have made clear that the most salient category for apprehending the series was either Hoffmanesque or Lovecraftian "cosmic horror" in the manner of *Twin Peaks* (1990–1991) or "metaphysical detective thriller" as pioneered by *The X-Files* (Fox 1993–2002; 2016).[39] Perhaps Hart was a Satan-worshipping sociopath and would kill his own daughter, or Hart would have to become a monster, or at least as spiritually empty as Cohle, to catch the killer, or Cohle was experiencing all of the narrative events for a second time in some sort of flat circle of time. But the shock was that the final episode—and, in particular the final scene—resolved the ambiguity that had cued such expectations by revealing *True Detective* to be a relatively traditional buddy-cop series complete with a "good triumphs evil" happy ending and, even, a spiritual awakening for Cohle. For many critics, this was a significant disappointment.[40]

Although a full discussion of evaluative judgments of television will have to wait, I raise the issue here because *True Detective* nicely illustrates the ways in which evaluative judgment partly depends upon the interpretation of work meaning, which in turn partly depends upon the interpretation of a work's category. Bridging the disclosure of *True Detective*'s genre in the final episode and the largely negative evaluative judgments of the show that followed are interpretations about the show's broader work meaning—in particular the attitudes it conveys—that critics formulated in large part on the basis of how the narrative ended, but also, relatedly, in large part on the basis of seeing the work in a particular category.

Many of those expecting *True Detective*'s genre to be confirmed as cosmic horror were disappointed that the show's narrative structure and genre ultimately worked together to undermine Cohle's initial pessimism, emphasizing instead the power of companionship. As critic Spencer Kornhaber neatly put it, "my suspense heading into the finale came less from the storyline and more from my continuing befuddlement at what *True Detective* really *is*. The answer is a letdown: a high-budget genre retread with the false veneer of profundity. (As opposed to what I'd hoped for: high-budget genre experiment with *actual* profundity) ... But no: Turns out [the "cosmic horror" build-up] was all in the service of pure *character study*."[41]

Many of those wagering that the series was, at bottom, firmly ensconced in the buddy-detective genre, took the final episode's confirmation of this as support for the interpretive hypothesis that *True Detective*'s attitude towards Cohle and Hart's mistreatment of women was more accurately characterized as the valorization of a "necessary sacrifice" than self-reflexive interrogation of that mistreatment. Again, these critics were not surprised by the revelation that *True Detective* was a "character study," but were disappointed by the consequences they took that to have for the show's broader meanings. Unsurprisingly, these critics generally judged the series to be an artistic failure. For example, critic Lilli Loofbourow wrote: "Let's put my inattention to Cohle's philosophizing in a more flattering light: I accepted it as atmospheric rather than substantial. What saddens me is that I was right. My laziness (or ungenerousness) was rewarded. Cohle's speeches didn't much matter—I was right about that—but I was wrong about the show's self-knowledge: It loves Cohle, really loves him, and thinks he's pretty much as awesome as he thinks he is. It was all a character study! [...] Cohle's rants reduce to signs of his much-vaunted complexity—or brokenness, which, in this narrative universe, amounts to the same thing—but they don't add up to much on their own merits."[42]

On the other hand, a minority of critics who also correctly hypothesized that *True Detective* was properly located in the buddy-detective genre took the finale to be an artistic success on the basis that the early-sown seeds of Cohle's need for companionship and hope bore fruit in the finale in a manner prescribed by the genre. In the words of critic Ben Travers, "*True Detective* was a *character study* through and through. It stayed true to those roots in the end by devoting the final 10 minutes to Rust and Marty, both unbelievably alive and now bonded over their shared experience. Anyone who didn't get choked up when Marty said the last thing he remembered about being in the put was 'saying my friend's name' hasn't been watching the show *right*."[43]

Now, there is a lot to be said about what these three critical analyses of *True Detective* might indicate about the nature of the artistic evaluation of television, but because my focus here is on interpretation I'll just flag some points to be picked up in the next chapter. In at least one case, an overall artistic judgment of the work is tacitly informed in part by a moral appraisal of the work; in that instance, especially, but also in the other two analyses, overall artistic judgment is informed in part by the attitudes critics take the work to actually express and in part by the category to which they think the category actually belongs. Importantly, the critics take these latter two features to be objective matters of fact (even Mittell, who, in his scholarly publications, advocates interpretive relativism). If the critics are right about this, then there are at least two objective grounds upon which they base their evaluative judgments. And, of particular significance, even though the critics diverge in their interpretation of work meaning and the judgment of artistic merit, they *agree* upon the *actual* categories in which *True Detective* is situated: it is a character study in the buddy-detective genre (in the serialized, mini-series/anthology format of the mode fictional drama of the art of television). The third critic is quite clear about the underlying premise here: One's apprehension of a work in a particular category can be correct or incorrect.

These considerations regarding the nature of artistic categories—how a work's category is determined and whether interpretations of categories admit of truth and falsity—lead us back to the questions with which we began regarding the plausibility of interpretive constructivism and interpretive relativism when we are dealing with categories of art that involve at least a minimal degree of semantic content.

Clearly Walton's "guernica" case and the *True Detective* case indicate that it is possible for people to apprehend a single work in different categories; is this a reason to think that viewers in any way construct those categories? I think it is in one sense, but not in a sense that supports the more ambitious claims of interpretive constructivism. Specifically, we should acknowledge that categories of art are fundamentally social constructs; they emerge out of shared artistic practices. In fact, in the absence of shared artistic practices that constitute pre-existing categories such as "cosmic horror" and "bro-mance," there simply would not be any way appreciators *could* apprehend a work in one of those categories, let alone interpret its higher-order meanings. As David Davies puts it, "in order to grasp the work's content, the properties resulting from the artist's activity must be perceived in terms of an artistic practice that classifies certain properties as standard and others as variable."[44] Hence, the idea that viewers or interpretive communities of viewers construct meaning in this first-order sense of constructing artistic categories is not a cogent one.

Yet might it still be the case that, since individual viewers and interpretive communities of viewers can apparently perceive a work in different categories, they also *determine* the work's category? We can think of this idea as a strong meaning-relativist thesis about the interpretation of categories of art. We can also consider a weaker relativist thesis—that interpretations of categories of art are not truth evaluable, that there is no fact of the matter about whether, say, *True Detective* is a cosmic horror or bro-mance. In response, I would first emphasize the fact that these sorts of proposals—call them instances of category relativism—are deeply at odds with our standard critical and appreciative practices. The example of *True Detective* criticism hardly settles the matter, but it lends some prima facie plausibility to the idea that critics take a work's category to be determinate and, moreover, determined independently of how various audiences perceive the work.

Moreover, to borrow a point Walton himself makes, it seems natural to think that appreciators can simply be mistaken about a work's category. This is perhaps clearer if we shift our thinking from genre to mode. If we read a student essay condemning Jonathan Swift's "A Modest Proposal" for putatively conveying callousness and barbarism, we are warranted in telling the student he has misinterpreted the work—more specifically that he has misinterpreted the overall work meaning, or what attitudes the work conveys, as a result of misinterpreting the work's category. So, too, it goes with television. There are (or at least were at one point) a perhaps surprising number of politically conservative viewers who thought that *The Colbert Report* (Comedy Central 2005–2014) straightforwardly conveyed pro-conservative attitudes on all sorts of topics ranging from gay marriage to corporate tax legislation.[45] Plausibly, these viewers misinterpreted the show's *actual* attitudes toward those topics as a result of misinterpreting the show's satire as straight political commentary. And, plausibly, we are warranted in saying that such interpretations—both of work meaning and category meaning—are simply wrong.

These considerations of satire lead to my preferred counterargument to relativism about category meaning as well as the other sorts of meaning to be discussed presently. Irony and satire are two modes that strongly suggest that appeal to intentional agency (authorial or otherwise, as argued in Chapter 1) is necessary for interpreting both "category meaning" as well as work meaning more broadly. I will address the latter issue presently, but at the moment, suffice it to say that in the absence of an alternative account of irony and satire, the burden of proof is on the proponent of relativism to show that (successfully realized) intentions are *not* determinative of a work's category.

Especially given the industrial context of television production, which involves enormous amounts of money, it is hard to imagine a work of a particular kind—whether a science-fiction thriller, an ironic comedy, a serialized soap opera, or a short dramatic mini-series—belonging to its category by accident. This is not to rule out cases of generic or categorical ambiguity, of which *True Detective* seemed to be an example before its ending. But such cases do not lend support to the relativist. Generic ambiguity is plausibly explained in terms of successfully realized intentions to create a generically ambiguous work or in terms of unsuccessfully realized intentions. In the latter case, there are several other principles to which we can resort as theorists—and to which we do resort as critics—before concluding that the work's genre or other category is simply indeterminate. For example, Walton suggests the following considerations: the work's having "a relatively large number of features" that are standard for a category; the work being "better, or more interesting or pleasing aesthetically, or more worth experiencing" when grouped in a given category; and a category being "well established in and recognized by the society in which [the work] was produced."[46] So, even if there are cases where intentions fail to establish a work's category, there are other plausible ways in which category membership may be determined, and the relativist still has a large burden of proof to shoulder.

Finally, my claim is not that intentions necessarily determine how a work can be perceived. We can all think of instances of dramas that are more enjoyable perceived as comedies and comedies that are better perceived as avant-garde experiments. But this is consistent with the claim that there is a fact of the matter about the work's category that is determined by successfully realized intentions.

Fictional Truth

Not all television artworks are fictions, of course, but many are. The second aspect of work meaning up for analysis is what I will call "fictional truth," by which I mean to refer to that which is true in any given fiction. An initially intuitive thought, neatly expressed by Peter Swirski, is, "figuring out what happens in the story—which is to say, what is true in it—is the first step in contact with any work of fiction."[47] It turns out, however, that matters are not quite so simple all the time—and even less so in the context of serial television.[48]

But the nature of fictional truth is hardly an academic question. On the contrary, it is central to the study of television reception, because it is one of the stable elements in the relationships between viewers and television works that Hirsch describes as "significance." Stecker notes that Hirsch puts things somewhat too strongly by suggesting that discerning a work's overall meaning necessarily antecedes analysis of its significance. Rather, he writes, "What is needed is some conception of what is going on in the work. One has to form *an* understanding, identify something the work could mean. On the basis of any of these things, as well as a (typically partial) identification of what a work does mean, one may legitimately find significance in a work."[49] Minimally, in my view, it is necessary for viewers to first identify what is true in the fictional world of the work. Only on the basis of this element of work meaning, can claims about a work's significance or "readings" of the work rationally proceed. In this way, the account of interpretation I offer here is fundamental to the sort of interpretative work that is the bread and butter of television studies; we just have not recognized at such.

At least two peculiarities with regard to the establishment of fictional truth in television are worth noting here. One is that, in virtue of their temporal prolongation, televisual serial fictions, much like other arts that involve expansive story worlds, face the challenge of not contradicting previously established fictional truths.[50] This challenge differs from that facing other forms of narrative fiction in degree rather than in kind. One classic example here is from Sir Arthur Conan Doyle's Sherlock Holmes stories, in which Watson's war wound is sometimes described as being on his leg and sometimes on his shoulder. This sort of problem becomes particularly acute in long-form television fictions. In *Friends* (NBC 1994–2004), for example, the protagonists' ages and birthdays are described differently on different occasions, as are the number of sexual partners Ross had before marrying his first wife. In the first season of *The X-Files,* Mulder says he was temporarily paralyzed during the abduction of his sister and thus did not see exactly what happened; however, in flashbacks in later seasons, Mulder is not paralyzed and does see the abduction. The epistemic question of how we can know what is true in such cases aside, there is a metaphysical question about what is sufficient for determining fictional truth in both complicated and more straightforward situations.

The second peculiarity regarding the generation of fictional truths in serial television similarly involves difficult epistemic and metaphysical questions. In some cases, we can only determine what is fictionally true with some degree of hindsight. In *Homeland* (Showtime 2011–present), for example, we do not know whether it is fictionally true that Brody is an al-Qaeda agent until the ninth episode of Season 1. So, there is a way in which our *knowledge* of what is fictionally true in serial television is always provisional until the series is complete. An extreme case here is the final episode of *St. Elsewhere* (NBC 1982–1988), in which it seems to be revealed that it is fictionally true that the narrative events of the entire six-season series up to that point occurred in the imagination of an autistic boy named Tommy—at least on a plausible interpretation of the final scene. However, from the fact that our knowledge of fictional truth is provisional until the completion of a series, it does not straightforwardly follow that what is fictionally true is *itself* provisional or, perhaps more accurately, indeterminate. We still face difficult metaphysical questions about when and how fictional truths are generated. With regard to the former question, we might ask, for example, is Brody's connection with al-Qaeda merely indeterminate until the ninth episode? If not, when is that fictional truth created? With the latter question in mind, we might ask what, if anything, generates the fictional truth that Brody works for al-Qaeda prior to the explicit representation of this in the ninth episode. Or we might ask how one scene could be sufficient to establish the fictional truth that 149 episodes worth of narrative events were imagined by an autistic child.

The other important point I think the preceding discussion establishes is that the common thought—expressed by Swirski in the context of literary studies and by David Bordwell in the context of film studies—that narrative comprehension precedes interpretation also puts things a bit more simply than they actually are.[51] As Bordwell himself argued in his seminal work on narrative comprehension in film, there is a minimal sense in which both film and television viewers are constantly doing some work that, in my view, qualifies as interpretation: to understand what's going on in a narrative, we need to mentally fill in what we are shown with plausible interpretations about what happens in the story world that we don't see. It is important to emphasize that we successfully infer fictional truths all the time—and in most cases without a moment's hesitation or a second thought. In contrast to the difficult cases I mentioned above, our typical inferences about fictional truths involve much more mundane matters, such as characters eating, sleeping, bathing, and so forth at moments in the story, or *fabula*, that are not explicitly represented on screen in the plot, or *syuzhet*. Nevertheless, the hard cases indicate, I think, that this inferential activity is oftentimes interpretive in a substantive sense, rather than merely a matter of comprehending what is straightforwardly "given."

Bordwell emphasizes the significance of this inferential activity—despite distinguishing it from interpretation—and he and others have concluded that viewers actually construct the *fabula* itself. Thus, it might be thought that Bordwell's work supports interpretive constructivism, when the relevant sense of "meaning" is fictional truth. In his words, "The *fabula* is thus a pattern which perceivers of narratives create through assumptions and inferences. It is the developing result of picking up narrative cues, applying schemata, framing and testing hypotheses."[52] However, Bordwell hastens to add that inasmuch as the process of constructing the *fabula* involves the application of intersubjective cognitive processes to mind-independent narrative cues and mind-independent narrative schemata, the *fabula* is also intersubjectively accessible. Therefore, he concludes, "In principle, viewers of a film will agree about either what the story is or what factors obscure or render ambiguous the adequate construction of the story."[53]

It is important to see here that on Bordwell's account of narrative comprehension—which, I am claiming, involves the interpretation of fictional truth—viewers "construct meaning" in the weak sense of inferring various fictional truths about the *fabula* in order to make sense of the *syuzhet*, but this is *not* the same idea underlying typical constructivist claims regarding viewers' interpretive activity. Based on Bordwell's account, a film narrative does not vary depending on who the viewers of the film are on different occasions, and it *is* open to correct and incorrect interpretations.

My own view is that while we may not want to accept Bordwell's account wholesale, it starts the inquiry in the right direction by acknowledging a normative dimension to the interpretation of fictional truth. Central to all extant analyses is something like the *fabula/syuzhet* distinction noted above, which bears some relation to the distinction between what Kendall Walton has termed "primary fictional truths," which are generated by "principles of direct generation," and "implied fictional truths," which are generated by "principles of implication."[54] Roughly, the idea here is that, in many standard cases, certain explicit representations in a text or audio-visual display are sufficient (but not necessary) for the generation of primary fictional truths; these fictional truths then tacitly specify further (implied) fictional truths. This is putting things somewhat simplistically because, for reasons we shall soon see, Walton explicitly "resist[s] identifying directly generated fictional truths with those the works make *explicit*" and casts some doubt upon the boundary between primary fictional truths and implied fictional truths. But this rough-and-ready characterization is a helpful place to begin our analysis and it probably strikes readers as intuitive, if not familiar. The two difficult questions are, in Walton's terms, By what principles of direct generation are primary fictional truths established? and By what principles of implication are implied fictional truths established?

Although my primary focus here will be with difficulties posed by the latter question, we should heed Walton's warning that the generation of primary fictional truths is not always straightforward either. Although what is explicitly stated in literature or shown in a television show, respectively, may be sufficient to establish fictional truth in many cases, there are important instances in which it is not. For example, in historical epics about ancient Rome, such as *I, Claudius* (BBC 1976), *Empire* (ABC 2005), and *Rome* (HBO 2005–2007), the actors speak English, but this does not make it fictionally true that the characters speak English. Rather, it is fictionally true that the characters speak Latin even though there is no explicit indication to this effect. Likewise, although the original *I Love Lucy* (CBS 1951–1957) shows us the narrative events in black and white, this does not make it fictionally true that Lucy and Desi's world is devoid of color. On the contrary, it is fictionally true that the *I Love Lucy* story world contains color just as our own world does, even though there is no explicit indication of this. Of course, there is an air of paradox here. Are matters really as simple as my claims suggest and, if so, how are these fictional truths established?

Alongside these metaphysical puzzles, we face epistemic ones. Of relatively straightforward cases such as those mentioned above, when it is an implied fictional truth that characters have eaten and bathed, we may still ask, How do we know the characters have eaten and bathed and what makes it fictionally true that they have? At the other end of the spectrum, there are much more contentious cases—perhaps the most gripping of which in recent times is that of Tony Soprano's fate in the series finale of *The Sopranos* (HBO 1999–2007). When the screen cuts to black, is it fictionally true that Tony is dead or alive? Is this even a germane question? Might there simply be no fact of the matter about it?

One point worth emphasizing at the outset is that on *any* plausible analysis of the generation of implied fictional truths, the *inference* of implied fictional truths appears to have an important normative dimension.[55] If all that a meaning constructivist would want to claim is that some narrative meaning is "constructed" in the sense that many fictional truths are not directly generated in virtue of explicit representation but rather need to be inferred by audiences, then there is nothing objectionable about the proposal. But we should not confuse this innocuous idea with the erroneous suggestion that fictional truths are constructed—in the sense of *determined*—by readers or viewers simply because they are not explicitly represented or otherwise directly generated. So, too, we should reject the relativist proposal that interpretations of fictional truths are not truth-evaluable.

First, note that strong versions of constructivism and relativism cannot account for the significant agreement amongst viewers (or communities of viewers) about what is fictionally true in a given television work. Although, as I have been stressing, there are difficult philosophical questions about the generation of fiction truths and there are, quite obviously, cases when viewers do *not* agree about fictional truth, we need to remain cognizant of the sea of fictional truths we do agree upon without even noticing it. Jerry, George, Elaine, and Kramer are humans, not space aliens taking the form of humans. Carrie, Samantha, Miranda, and Charlotte take cabs everywhere because they can't fly or teleport themselves. Sam, Coach, and Woody aren't constantly sneaking drinks behind the bar and just pretending to be sober. Lucy and Desi live in a world with color despite the fact that our only access to that world comes from black and white photographic representations.

These are all merely implied fictional truths, which we could go on to list indefinitely. Even though they are never explicitly established, hardly anyone would try to deny them. True, that is because the examples I offer above are banal, but the principle established by even banal examples has far-reaching consequences: Numerous semantic properties of television works are determinate in such a fundamental way that we scarcely recognize the degree to which they underpin our higher order interpretations. The frequency with which our inferences of fictional truth converge is a serious hurdle for interpretive constructivists and interpretive relativists who claim to be analyzing "texts," where "texts" are defined as the product of interaction between a program and a viewer. If viewers actually engaged with different texts, they would, of necessity, infer different fictional truths because many fictional truths are merely implied by the "text" (or work, as I would prefer) rather than explicitly represented within it.

In other words, insofar as implied fictional truths depend at least partly on "texts," differences in "texts" constitute differences in what fictional truths are implied. However, if this view were correct, it would be hard to see how we could possibly engage in coherent, meaningful conversation about television "texts" on a very basic level. Rather, it seems that viewers would have drastically divergent conceptions of what was fictionally true of television "texts," making this yet another level at which, as I indicated in the previous chapter, the constructivist view would have television viewers simply talking past one another. To raise an example to be explored in more detail presently, if you think it is fictionally true of *Star Trek* (NBC 1966–1969) that Kirk and Spock are lovers and I think it is fictionally true that they are merely good friends, it seems that there is a fundamental level at which we can't engage in meaningful conversation about the "text." The problem for constructivists is that while we don't always agree about fictional truth, the fact is that we successfully communicate with each other about television texts almost all of the time. The ubiquity of episode recaps, in which what is fictionally true of an episode is simply summarized, is itself enough to suggest that we typically do agree on fictional truth and, at the very least, lays the burden of proof on the constructivist and relativist to show otherwise.

General convergence on the interpretation of fictional truths is not, itself, a source of the normativity I want to stress here, but it is indicative of it. More specifically, convergence around the acceptance of implied fictional truths plausibly results from various principles and conventions in currency within the informal institutions of television art and fiction in general. I cannot review the literature on fictional truth here, much less offer a full analysis, but I will briefly outline and defend an account that meshes with my overarching arguments in this book.[56] Of particular importance here is Walton's observation about the nature of fiction in general: "Fictionality is not *defined* by the principles of generation; it consists rather in prescriptions to imagine."[57] A central, perhaps essential, convention of the institution of fiction is that fictions are created for the purpose of directing our imaginings and are properly appreciated by imagining in the ways they specify. Thus, there is normative pressure on appreciators to treat fictions as, indeed, *prescribing* their imaginings. And, *pace* interpretive constructivists and interpretive relativists, we typically think—and are rationally justified in thinking—that someone who has offered an interpretation of fictional truth that is not so prescribed by the fiction has either misunderstood the fiction, misunderstood the nature of fiction, or is knowingly engaging with the fiction from outside the boundaries of the institution of fiction, which is governed by various norms and conventions, including that audiences are to imagine in the ways prescribed. In Walton's words, "Anyone who refuses to

142 Interpretation I

imagine what was agreed on refuses to "play the game" or plays it improperly. He breaks a rule."[58]

Similarly, in Paisley Livingston's terms, "Elucidating the problem of fictional truth in terms of appropriateness of make-believe in response to a work's content has the advantage of foregrounding the issue's normative character (in a broad, axiological, and not exclusively moral sense)."[59] As Livingston explains, couching the analysis of fictional truth in terms of appropriateness allows for what he calls "a sensible pluralism about the value of divergent interpretive projects."[60] Assuming one approaches a work as a purposive artifact, it is the author(s)' or creator(s)' intentions (when successfully realized in the work or otherwise compatible with the structural features of the work) that determine what is appropriate or inappropriate to imagine and, thus, what is fictionally true of the story.[61]

Such a principle parsimoniously explains the generation of the sorts of fictional truths we typically take for granted, because it is plausible to suppose that the creators of *Seinfeld* (NBC 1989–1998) intended that the characters were human rather than aliens in disguise, that the creators of *Sex and the City* (HBO 1998–2004) intended that the characters took cabs because they couldn't teleport themselves—not because cabs are more fun–and that the creators of *Cheers* (CBS 1982–1993) intended that the bartenders really were sober and not merely pretending to be sober. Furthermore, although there are no hard and fast rules on this count, it seems plausible that Roman epics involving English-speaking actors and black and white television shows are compatible with what is likely the best explanation of creators' intentions—to wit, that viewers are to imagine that the Roman characters are speaking Latin and that the characters represented in black and white images live in a world as colorful as our own. Related to the matter of color, the intentionalist principle advocated here avoids the implausible view that all of the details of a fictional world are fully determinate. Although we would want to say that it is fictionally true in ordinary black and white television shows that, say, avocados are green and oranges are orange, there simply is no fact of the matter about the specific color of carpets or wallpaper unless a character indicates as much. The intentionalist principle accounts for this intuition, according to which *some* claims about fictions are not truth-evaluable.

Another benefit of the approach advanced here is that it offers a way to ensure the coherence of fictional worlds in cases where we are presented with incompatible fictional truths. Most advantageously, we have a principled way of maintaining the coherence of fictional worlds in the face of basic continuity errors that are an unavoidable part of film and television production. Based on this theory, for example, a shot/reverse-shot dialogue sequence that reveals a logically impossible change of body position, jewelry, hairstyle, and so forth is nevertheless sufficiently compatible with the creators' intentions that we can explain away the continuity error in a way that meshes with our intuitions—that is, as an unintended mistake that we are not to imagine has any bearing on the fictional world. Of course, many cases are more complex, such as those mentioned earlier involving *Friends* and *The X-Files*. In such instances, there may be no principled way to determine which fictional truth is more likely compatible with the creators' intentions or the creators' intentions appear so scattershot with regard to a particular fictional truth that no particular imagining seems best justified. In such cases, I suggest, someone with the requisite authority may sanction the imagining of a particular fictional truth. That is to say, in the case of *The X-Files*, given the absence of "textual" reasons to favor accepting either one of two incompatible fictional truths—that Mulder saw and did not see his sister's abduction—we could, as a last resort, ask Chris Carter (and any other production team members with the requisite authority) which scenario is in fact fictionally true. That answer, if sincere and not self-deceived, would be decisive. Why? Because the creators of fictional worlds enjoy a certain amount of epistemic privilege with regard to their creations, just as the creators of all artifacts do.[62]

To be clear, this claim does not entail the rather more contentious and implausible ideas that creators' intentions are always successfully realized, that fictional truth can be determined by what creators say or intend despite overwhelming evidence to the contrary within the work itself, or that creators' post hoc declarations actually *determine* rather than simply clarify what is fictionally true. In the case of *The X-Files*, Carter's testimony carries decisive weight not only because of his authority but because he is attesting to a fictional truth that is as well supported as any other by the work itself. Call the fictional truth that Mulder saw his sister's abduction *p* and the fictional truth that he did not see the abduction not-*p*. It seems preferable to take a pragmatic approach here, accepting that the creators were largely successful in their attempts to imbue the series with features generating *p*, and that they simply made a mistake in giving the series features that seemed to generate not-*p*. The alternative, that in the fictional world of the *X-Files*, both *p* and not-*p* obtain seems far less palatable. In other cases, however, we are warranted in denying creators' assertions regarding what is fictionally true, because those statements are manifestly contradicted by the features of the work.

Here an interlocutor might object that, in contrast to what I have claimed, we accept that fictional truth is simply established by the work itself and that creators' intentions have no power whatsoever. However, the real test of my argument is not a case in which creators' claims regarding fictional truth belie the evidence manifest in the work itself, but rather a case in which there is significant ambiguity among multiple incompatible options regarding what is fictionally true. Let us take a close look at the infamous finale scene of *The Sopranos*.

As is well known, this ending caused a significant amount of consternation amongst viewers who thought the smash cut to black was actually a technical glitch or simply felt entitled to a clear narrative resolution to the series. In any case, there was a significant degree of consensus that whatever happened in terms of the narrative, the smash cut to black made things ambiguous and necessitated interpretive work on the part of viewers. Importantly, this interpretive work involved attempting to discern not only higher-order meaning—that is, what was expressed or symbolized by ending the series in this way—but also "meaning" in the sense of fictional truth—in particular, what happened to Tony Soprano after the smash cut to black?

With regard to the latter, it is worth beginning an analysis by remarking upon one possibility that nobody, to my knowledge, even canvassed: Nobody suggested as a live option that the fictional truth about Tony Soprano's fate was simply indeterminate, because it was not explicitly represented in the *syuzhet*. And rightly so, for such a view would then implausibly entail indeterminacy about fictional truth in a wide variety of cases in which we are justified in thinking there are certain fictional truths that obtain in the *fabula* in narrative time past what is represented in the *syuzhet*. Such fictional truths are generated by implication. Oftentimes the implication is fairly obvious and viewers can easily infer the implied fictional truths that obtain in narrative time beyond what is represented in the *syuzhet*; the ending of *North by Northwest* (1959) is a well-known, if hackneyed, example. But the problem raised by *The Sopranos* is that sometimes such implications are fraught with ambiguity. And supposing that fictional truth is thus simply indeterminate seems like an inadequate response.

The presumption that there is a determinate fictional truth about narrative events following the end of the *syuzhet* partly explains the widespread entreaties for David Chase to simply tell everyone what happened to Tony Soprano. However, these appeals are also indicative of another important tacit assumption—namely, that given the ambiguity of the final scene, Chase's explanation could clarify what was fictionally true (so long as his explanation meshed with the evidence of the scene) precisely because his creative authority on the series afforded him a distinct epistemic privilege. Simply put, the important assumption underlying requests for an explanation was that Chase *knew* what happened to Tony because it was *his* story and he had made up his mind about it. Both of these assumptions, I have been arguing, are sound. The problem, which anti-intentionalists are right to identify, is that it does not follow that we can necessarily trust Chase or any other artist to proffer a truthful and accurate report of his intentions and, thus, what fictional truths are implied in the work. Chase has been especially coy, hinting in various contexts that Tony is dead, that he is not, that it is indeterminate, and that it doesn't matter whether he's dead or not. It is important to emphasize that this does not present an insurmountable challenge for intentionalism of a moderate variety. For the moderate intentionalist simply draws a distinction between a metaphysical problem and an epistemic one, noting that from the fact that Chase's unreliable self-report stymies our knowledge of what is fictionally true, it simply does not follow that Chase's successfully realized intentions did not determine it.

Indeed, the moderate intentionalist should not want to deny that the best evidence of what fictional truths obtain is always what is implied by the work itself. Generally speaking, the assumption amongst fans and critics is that the work supports two apparently incompatible interpretations. One the one hand, some have argued that after the smash cut to black the fictional world of *The Sopranos* continues as normal, with Meadow sitting down and the family eating dinner together with Journey's "Don't Stop Believing" playing in the background. In this theory, the cut to black simply signals that end of the viewer's access to the story world in a way that calls attention to the constructed or artificial nature of that world, thus flaunting network television's norms of narrative closure and clarity. There are two central ideas motivating this interpretation. The first is defensive: Challenged that the ending implies that Tony is dead, the advocate of this account replies that, in the wake of the peace treaty with the Lupertazzi crime family, there is simply insufficient narrative motivation to infer that Tony was murdered. And, after all, he is alive the last time we see him, so the "end of narrative access" interpretation is a kind of inference to the best explanation, and the burden of proof is on opponents to provide compelling evidence that Tony was whacked. The second idea motivating the "end of narrative access" interpretation is that throughout its run, *The Sopranos* often flaunted conventionality and either sought to deny viewers what they appeared to want (e.g., with extended dream sequences) or gave it to them with some degree of distaste and condescension, suggesting a kind of complicity on their part (e.g., the brutality of Ralph Cifaretto). Asked to explain the ways in which the final scene's formal structure cues us to think something dramatic is about to happen (as I shall show presently), the critics in this camp claim that the pattern should be understood as implying that Tony will still always have to look over his shoulder and sleep with one eye open.

The second dominant interpretation claims that the smash cut to black should be understood as the end of Tony's life. That is, the viewer's access to the story world ends *because* Tony's life ends. The idea here is that the black silence is a moment of subjective narration, representing Tony's death from his own perspective as it were. To support this claim, critics refer to a conversation from the first episode of Season 6, Part II, "Soprano Home Movies," in which Tony's brother-in-law, Bobby Baccalieri, points out that men like him and Tony could die at any moment. "You probably don't even hear it when it happens, right?" Bobby remarks. Interestingly, there is a flashback, from Tony's perspective, to this moment at the very end of the penultimate episode, "The Blue Comet," which is stylistically atypical for *The Sopranos*. Moreover, advocates of the "death of Tony" interpretation point out that the cutting pattern and sound design leading up to the smash cut to black cues viewers to expect a dramatic event and a point-of-view shot from Tony's perspective at just the moment that the smash cut to black occurs.

Figure 4.1 "Made in America," the final episode of *The Sopranos* (HBO 1999–2007). Tony's first glance up at the door of Holsten's, motivated by the sound of the bell.

Figure 4.2 Tony's point of view: A female customer entering the restaurant.

Figure 4.3 A "reverse shot" matching 4.1 and emphasizing the subjectivity of 4.2.

Figure 4.4 Tony glances up at the door of the restaurant, again motivated by the sound of the bell.

Figure 4.5 Tony's point of view: A male customer entering the restaurant.

Figure 4.6 A "reverse shot" matching 4.4 and emphasizing the subjectivity of 4.5.

Figure 4.7 Tony glances up at the door of the restaurant, again motivated by the sound of the bell.

Figure 4.8 Tony's point of view: Carmela enters the restaurant.

Figure 4.9 A "reverse shot" matching 4.7 and emphasizing the subjectivity of 4.8.

Figure 4.10 Tony's point of view: Carmela approaches and makes eye contact.

Figure 4.11 A "reverse shot" matching 9.9 and 4.7, a gain emphasizing the subjectivity of 4.10 and 4.8.

Figure 4.12 Tony's ostensible point of view of the "Members Only man," although likely not a literal POV shot because the door has yet to open and ring the bell, cuing Tony's glance.

Figure 4.13 A "reverse shot" of Tony's gaze, ostensibly revealing the source of the apparent POV.

Figure 4.14 A "true" point of view shot of the "Members Only man" and of A. J. from Tony's perspective.

Figure 4.15 A "reverse" shot indicating the source of the point of view in 4.14.

Figure 4.16 A wide shot, revealing the men's room, which the "Members Only man" is entering, in relationship to Tony.

Figure 4.17 Tony glances at the restaurant door, cued by the sound of the bell.

Figure 4.18 The final "shot"; arguably Tony's "point of view."

Asked to explain what narrative evidence supports the interpretation that Tony is whacked, supporters of the "death of Tony" interpretation point out that the narration focuses our attention more on the "Man in the Members Only Jacket" than any other restaurant patron and, moreover, "Members Only" is clearly staring at Tony from his seat at the counter and as he passes him to use the toilet.

Figure 4.19 An earlier shot of the "Members Only man" looking (at Tony's table?).

Figure 4.20 A shot of Tony following 4.19, ostensibly revealing what the "Members Only man" is looking at.

Further, his use of the restaurant's toilet is plausibly understood as an allusion to Tony's favorite scene from *The Godfather* (1972), in which Michael Corleone excuses himself from the dining table, retrieves a planted gun from the men's restroom, returns to the table, and shoots Sollozzo and McCluskey. The scene in "Made in America" also parallels that in *The Godfather* by foregrounding a high-pitched screeching sound in the audio mix before the climactic moment. Finally, advocates of this interpretation point out that "Members Only" is also the title of the first episode of Season 6, Part I, in which Tony is shot by his Uncle Junior.

Both interpretations strike me as having a good deal of plausibility. Both mesh fairly well with the structural features of the work(s)—the salient work being not just the "Made in America" episode, but Season 6 as a whole, and the series overall. And both interpretations mesh with sound hypotheses regarding the intentions behind the creation of the episode. Given the unreliability of Chase's testimony, do we have reason to prefer one over the other? In my view, the "death of Tony" interpretation fits better with the structural features the episode—in particular the use of editing and sound—and is well supported by Tony's odd flashback to his conversation with Bobby at the end of "The Blue Comet."

However, there seems to me a way in which certain elements of both interpretations might be combined in a way that respects the evidence in the work and the best guess as to the intentions with which the episode was created. The "death of Tony" interpretation seems right in terms of what is fictionally true, but that this is compatible with, perhaps even better supported by, the opposing camp's emphasis on Chase's grudge against network television and its attendant narrative norms, his oft-expressed distaste for his viewership's apparent bloodlust, and his documented embrace of various art-cinema conventions. Based on my unified account, then, it is fictionally true that Tony dies at the end of *The Sopranos* because the show's creators successfully realized their intentions to structure the episode in such a way that his death is implied strongly enough that alert viewers are able to infer it and that "bad" viewers will not only overlook the implication but also be frustrated by the lack of clear narrative closure and a graphic shooting scene. And there is nothing suspect with the claim that this is all determinate or established in a metaphysical sense, even if we never have reliable access to the creators' intentions.

There is, then, an important way in which creators' successfully realized intentions determine what is fictionally true in their televisual works and, furthermore, an important cogency in the standard practice of asking creators what they intended when fictional truth is ambiguous. Fans and critics are not naïve; they also know that creators' declarations on such matters cannot be accepted blindly and do not have the power to change what is fictionally true post-hoc. But the reliability of creators' testimony is an epistemic problem rather than a metaphysical one.

In this way, our analysis of fictional truth in television offers a response to what Livingston has characterized as the best argument for anti-intentionalism.[63] The argument can be stated as a dilemma: Either the creators' intentions are successfully realized in the work or they are not. If they are not, they cannot determine what the work means and we should not take them into account in interpreting the work. On the other hand, if the creators' intentions are successfully realized in the work, then all the evidence we need to determine what the work means is in the structural features of the work itself, making the creators' intentions redundant.

On the moderate intentionalist account offered here, we should accept the first horn of the dilemma but challenge the second. Evidently, part of what viewers need to interpret are fictional truths that are merely implied by rather than manifest in the structural features of the work. So, strictly speaking, not all of the creators' successfully realized intentions are manifest in the structural features of the work itself. Moreover, when there is ambiguity in those structural features as to what is fictionally true by implication, viewers are rationally warranted to appeal to the creators' intentions in order to disambiguate what is fictionally true. For in such cases, the work underdetermines what is fictionally true, and even in a fiction it is implausible that both p and not-p obtain simultaneously. This appeal to creators' intentions may be active or explicit, taking the form of a Google search or the like, but it may also be implicit. In the latter case, viewers may simply make an inference as to what the creators most plausibly intended—and this without necessarily having a well-developed notion of who the creators are but rather a general sense of intentional agency behind the work.[64]

Conclusion

The primary aim of this chapter has been to argue that two often overlooked components of work meaning, category and fictional truth, are determined by creators' successfully realized intentions. I believe that even many avowed interpretive constructivists and relativists would assent to this view, but they have not sufficiently acknowledged the dilemma this raises for them. Constructivist and relativist approaches to interpretation almost always ultimately make reference to category and/or fictional truth, because they need *some* stable foundation on which to ground their interpretations. But if this is right, then meaning is more determinate than constructivists and relativists often allow. Furthermore, it follows that the popular project of analyzing the significance of television works for various audiences is implicitly subtended by viewers' activity of *detecting* creators' intended meaning in terms of category and fictional truth. For this reason, moderate intentionalism is a necessary supplement to approaches that seek to understand the interpretive activities of viewers in terms of "constructing meaning." It is time for the field to recognize it as such.

    I want to close by highlighting one more way in which this line of thought is compatible with cultural studies approaches to interpretation. Sometimes such approaches emphasize the fact that viewers (or readers or listeners) can refuse to abide by the norms of the institution of fiction; in Walton's terms, they "refuse to play the game." Let's return to the example of *Star Trek*. As is well documented in the cultural studies literature, there is a significant community of *Star Trek* fans that write fan-fiction—stories based, to a greater or lesser degree, on the *Star Trek* story world. A sub-set of these fans write homoerotic fan-fiction known as "slash," because the subgenre is informally referred to as "Kirk/Spock" or "K/S."[65] In what I take to be standard analyses of slash, fan-fiction authors produce a new piece of fiction that prescribes the imagining of a homosexual relationship that is *not* part of the fictional truth of the original work. Lynne Segal, for example, refers to K/S stories as involving "female fans ... writing their own erotic fantasies over Star Trek characters and narratives ... [They] enthuse over the explicit sexual and romantic bonds they construct between Captain Kirk and Mr. Spock ..."[66] Now, there is a somewhat distinct view, premised on a weak version of interpretive constructivism, according to which Kirk and Spock's romance is not merely an audience fantasy, but a *possible* way of "decoding" the polysemic "text." As Sara Gwenllian Jones summarizes this view, "Reading 'innocent' same-sex relationships between characters such as Kirk and Spock ... as homoerotic appears to directly contradict the explicit evidence and 'preferred meaning' of the text, taking characters in 'unauthorized' directions;" thus, such interpretations are characterized as "against-the-grain readings"—that is, interpretations that are "oppositional" or "resistant" to the "preferred" or "dominant" "decodings."[67] But as we have seen—and as I suspect the scholars I discuss below have noticed—such interpretations don't carry much force, because the "text" has already been defined as polysemic. For if the text is polysemic why should it be of surprise or interest that some viewers "decode" in divergent ways?

Hence, we arrive at the view with which I am really concerned here—namely, that, in my terms, it is an implied fictional truth of *Star Trek* that Kirk and Spock are lovers, or, in Sara Gwenllian Jones's terms, that such an interpretation (manifested in slash) is "an actualization of latent textual elements"[68] Although I ultimately disagree with her view, it seems to me that Elizabeth Woledge is on the right track in asserting that "a major problem for interpreters is that the existence of K/S suggests that there are homoerotic elements in *Star Trek*, but since these elements are not an overt part of the show they must be explained as "subtextual" and "latent.""[69] I would tweak this analysis slightly: It seems to me that views according to which Spock and Kirk are lovers are possible in part because of ambiguity regarding what is fictionally true regarding their relationship.

As I set up the problem in this chapter, I assumed that we were interested in television works as artworks—intentionally designed communicative utterances—and, moreover, that in approaching those works within the institution of fiction, the aim of interpretation was normatively constrained. It is, specifically, to figure out, what the creators have asked us to imagine is fictionally true and what we *should* imagine as fictionally true—if we are playing by the rules of the game. In such cases, we ought to seek to disambiguate what is fictionally true by closely analyzing the structural features of the work in conjunction with attempting to determine the creators' intentions.

But this is compatible with recognizing that some viewers aren't interested in engaging with *Star Trek* and other television works *as* works of fiction—that is, as intentionally designed communicative utterances that prescribe certain imaginings. Some viewers are simply interested in the sorts of imaginings or fantasies that *Star Trek* can afford them. And in such cases, viewers' interpretive aims are not normatively constrained in the same way. Such viewers are invested neither in the project of trying to determine what the creators asked us to imagine as fictionally true nor in the project of imagining in accordance with those prescriptions.

So, when implied fictional truths are ambiguous, it is entirely coherent for these viewers to disambiguate them without regard for what the creators intended. Specifically, it is coherent for the sort of *Star Trek* viewer I have described to *use* the work for the purpose of imagining that it is fictionally true that Kirk and Spock are lovers, because the work itself is sufficiently ambiguous that such a proposition is not explicitly ruled out as an implied fictional truth. Nevertheless, these viewers cannot completely ignore the intentional agency of *Stark Trek*'s creators. For they still require *some* determinate facts to ground their fantasies about Kirk and Spock, and once again reference to the successfully realized intentions of creators offers the most plausible account of how such facts are established. To use a banal example for the purpose of clarity, these fans accept that it is true of the fiction that the characters' names are Kirk and Spock; these determinate fictional truths that have been established by the creators' successfully realized intentions.

In summary, while I have tried to show that in fundamental interpretive matters regarding a work's category and fictional truth, there is no avoiding the intentional agency of creators, I am happy to accept that there is something correct and important about cultural studies approaches to television interpretation which focus on the activities of viewers. As we shall see in the next chapter, however, such approaches often encounter problems when what is at stake in interpretation is not merely fictional truth, but the views or attitudes expressed, endorsed, or advocated in a work.

Notes

1. There is something of a normative component to this conception of works as well: creators can, of course, fail to realize their intentions and fail to make a work. In this way, all works are achievements in at least the very minimal sense of being successful realizations of intentions to make *something*. The important point, though, is that while the concept of work does have this normative component, it is nevertheless not an honorific term that applies only to *good* works or, more generally, works of a particular value.
2. As Noël Carroll puts it in characteristically pithy fashion, "Artworks ... are the products of human action. Typically, our understanding of artifacts is enabled by grasping how and why they were made. Understanding how [and for what] an artifact is made—which involves grasping the maker's intentions—is generally relevant to understanding the artifact. Prima facie, what is appropriate to the understanding of the results of human action in general is appropriate to the understanding of artworks ..." See Noël Carroll "Anglo-American Aesthetics and Contemporary Criticism: Intention and the Hermeneutics of Suspicion," in *Beyond Aesthetics*, (Cambridge, UK: Cambridge University Press, 2001), 183.
3. E. D. Hirsch, *Validity in Interpretation* (New Haven, CT: Yale University Press, 1967), 8. For an excellent critical discussion of how television studies has sought to analyze "significance" in the sense I am using it here, see, especially, Sonia Livingstone, *Making Sense of Television: The Psychology of Audience Interpretation*, 2nd ed. (London: Routledge, 1998).
4. This dilemma is related to and inspired by Robert Stecker's "constructivist's dilemma," but raises a distinct challenge. See Robert Stecker, *Interpretation and Construction: Art, Speech, and the Law* (Malden, MA: Blackwell, 2003), 126–135.
5. On this point, again see Carroll, "Anglo-American Aesthetics and Contemporary Criticism" Although I use Carroll's term, "moderate intentionalism," to describe the view I advocate, this view has important affinities with what Stecker calls "the unified view" and what Livingston calls "partial intentionalism." See Stecker, *Interpretation and Construction*, 42–50; and Paisley Livingston, *Art and Intention: A Philosophical Study* (Oxford: Oxford University Press, 2005), 142–43; 149–52.

152   *Interpretation I*

6. Stecker, *Interpretation and Construction*, 52.
7. As Stecker puts it, "Critical pluralism is, or should be, founded on the idea that there are various legitimate, interpretive projects that concern what works could (can be taken to) mean or the work's significance for various audiences. This leaves logical space for the question, 'Is there something the work does mean?'" Ibid., 58.
8. This brief summary necessarily glosses over some difficult epistemological issues. The philosopher Hilary Putnam offers a helpful discussion in which he endorses a view, "interest relativity," which is in some respects similar to Stecker's. According to Putnam, "It can be objective that an interpretation or an explanation is the correct one, *given* the context and the interests which are relevant in the context … A sane relativism can recognize there is a fact of the matter in interpretation without making that fact of the matter unique or context-independent." Importantly, Putnam adds, not all interests are equal: "There are silly interests, deluded interests, irrational interests, and so on, as well as reasonable and relevant ones." See Hilary Putnam, "Is There a Fact of the Matter about Fiction?" in *Realism with a Human Face*, ed. James Conant (Cambridge, MA: Harvard University Press, 1990) 210–11. For a critical discussion of framework relativism, according to which there is no possibility of adjudicating between different interests or frameworks, see Paisley Livingston, *Literary Knowledge: Humanistic Inquiry and the Philosophy of Science* (Ithaca, NY: Cornell University Press, 1988).
9. Again, there are complexities here that I must pass over to address the central matter at hand. Nelson Goodman advocates a unique form of constructivism and relativism, according to which truth is relative to "world-versions," the contents of which (including everything from pictures to scientific theories) may nevertheless be appraised for "rightness." See Nelson Goodman, *Ways of Worldmaking* (Indianapolis, IN: Hackett, 1978).
10. For example: "A segment of the television flow, whether it be an individual program, a commercial, a newscast, or an entire evening's viewing, may be thought of as a television text—offering a multiplicity of meanings or polysemy." Jeremy Butler, *Television: Critical Methods and Approaches*, 4th ed. (New York: Routledge, 2012), 10.
11. Alan McKee, *Textual Analysis* (London: Sage, 2003), 2.
12. Ibid., 63.
13. Ibid., 73.
14. Elliott Logan pointed out to me that one still might worry that this approach still imposes meaning upon a work or, at least, restricts the critic's focus in such a way that may blind her or him to more salient meanings within the work. I agree that this is a potential pitfall, but whether it constitutes a problem in any particular instance depends upon the critic's research questions. If one wants to know, for example, what broad themes and attitudes are expressed in *Dexter*, then approaching the work with the aim of analyzing it to see how it constructs heteronormativity is likely to skew the findings. On the other hand, one might ask about the extent to which heterosexuality is normalized (and how this happens) in contemporary American television drama and, reasonably enough, analyze *Dexter* and similar series with a focus on elements that are salient to this particular question while more or less ignoring other themes that might be more prominent or salient within the work itself. In each case, the aims of interpretation are different and warrant distinct interpretive procedures.

15. McKee, *Textual Analysis*, 70.
16. Matt Hills, "Television and Its Audience: Issues of Consumption and Reception," in *Tele-Visions: An Introduction to Studying Television*, ed. Glen Creeber (London: BFI, 2006), 93.
17. Gray and Lotz represent the view I criticize here, because their recent introductory textbook advances it with admirable clarity. See Jonathan Gray and Amanda D. Lotz, *Television Studies* (London: Polity, 2012). But the view itself is both an old and a pervasive one in television studies. For seminal discussions, see the work of John Fiske, who claims: "Programs are stable, fixed entities … A text is a different matter altogether. Programs are produced, distributed, and defined by the industry: texts are the product of their readers. So a program becomes a text at the moment of reading, that is, when its interaction with one of its many audiences activates some of the meanings/pleasures that it is capable of provoking," *Television Culture* (London: Routledge, 1987), 14.
18. Gray and Lotz, *Television Studies*, 44.
19. Stecker, *Interpretation and Construction*, 82.
20. Gray and Lotz, *Television Studies*, 44.
21. Ibid., 46.
22. Cf. Stecker's "constructivist's dilemma": "Either interpretations make statements that are truth valued (true or false), or they do not. If they do, then, when they are true, their objects already have the properties attributed to them; while, if they are false, their objects do not have those properties and will not acquire them in virtue of such false ascription. What if interpretations lack truth value? … I cannot change an artwork by issuing a commend, recommendation, or by imagining something with regard to it. The best I can do is bring about a change in myself or another human being by doing these things … So, it appears, that on either supposition, interpretations do not change their objects." *Interpretation and Construction*, 126.
23. Ibid., 76. Needless to say, this view is indebted to Hirsch.
24. Ethan Thompson and Jason Mittell, "Introduction: An Owner's Manual for Television," in *How to Watch Television*, ed. Ethan Thompson and Jason Mittell (New York: New York University Press, 2013), 4.
25. Thompson and Mittell, "Introduction: An Owner's Manual" 6.
26. Butler, *Television, Critical Methods and Approaches*, 363.
27. Kendall L. Walton, "Categories of Art," in *Marvelous Images: On Values and the Arts* (Oxford: Oxford University Press, 2008), 195–220.
28. David Davies, "Categories of Art," in *The Routledge Companion to Aesthetics*, 3rd. ed., ed. Berys Gaut and Dominic McIver Lopes (New York: Routledge), 229.
29. Walton, "Categories of Art," 199. As Walton acknowledges, in practice these are not always clear distinctions, and, furthermore, works usually belong to several different categories.
30. Ibid., 204.
31. Ibid., 205.
32. Emily Nussbaum, "Cool Story, Bro," *The New Yorker* (March 3, 2014). Accessed February 18, 2015. http://www.newyorker.com/magazine/2014/03/03/cool-story-bro.
33. Willa Paskin, "The Horrible Things that Men Do to Women," *Slate* (February 23, 2014) Accessed February 18, 2015. http://www.slate.com/articles/arts/television/

154　　*Interpretation I*

2014/02/true_detective_the_women_on_the_show_are_treated_badly_but_there_s_a_good.html.
34. For discussion, see Anthony N. Smith, "*True Detective* and the Pleasures of Genre Uncertainty," *CST Online* (April 11, 2014). Accessed February 18, 2015. http://cstonline.tv/true-detective-and-the-pleasures-of-genre-uncertainty.
35. Jason Jacobs, "*True Detective* and Practical Criticism," *CST Online* (April 11, 2014), available at http://cstonline.tv/true-detective-and-practical-criticism (accessed February 18, 2015).
36. It is also worth flagging here, although I cannot discuss it, the fact that the divergence in evaluative judgments of the show is explicable in terms of genre or category more broadly. Those who thought *True Detective* was a metaphysical horror finally found the series an artistic disappointment; those who thought it was an update on the detective procedural tended to assess it more positively.
37. Thanks to Elliott Logan for pushing me to elaborate this point.
38. I am skipping over some ontological complexities here that I flagged in the previous chapter: it may be the case that the work was in fact complete earlier—say when those with the relevant authority (e.g., the executive producers) decided it was, or, perhaps when they acted on that decision by sending the master to HBO, and so forth. But these technicalities are not so important for the present argument.
39. For discussion, see Joseph Laycock, "*True Detective* vs. H. P. Lovecraft's 'cosmic horror,'" *Salon.com* (March 17, 2014), http://www.salon.com/2014/03/16/the_dangerous_mythology_of_true_detective_partner/ (accessed February 19, 2015).
40. Emily Nussbaum, "The Disappointing Finale of *True Detective*," *The New Yorker* (March 10, 2014), http://www.newyorker.com/culture/culture-desk/the-disappointing-finale-of-true-detective (accessed February 19, 2015); Jason Mittell, "True Disappointment," *Just TV* (March 10, 2014). Accessed February 19, 2015. https://justtv.wordpress.com/2014/03/10/true-disappointment/.
41. Spencer Kornhaber, Christopher Orr, and Amy Sullivan, "The *True Detective* Finale: That's It?" *The Atlantic.com* (March 10, 2014). Accessed February 19, 2015. http://www.theatlantic.com/entertainment/archive/2014/03/the-em-true-detective-em-finale-thats-it/284312/. Emphasis on "character study" mine.
42. Lili Loofbourow, "Marty, the Monster," *Los Angeles Review of Books* (March 11, 2014). Accessed February 19, 2015. http://lareviewofbooks.org/essay/true-detective-finale.
43. Ben Travers, "*True Detective* Finds the Light in a Truly Surprising Season Finale," *Indiewire.com* (March 10, 2014). Accessed February 19, 2015. http://www.indiewire.com/article/television/true-detective-finds-the-lights-winning-in-a-truly-surprising-season-finale. Emphasis mine.
44. Davies, "Categories of Art," 230.
45. Heather L. LaMarre, Kristen D. Landreville, and Michael A. Beam, "The Irony of Satire: Political Ideology and the Motivation to See What You Want to See in *The Colbert Report*," *The International Journal of Press/Politics* 14, no. 2 (April 2009): 212–31.
46. Walton, "Categories of Art," 212.

47. Peter Swirski, *Literature, Analytically Speaking* (Austin: University of Texas Press, 2010), 111.
48. For a seminal discussion of this complex topic, see David Lewis, "Truth in Fiction," *American Philosophical Quarterly* 15, no. 1 (January 1978): 37–46.
49. Stecker, *Interpretation and Construction*, 77.
50. As Walton colorfully puts it, "Fictional truths breed like rabbits." Kendall L. Walton, *Mimesis as Make-Believe* (Cambridge, MA: Harvard University Press, 1990), 142.
51. In *Literature, Analytically Speaking* (Austin: University of Texas, 2010), Swirski writes, "After all, we must first know what the story is in order to interpret it" (111). Also see David Bordwell, *Making Meaning: Inference and Rhetoric in the Interpretation of Cinema* (Cambridge, MA: Harvard University Press, 1989). For sympathetic but sharp criticisms of this view, see George Wilson, "On Film Narrative and Narrative Meaning," in *Film Theory and Philosophy*, ed. Richard Allen and Murray Smith (Oxford: Oxford University Press, 1997), 221–238.
52. David Bordwell, *Narration in the Fiction Film* (Madison: University of Wisconsin Press, 1985), 49.
53. Ibid.
54. Walton, *Mimesis as Make-Believe*, 140.
55. For further discussion, see Livingston, *Art and Intention*, 192.
56. For clear, critical reviews of the literature, see Livingston, *Art and Intention*, 186–200; Swirski, *Literature, Analytically Speaking*, 110–31; and Richard Woodward, "Truth in Fiction," *Philosophy Compass* 6, no. 3 (2011): 158–67.
57. Walton, *Mimesis as Make-Believe*, 185. Also see Livingston, *Art and Intention*, 194–96.
58. Walton, *Mimeses as Make-Believe*, 39.
59. Livingston, *Art and Intention*, 196.
60. Ibid., 197.
61. This claim lines up with the accounts offered by Livingston and Swirski, to which it is indebted. See Livingston, *Art and Intention*, 197–200; and Swirski, *Literature, Analytically Speaking*, 126–28.
62. See Amie Thomasson, "Artifacts and Human Concepts," in *Creations of the Mind: Theories of Artifacts and Their Representation*, ed. Eric Margolis and Stephen Laurence (Oxford: Oxford University Press, 2007), 63–69.
63. Livingston, *Art and Intention*, 146.
64. I am grateful to Sarah Cardwell for a helpful discussion on this point.
65. The seminal study is Henry Jenkins, *Textual Poachers: Television Fans and Participatory Culture* (New York: Routledge, 1992).
66. Lynne Segal, *Straight Sex: Rethinking the Politics of Pleasure* (Berkeley: University of California Press, 1994), 236.
67. Sara Gwenllian Jones, "The Sex Lives of Cult Television Characters," *Screen* 43, no. 1 (Spring 2002): 79–90, cited at 81. For an example of this sort of analysis, see Camille Bacon-Smith, *Enterprising Women: Television Fandom and the Creation of Popular Myth* (Philadelphia: University of Pennsylvania Press, 1992), 232–33.
68. Jones, "Sex Lives," 82.
69. Elizabeth Woledge, "Decoding Desire: From Kirk and Spock to K/S," *Social Semiotics* 15, no. 2 (August 2005): 237.

5 Interpretation II

Introduction

With a particular focus on discerning a television work's salient artistic category and what is fictionally true in a work of television, I argued in the previous chapter that constructivist and relativist approaches to the interpretation of television face substantial obstacles and that we have good reasons to embrace a moderate form of intentionalism in those contexts. I also indicated that moderate intentionalism offers a better account of interpretation when the critic's aim is to grasp the higher order meanings of television artworks, and I suggested that one advantage of this view is its ability to account for some of the ways in which interpretation and evaluation interact in our ordinary appreciative practices.

The goal of this chapter is to make good on these latter two claims. My argument is that, *pace* interpretive constructivists and interpretive relativists, the themes, ideas, and attitudes conveyed by television artworks are determined in part by their creators' successfully realised intentions. If, as interpretive constructivists and interpretive relativists would have it, the attitudes conveyed by television works were in any substantive sense constructed by viewers or were simply indeterminate or not truth evaluable, all sorts of criticism in which we regularly engage would turn out to be incoherent.

In this chapter, my focus will be on the relationship between interpretation and ethical criticism, in particular. The discussion of ethical criticism owes to my personal interest in ethics, but I hope to show that my concerns and arguments in the context of ethical criticism have parallels in the context of ideological criticism commonly practiced in television studies. I argue that the widespread activity of criticizing television artworks (and their creators) for endorsing or advocating ethically flawed attitudes is tacitly underpinned by the assumption that "meaning" in this sense is neither constructed by viewers nor relative to differing interpretations but rather something that objectively exists *in* the work as a result of creators' successfully realized intentions. The final section of this chapter attempts to segue to the book's concluding chapter on evaluation, laying some initial groundwork for the discussion there with this argument: To the extent that work meaning obtains in a real, objective sense as the result of successfully realized semantic intentions, there are some ways in which the artistic evaluation of television is objective. Most basically, the successful realization of semantic intentions is a particular kind of achievement and, as such, constitutes a good-making feature or *pro tanto* artistic merit. In addition, if a television artwork objectively expresses or endorses attitudes in a way that constitutes an ethical merit or flaw, this too may serve as the basis of an objective evaluation of the work's ethical and, plausibly, artistic value.

Higher-Order Meaning in Television Interpretation

Although I spent the previous chapter exploring interpretation as it relates to the categories of television works and what is fictionally true in them, most viewers, critics, and scholars who engage in interpretation conceive of that practice in a rather different way. The interpretation of television is commonly thought of as the practice of either attributing or discerning higher-order meanings. By higher-order meanings, I have in mind roughly the sorts of things that, in the context of film interpretation, David Bordwell classifies under the categories of "implicit meaning" and "symptomatic meaning"—in particular, the broader themes and attitudes expressed by the work as a whole. Such higher-order meanings are, I take it, the primary focus of concern in scholarly volumes typified by I. B. Tauris's Reading Contemporary Television series, which includes, for example, *Reading* 24: *TV Against the Clock,* and *Reading* CSI: *Crime TV Under the Microscope.*

One initial question is whether the constructivist and relativist approaches canvassed in the previous chapter have any more plausibility when the interpretive focus is upon higher-order meanings. Here it is important to bear in mind the plurality of aims with which we interpret television works and other cultural objects. The diverse reading "strategies" with which the contributors to books in the Reading Contemporary Television Series approach particular television series are indicative of this pluralism. These books, and the essays that constitute them, are part of a critical institution in which one valid interpretive aim is to diagnose the ways in which a series is symptomatic of the social and political concerns of the context in which it was created. Another valid interpretive aim is, in McKee's words, "to understand the likely interpretations of texts made by people who consume them."[1] And still another valid interpretive aim is, as discussed in the previous chapter, the construction of significance for a particular viewer or group of viewers. According to the doctrine of critical pluralism, advocated in the previous chapter, the plausibility and success of any given interpretive project ought to be assessed relative to its particular interpretive aim.

Note, however, that all of the above-mentioned, commonly embraced interpretive aims seek to describe what a television work (or "text") *could* mean. That is, interpretive projects guided by each of those interpretive aims respectively would likely result in a conclusion about what a television work (or "text") could mean given a particular set of circumstances—that is, what it could mean against the backdrop of increasingly digitized social relations, or what it could mean to Australian audiences, or what it could mean to viewers that identify as queer, or what it could mean to fans of the series, or what it could mean to viewers who know it's an adaptation, and so forth.

Given that the aim of interpretations in the loose institution of contemporary television criticism and scholarship is to describe what a television work (or "text") *could* mean, constructivists face a dilemma similar to the one described in the previous chapter. On the one hand, constructivists could insist that viewers construct what works actually *do* mean, which would give their central claim ambition but render it implausible. As I argued in the previous chapter, it is just unclear how an interpretation alone could change its object.[2] On the other hand, constructivists may settle for the plausible idea that viewers either construct *possible* meanings (or significance) for themselves or the actual meaning of "texts" where texts are simply stipulated as constructed in the process of viewing anyway. But this latter view is theoretically uninformative and seems weaker than what some constructivists would want to claim. So, the shift in focus from the interpretation of categories and fictional truth to higher-order meaning lends no help to constructivists.

However, relativism might seem to be on stronger ground. Why? With regard to the interpretation of artistic category and fictional truth, there is no substantive institutional practice of interpreting with the *intrinsic* aim of describing what category a work *could* be apprehended in or what *could* be fictionally true in a work. (This is not to say there is no substantive institutional practice of *imagining* such possibilities, for in fan-fiction there surely is.) On the contrary, there tends to be a high degree of critical convergence upon the matter of artistic categories and fictional truth. But things are rather different when it comes to the interpretation of higher-order meanings, for, as I have just observed, there clearly is a critical institution that supports a variety of thriving interpretive practices, often pursuing different aims and often rendering divergent and apparently incompatible interpretations of the meaning of a single television work (or "text"). These circumstances may appear to lend weight to the relativist contention that meaning cannot be "fixed" or "closed" such that we can speak of what a work *does* mean and, thus, evaluate for truth and falsity at least those interpretations that seek to track work meaning. For, as we saw in previous chapters, many prominent scholars—Jeremy Butler, John Hartley, Matt Hills, Alan McKee, Jason Mittell—take it as axiomatic that there simply is no "right" way to interpret television, despite their somewhat diverse theoretical backgrounds.

Despite the pervasiveness of interpretive relativism in contemporary television studies, it is actually hard to find recent sustained arguments in favor of the view—particularly when it is not also hitched to some version of constructivism.[3] In recent years it is more common for the relativist view to simply be asserted, perhaps with a brief nod to the concept of "polysemy" and the idea that people in different social or cultural contexts interpret television in different ways.[4] As far as I can tell, the most sustained argument for relativism is still John Fiske's *Television Culture* (a book that is approaching its thirtieth anniversary) and the vast majority of explicit defence for the doctrine invokes both of Fiske's points—polysemy and what I'll call "interpretive incompatibility."[5] Therefore, I want to engage with Fiske's account as representative of contemporary views.

Fiske commences his brief with an emphasis on polysemy—which he simply asserts is "an essential characteristic of television." In his words:

> A program provides a potential of meanings which may be realized, or made into actually experienced meanings, by socially situated viewers in the process of reading. The polysemic potential is neither boundless nor structureless [sic]: the text delineates the terrain within which meanings may be made and proffers some meanings more vigorously than others.[6]

As a result, Fiske claims, "Analysis has to pay less attention to the textual strategies of preference or closure and more to the gaps and spaces that open television up to meanings not preferred by textual structure but that result from the social experience of the reader."[7]

Immediately, we see a tension here between the claim that polysemy is "an essential characteristic of television," in which case it seems that any particular instance of television possesses multiple meanings, and the claim that polysemy describes the fact that a given instance of television has the potential to be interpreted in myriad ways by readers in different social contexts. Later in the book, it becomes clear that Fiske wishes to advance the latter claim. For, he states, "Meanings are determined socially: that is, they are constructed out of the conjuncture of the text with the socially situated reader."[8] Therefore, polysemy and interpretive incompatibility collapse into just one consideration in favour of relativism, as is clear from Fiske's own summary of his argument:

> the television audience is composed of a wide variety of groups and is not a homogenous mass [premise 1]; these groups actively read television in order to produce from it meanings that connect with their social experience [premise 2]. These propositions entail the corollary that the television text is a potential of meanings capable of being viewed with a variety of modes of attention by a variety of viewers. To be popular, then, television must be both polysemic and flexible [conclusion].[9]

This is an unconvincing argument. As we have seen on several occasions now, the problem is the ambiguous use of "text." Fiske's earlier characterization of "meaning" and his second premise in this argument make it patently clear that, on his account, viewers construct meanings in their interactions with television. But if that's the case, the conclusion only follows from the premises if "the television text" is disambiguated, in a question-begging way, as something that is produced in the audience's interactions with television. And this leads to a conclusion that is true but trivial, as it merely affirms what is asserted in the second premise—namely, that viewers produce meanings in their interactions with television. If, on the other hand, "the television text" is disambiguated as "the television work," then the argument is formally invalid, because the conclusion that "the television text is a potential of meanings ... [and is] polysemic" simply does not follow from the premises. For the meanings that viewers produce in their interactions with the television work are not properties of the work itself—or, at least, the burden is on Fiske to provide an additional argument to show how such meanings become properties of the work itself.[10]

Better arguments for interpretive relativism are on offer in philosophical aesthetics. Because my focus here is not the interpretation of art in general, but rather of television *works*, I will only briefly make a few general points before moving on to some more detailed pragmatic reasons why relativism about the interpretation of television works is unappealing. As I have already indicated, if relativism has any prima facie plausibility as a doctrine about the interpretation of higher-order meanings, this seems to stem from the fact that such interpretations often do *not* converge—indeed, they sometimes seem irresolvable. Perhaps it will turn out that there is no critical consensus about what attitude *Mad Men* (AMC 2007–2015) takes to its protagonist, Don Draper: Some critics claim the show takes a distanced, critical view of him, others claim that it endorses his behaviour, and others claim that the truth is somewhere in between, because the show revels in Don's complexity. Closely related to this sort of practical dilemma regarding intractable debates about higher-order meaning is an epistemic worry: We appear to have no way of knowing which interpretation is the best one or the right one.

Stephen Davies has neatly summarised this sort of argument, which is advanced, most notably, by Joseph Margolis:

1 No work of literature can be interpreted truly as *p and not-p* (nor as *p and q* where *p* and *q* are contraries).
2 Many a work of literature admits of equally plausible (convincing, revealing) but contradictory or contrary interpretations; so
3 Interpretations of works of literature cannot be assessed for truth (nor can they be assessed for falsity).[11]

If we substitute "literature" with "television," this argument is one that, I think, tacitly underpins the views of interpretive relativists in television studies—or at least perhaps it should, because something like this is probably their best argument. Davies offers a good analysis of it, and so I will merely summarize a few of his points here.

First, we might, with Monroe Beardsley, accept both the premises but reject the conclusion. For the conclusion arguably illicitly shifts the problem from an epistemic one to a metaphysical one. The fact that we cannot identify the best interpretation of a television work hardly shows that one doesn't exist. As Beardsley argues, we need not—and should not—"deny that there are cases of ambiguity where *no* interpretation can be established over its rivals; nor ... that there are many cases where we cannot be sure that we have the correct interpretation."[12] But this does not entail the conclusion that the relativist draws—namely, that interpretations are not truth evaluable *in principle*.

Not only do relativists owe an additional argument for the epistemic worry to carry any weight, they also owe an account of why the epistemic worry fails to impede our ordinary interpretive practices. In other words, the relativist should be able to explain how and why it is we often advance interpretations of higher-order meanings in conversation, informal writing, or scholarly essays *as if* those interpretations were truth evaluable. In particular, we offer supporting evidence and reasons in defense of our interpretations. But if interpretations of higher-order meaning are not evaluable for truth or falsity, why do we support them with evidence and reasons?

Here television scholars frequently claim that what is at stake is not "truth" or "falsity" *per se,* but "reasonableness" or "persuasiveness." For example, Jeremy Butler writes, "Remember, critical analyses are, by their nature, subjective. There can be therefore no claims for objective truth, but some claims are still more reasonable and compelling than others."[13] There are two problems with this statement. First, the conclusion that there can be "no claims for objective truth" is unsound, because it follows from a bad inference involving an ambiguous use of "subjective." The sense in which a critical analysis is subjective here—that is, I take it, mind-dependent—does not preclude the possibility that the analysis could itself describe an objective (in the sense of mind-independent) truth. But it's the second problem that is most important here—namely, that it is not clear what the measure of being "reasonable" or "compelling" could be in the absence of truth. By what other measure could an interpretation *of a work* be judged reasonable or compelling other than its approximate correspondence to what the work actually means? If Butler were to maintain that the object of interpretation is a "text" rather than a work, or the aim of interpretation were, say, describing its significance for a particular group of people, then he could reasonably proffer other criteria of being reasonable or compelling. But then, of course, we would be talking about *possible* meanings derived from different interpretive aims—something with which critical pluralism is compatible, but which is not our focus in interpreting instances of television as *works*.

Remember: Of the various interpretive aims with which we could approach television, an interest in television artworks—intentionally designed communicative utterances—demands that we focus on what the works actually do mean. And in fact our standard interpretive practices with regard to television suggest that our interest in television is frequently (but not always) as an art form comprising works. This interest is tacit in just the sort of activity I mentioned above—arguments, supported by evidence and reasons, about whether a work does, as a matter of fact, convey x or y attitude toward its characters.

Note that this claim is entirely compatible with the idea that there are a variety of interpretive practices that embody different interpretive aims. Sometimes, of course, we do advance interpretations that describe a way in which a particular group of people make sense of—that is, find significance in—a television series. In such cases, it may *not* be the case that interpretations are truth evaluable. Thus it is possible to acknowledge the diversity of our interpretive practices, which sometimes involve both claims that are advanced as if they are truth evaluable and claims that are not, without embracing relativism.

Davies puts this point somewhat more formally in denying the first premise of the relativist's argument above. Specifically, he identifies an implausible assumption tacit in that premise, to wit: "if any interpretation of a work can be true, then only one interpretation of it can be true."[14] As Davies and several other aestheticians have pointed out, there are several ways one can reject this assumption. I favor the option outlined by Robert Stecker, which emphasizes the point above regarding the myriad aims with which we interpret works. As we have seen in the varying conceptions of textual analysis among television scholars, some writers offer interpretations with the aim of describing a work's "significance" to a specific social group, while others are offering accounts of what the works *could* mean, and still others merely claim that it is interesting or aesthetically rewarding to interpret the works in particular ways. And in the present context, where the focus is on the appreciation of television artworks as *works*, the aim of interpretation is to identify what works actually *do* mean.

As Stecker argues, if we accept the plausible premise that interpretations should be evaluated relative to their aim, then we should embrace critical pluralism—that is, the idea that "there may be a multiplicity of acceptable interpretations of the same item."[15] He explains as follows:

> The many ways of *taking* works for the sake of the many different interpretive aims that critics … bring to the task of understanding and appreciation guarantee a plurality of acceptable interpretations for just about any work. Given these different aims, the interpretations in question include those that speak to what a given work could mean, as well as what it does mean. It includes those with instrumental aims that attempt to find a significance in the work for the audience the interpreter addresses. *Despite this diversity, it does not follow that these interpretations are strictly logically incompatible, as is sometimes claimed* …[16]

In short, the irresolvable nature of some interpretive debates is insufficient to motivate relativism. The apparent problem can be explained away by appealing to the idea that interpretive disputes can be understood as manifesting confusion about different interpretive aims. That is, the evidence proffered by the relativist is just as well explained by critical pluralism.

Interpretation and Ethics 1: A Critique of Relativism

This is all rather abstract, and while it might strike some readers as a decent opening defense against relativism, it also does not present any significant challenges to that view. At this point, then, I'd like to make the discussion somewhat more concrete with a challenge. The challenge, as indicated in the previous chapter, takes the form of a dilemma: Confronted with an apparently ethically flawed television artwork—say, an episode that appears to endorse racist attitudes or a series that appears to sanction torture—the relativist has two unappealing options.

One option is to stand fast and deny that the television work is indeed ethically flawed in any objective sense, maintaining that interpretations of the work as, say, racist or sexist, are not evaluable for truth or falsity, correctness or incorrectness. The consequences of this option are obviously dire. The relativist is left without any rational basis to critique a television work for the attitudes it appears to convey—indeed, whether those are characterised as ethical, ideological, political, or whatever. Practically speaking this is a problem because very few advocates of relativism, I suspect, actually behave as if television works are truly bereft of objective, higher-order meanings. That is, I doubt most of the scholars who deny the existence of correct and incorrect interpretations actually refrain from critiquing the ethics, ideology, or politics of various television works—the latter activity rendered incoherent by the doctrine of interpretive relativism.

So, the relativist's second option is to embrace the position *tacitly* endorsed in lodging such critiques—namely, that at least some television works actually do possess objective, higher-order meanings. (For if they don't, whence the critique?) Needless to say, though, this option simply makes the relativist's position unsustainable. For it means that the self-professed interpretive relativist is not really one after all. Call this "the relativist's ethical dilemma."

The relativist's ethical dilemma strikes me as a fairly obvious problem—obvious in the sense that it seems inescapable for anyone who regularly engages with popular artworks, including television, and experiences moral emotions or makes moral judgments. An interlocutor may object here that I am illicitly assuming a universalized morality. However, my argument assumes neither a particular moral framework nor universal assent. Rather, it simply assumes *general* convergence of ethical judgment around some fairly noncontroversial issues such as torture, racism, sexism, and so forth. It seems hard to see how anyone who has any sort of ethical sensibility can rationally square this with a relativist view of the meanings of popular artworks. Nevertheless, for those who remain unconvinced, the same problem arises in the context of ideological criticism. Does the relativist really want to deny that, say, *24* (Fox 2001–2010; 2014) is ideologically (and ethically) flawed to the extent that it sanctions torture? Or that *The Newsroom* (HBO 2012–2014) is ideologically (and ethically) flawed to the extent that it endorses sexist attitudes? Of course, the answer is probably "no," not least because many television scholars have justifiably criticized such programs for these very reasons. The fact that so few, if any, of us are relativists in practice (for good reason) should be motivation to develop a subtler account of interpretation.

This is not to say relativists have no arguments for such a position at their disposal. But to my knowledge no interpretive relativists in television studies have acknowledged, let alone dealt with the dilemma, except for Alan McKee, in his characteristically lucid and explicit fashion. In contrast to my approach, McKee frames the problem as having to do with politics: "The linking of politics with certainty—here, the certainty of interpretation—is common in writing on culture which emerges from identity politics."[17] This parallels the ethical problem I am raising, and, in fact, we could also think of the ethical in broad enough terms that it incorporated the political and the ideological. In any event, McKee's defense of interpretive relativism in the political context can be applied *mutatis mutandis* to the ethical context.

McKee's strategy is, in short, to defend relativism by simply biting the bullet and denying that "texts" can be, as a matter of fact, politically noxious or (one presumes) ethically flawed. In his case study of *The Adventures of Priscilla, Queen of the Desert* (1994), he writes that the starting point of his argument is "a belief that the attempts by critical writing to label *Priscilla* as 'racist' or 'misogynistic' or 'homophobic' are sacrificing too much of our understanding of the polysemic nature of texts in order to gain their 'political' leverage."[18] Nevertheless, McKee writes, "I hope to demonstrate in my approach to these interpretations that a full acknowledgement of the potential polysemy of film texts and a refusal to make ontological statements which simply claim that it "is" [sic] racist, sexist, homophobic, do not lead to simple celebration, nor [sic] to the impossibility of critical engagement with these representations."[19]

My response to McKee's essay is to draw upon the above discussion of critical pluralism and suggest that while he does an excellent job of documenting how the film was actually interpreted by distinct social groups and suggesting possible meanings, he fails to show that there isn't something that the film really does mean. Neither does he show that there isn't a correct interpretation. As I argued previously, this is because the demonstrating that a work has been or can be interpreted in a variety of ways is insufficient for concluding that there is no correct interpretation and, thus, nothing that the work actually means. Moreover, the burden of proof is on McKee to argue for this conclusion, because the relativist view so deeply clashes with the ways in which we actually behave.

That is, the relativist view seems to render incoherent the fairly ordinary occurrence of people being offended by meanings they take to be properties of a particular work. If such meanings are merely properties that arise from the viewer's engagement with the work or are otherwise constructed by the viewer, then the viewer has no rational ground to be offended. A parallel point can be made regarding ethics. The relativist owes a plausible account of the fact that it is common for folks to judge the creators of apparently ethically flawed works to be blameworthy. And this has tangible consequences. In the best-case scenarios, the creators might apologize. Cynically, one might think that such apologies are merely attempts to placate an angry public. But are they always merely that? Or do the creators actually admit that they created a work that possess ethical flaws—that is, as a matter of fact, ethically flawed. For if these are merely properties that viewers have constructed, we need an explanation not only of why viewers blame the creators, but also of why creators apologize. And, of course, in more serious situations, the creators of ethically flawed works might face legal consequences such as being fined or going to jail.

It seems to me that the relativist doctrine depends on a mistake we have encountered previously—namely, ignoring the distinction between work and text I argued for in Chapter 3. In this context, it is important to recognize the tension between McKee's avowed "acknowledgment of the potential polysemy of film texts" and his rejection of "the impossibility of critical engagement with these representations." The difficulty for McKee is that if we are talking about mere *texts*, properly so called, then we can recognize that they *are* polysemic. Consider: "chat." Does this refer to an informal conversation or a furry feline? There is no answer because here we have just text, removed from a determinate set of linguistic conventions and the intentions of an utterer. But this means that here, "chat" doesn't represent *anything, per se*.[20]

Representation is only possible against a backdrop of convention and intention—at least, if the representation bears "non-natural meaning" in Paul Grice's sense. Grice contrasts "non-natural meaning" with "natural meaning," the latter of which includes "representations," broadly construed, such as spots on one's body, which "mean" measles. "Non-natural meaning," on the other hand, includes "representations" such as three rings of a bus's bell, which "mean" that the bus is full.[21] Clearly, it does not make any sense to be critical of representations bearing natural meaning, for in such cases there is nothing to be critical *of*. There is no intention, let alone agency, behind representations bearing natural meaning. So, if we are going to be critical of representations, these representations must be bearers of non-natural meaning.

However, for a representation to bear non-natural meaning, it *must* be the product of some minimally intentional action on the part of an agent— an agent who knows that the successful realization of her action will bear a particular (non-natural) meaning against a backdrop of conventions and shared understandings. Without an agent acting in such a context, in which her representation can be recognized *as* a representation in light of a web of conventions and shared understandings, representation is not possible. So, in a French novel, "chat" would typically be used to represent a feline, and in an English novel, "chat" is more likely to represent an informal talk. But now we are not talking about a polysemic text. Rather, we are talking about representations embedded in a *work* that is both the product of intentional agent acting within a network of conventions and shared understandings that serve to disambiguate her meaning.

The point here is *not* to deny that work meaning or specific "utterances" or "representations" within a work are sometimes ambiguous. Rather, it is that the sort of polysemy McKee describes is not logically compatible with the concept of representation (of non-natural meaning). If we are talking about polysemic texts, there is nothing, logically speaking, that could be the object of rational criticism. But if we are talking about representations in works of film and television, which we are rationally warranted to criticize, then this is because those representations bear meanings. I hasten to acknowledge that such representations do not necessarily bear the meanings their creators intended. But that does not entail they are not the products of intentional action. They are. They are simply not the products of entirely successful intentional action. And, of course, many representations *do* bear the meanings intended by their creators. In both cases, criticism of politically retrograde or ethically flawed representations is rationally warranted, in part because there is intentional agency behind the representations. This offers a partial explanation of why "moderate intentionalism" is an apt name for the view I endorse.

Interpretation and Ethics 2: In Defense of Moderate Intentionalism

As I have sketched it thus far, my view squares nicely, I believe, with the common critical practice of judging popular artworks ethically flawed and judging their creators to be blameworthy. (Or, if one prefers, it also squares with the common critical practice of judging popular artworks ideologically flawed and judging their creators to be blameworthy.) I say this is a prima facie rationally warranted practice and that moderate intentionalism offers the best account of interpretation that explains how and why it is rationally warranted. At this point, I want to offer a precise characterisation of moderate intentionalism and, using 24 as an example, show how this account of work meaning tacitly underpins the ethical criticism of television and its creators.

The sort of moderate intentionalism I advocate has been argued for at length by Noël Carroll, Paisley Livingston, and Robert Stecker, and, given that my primary audience here is television scholars, I will provide neither a full exegesis nor a defense of the view but simply outline it in broad strokes. To begin, recall the discussion of intentions pursued in Chapter 1, where

I followed Michael Bratman in characterizing (future-directed) intentions as planning states. In his words, "they are embedded in forms of planning central to our internally organized, temporally extended agency and to our associated abilities to achieve complex goals across time ... One's plan states guide, coordinate, and organize one's thought and action both at a time and over time."[22] It is this subtle view of intentions I have in mind in this context.

Given this view of intentions and the ways in which such intentions seem fundamental to our interests in interpreting and evaluating cultural artifacts in general and television artworks in particular, my sympathies lie with the family of accounts of interpretation and work meaning that are known collectively under the heading "actual intentionalism." The "actual" modifier refers to the actual intentions of real agents, distinguishing these versions of intentionalism from others, including "fictionalist intentionalism," which attributes intentions to an implied or postulated author, and "hypothetical intentionalism," which holds that work meaning is determined by those intentions that an "appropriate" audience would be warranted in hypothesizing that the creator of a work had.[23]

However, among varieties of actual intentionalism, still more nuance is needed in order to distinguish moderate intentionalism from rather more implausible views, such as "absolute" or "extreme" actual intentionalism, according to which the meaning of a work is simply equivalent to what its creator intended.[24] For surely we want to allow that sometimes work meaning comes apart from the creator's intended meaning. The creators of *24* may not have intended to create a work that sanctions torture, but arguably this is precisely the attitude the series endorses. Of course, there are also happier cases in which the creators of a television show *do* successfully realize their semantic intentions and an ethically meritorious work results: Think, for example, of *When the Levees Broke* (HBO 2006), *Angels in America* (HBO 2003), or *Alive Day Memories: Home from Iraq* (HBO 2007). However, individual cases in which semantic intentions are successfully realised are insufficient to secure the extreme actual intentionalist's thesis, which is, simply put, "intention is always sufficient for meaning."[25]

Thus, moderate intentionalism represents a middle position that avoids the polar extremes of anti-intentionalism (manifested, in the present context, in constructivism and relativism) and absolute intentionalism. There are still more subtleties that distinguish the sorts of moderate intentionalism developed by Carroll, Livingston, and Stecker, but for the present purposes we can regard the view as more or less unified. Common to these formulations is the basic thought that work meaning is, roughly, "a function of both the actual intentions of artists and the conventions in place when the work is created," as Stecker puts it.[26] In a similar vein, Livingston offers a helpful summary: "A moderate or partial intentionalist thesis holds that intentions determine some, but not all, of the semantic properties of at least some works of art."[27]

As Livingston explains, moderate intentionalism is motivated to a significant degree by our interests in artworks as *works*. Like Stecker, Livingston is careful to acknowledge the plurality of interpretive aims: "Texts and artefacts can be put to all sorts of uses having diverse values, and the satisfaction of curiosity concerning the work's actual meaning is only one possible goal."[28] However, he urges, "if one's goal is that of understanding and appreciating the work of art in a historically and artistically appropriate (that is, non-anachronistic) manner—or as we sometimes say, *qua*, or in its capacity as, a work of art, then a concern with intended meaning is necessary to the successful realization of one's project."[29] My present claim is that ethical criticism is one visible and important facet of the sort of appreciation Livingston describes.

However, there is a somewhat different way of putting this point that makes the claim more interesting and might have the additional benefit of supporting the moderate intentionalist view in an original way. Given the prima facie coherence of and warrant for the sort of ethical criticism we are discussing, one way of adjudicating the debate about intention and interpretation is by analysing how well competing views account for those critical practices. In other words, an inability to offer a plausible account of ethical criticism ought to constitute a serious strike against any prospective view of intention and interpretation, while the ability to offer a plausible account ought to constitute a significant merit.

To make this a bit more concrete, let's consider the case of *24*. This series is interesting because interpretations of its higher-order meanings generally tend to converge, while judgments of its political or ethical standing tend to diverge, along partisan lines. In particular, ordinary viewers, critics, and scholars have largely agreed that *24* endorses torture as a warranted means of obtaining information given certain circumstances. As one scholar puts it, "Routine interrogation and torture of suspects ... figure prominently here as tacitly condoned methods, especially when immediate information extraction is necessary to ensure public safety, which is always the case."[30] More specifically, *24* presents a series of "ticking time-bomb scenarios"—situations in which there is an imminent threat to public safety that can only be avoided (although not with certainty) if a piece of vital information is extracted from a terrorist *and* the only likely way to achieve this is through torture. As several scholars have commented, *24* literalizes the ticking time-bomb scenario in its narrative structure, which ostensibly takes place in real time with each one-hour episode depicting one hour of diegetic time. Indeed, viewers are reminded of the passage of real time—and, thus, the urgency for the protagonist, Jack Bauer, to take action—by the literal ticking of a digital clock that appears on screen prior to and subsequent to each commercial break.

In popular discourse and in the scholarly literature, the ticking time-bomb scenario has often been described as a kind of moral dilemma.[31] Here then is what typically divides judgment about the political and ethical standing of *24*. On the one hand, those who believe the series is politically and ethically meritorious cite, as evidence for their view, the putative fact that the series endorses Jack Bauer's frequent decision to make "the hard choice" of extracting the information by any means necessary to "protect" the greater good. As one critic wrote, "*24* as a whole is patriotic in its honesty about the nature of our adversaries and its refusal to indulge in the moral equivocation favored by most critically lauded television dramas."[32] Or as another critic, who describes Jack Bauer as an "American hero," put it, "The lesson of the show is not that Big Brother will keep us safe. The lesson is that we need ruthless bravery from Everyman to keep us safe."[33]

On the other hand, those who believe *24* is politically and ethically flawed cite, as evidence for their view, the very same interpretation of the series' political and ethical meanings, and, sometimes, further argue that the depicted dilemma is a false one that deceives viewers. For example, journalist Richard Kim claims, with reference to the ticking time-bomb scenarios, "the first three seasons of *24* stage torture as a kind of necessary evil and mark of resolve." "The problem with this scenario," he continues, "is not just that it starts down a slippery slope, but that it allows a plot dreamed up by Hollywood to determine the limits of moral authority." More broadly, Kim asserts, *24* "epitomize[s]" a tendency in the 2000s for American popular culture to "rationalize torture as necessary to preserve not just U.S. national security, but law, authority, and agency in general."[34] Writing in the same publication—the progressive *The Nation*—Jon Wiener claimed of the Season 6 premiere: "[It] again argued not just that torture is necessary, but that it works ... The show as usual made the 'ticking time-bomb' case for torture: We need to torture a suspect, or else thousands, or millions, will die in the next hour."[35]

Similar views are easily found in the scholarly literature. For example, in his incisive study of post–9/11 film and television, Stephen Prince writes, "Jack's behavior manifests the series' core political outlook, which verges on an authoritarian contempt for due process and a belief that methods of extreme brutality offer the best way to counter terrorism. The show, in other words, was in love with torture, which it depicted frequently, and always as something that produces good intelligence."[36] Of the many salient criticisms he makes, Prince notes in conclusion, "Jack never wonders whether his own behavior threatens the democracy that he should be sworn to protect. *24* creates a paradox it does not acknowledge. Jack runs frantically each and every season to save an America that the show itself depicts as possessing little inherent or enduring value."[37] Offering a complementary view with a greater emphasis on the problematic way in which *24* stages moral dilemmas, the ethicist John M. Parrish writes:

> The key to the ethical sleight of hand which *24* performs lies in recognizing its attempt to use the peculiarities of its real-time narrative structure to turn the ticking time-bomb scenario into a constant state of being ... The effect of this is to turn the extreme moral conditions of the

ticking time-bomb scenario into an everyday operating environment—such that our conclusions about the scenario, once reached, can be taken as a given in any future moral calculations without qualm, and without the necessity of having to rethink the quandary itself from the ground up.[38]

For Parrish, as for Prince, the manipulative ticking time-bomb scenario at once constitutes an ethical flaw narrowly, in terms its intimate connection to the Bush administration's rationalization of "enhanced interrogation techniques." But it also constitutes an ethical flaw in a broader sense:

> [W]hen 24 contributes to making it more difficult for us to see hard ethical cases as *being* hard cases, when it makes it easier for us to see murder and torture and betrayal as nothing more than necessary acts of statesmanship and survival, when it helps to deaden our sense of moral tragedy by stretching melodrama to the point of parody and farce, it does us a grave disservice. Such ethical revisionism can over time help to impair, not just our aesthetic sensibilities, but also those ethically sensitive judgments and practices out of which true citizen virtue alone can emerge.[39]

To be clear, my point here is not to offer a general account of 24's reception, which is undoubtedly more complex than I have described it here.[40] Instead, it is that (1) interpretations of the series' higher-order meanings—in particular, its attitudes towards torture—seems to converge to a significant degree and (2) these interpretations underpin both positive and negative political and ethical evaluations of the series. The primary interpretive aim of both sides of the debate about 24's politics and ethics is to identify the series' actual higher-order meanings because only those actual meanings can function in evidence or reasons supporting ethical evaluations of the series. That is, unless ethical judgments are supported by reference to 24's work meaning, it's not clear what rational force they could have. What is striking is that although each side of the debate has an interest in interpreting 24's higher-order meanings in a way that would favor its preferred ethical evaluation, those interpretations are largely the same. Thus, we have prima facie evidence to suppose that the two camps have successfully identified higher-order meanings the series does in fact possess. This counts as a strike against both constructivism and relativism.

However, there is still more insight to be gleaned from the case of 24. As I noted earlier, it is common in ethical evaluations of artworks to not merely judge the ethical praiseworthiness or blameworthiness of the work, but also of its creators. Moreover, there are good reasons to think that, common or not, ethical judgment of what the creators *did* to create the work, is rationally warranted.[41] We certainly see this here, along with a sustained interest (from both sides in the debate) in the creators' own political views and semantic intentions. As reported by Jane Mayer in *The New Yorker*, in 2007 the dean of the United States Military Academy at West Point at the time, Brigadier General Patrick Finnegan, visited the set of *24* along with three expert interrogators and representatives of Human Rights First. Their goal was to encourage the series' creators to alter their depiction of torture because, according to Mayer, "In their view, the show promoted unethical and illegal behavior and had adversely affected the training and performance of real American soldiers."[42] One of the interrogation experts, Tony Lagouranis, said of the meeting: "[The creators] were a bit prickly. They have this money-making machine, and we were telling them it's immoral."[43] The underlying assumption of the trip was, of course, that *24*'s creators had the ability to imbue the show with *different* meanings—meanings that would be grasped in such a way that might make viewers reassess its earlier tacit arguments justifying torture.

Despite a voluminous amount of academic theorizing, ordinary folks who work in and with the entertainment industry assume, with justification, that creators possess the sort of agency and abilities necessary to shape what a television show means—what attitudes it conveys, what ideas or principles it endorses. It is for this reason that both sides of the debate about *24*'s ethics and politics courted co-creator and executive producer Joel Surnow, respectively encouraging him to keep up the patriotic work or to stop glamorizing torture.[44] And it is for this reason that judging the actions of Surnow and the other creators of the series as ethically praiseworthy or blameworthy makes sense. Jane Mayer quotes David Nevins, the former Fox Television executive who bought the *24* pilot, as saying: "There's definitely a political attitude of the show, which is that extreme measures are sometimes necessary for the greater good ... The show doesn't have much patience for the niceties of civil liberties or due process. It's clearly coming from somewhere. Joe's politics suffuse the whole show."[45] I am not suggesting that we should blithely accept such claims regarding creators' abilities to successfully realize their semantic intentions, much less that we assume a single agent like Surnow has the creative control of an author in such cases. However, in this and many other cases, there ample evidence to justify thinking that at least some creators, like Surnow, are able to successfully realize their semantic intentions to a degree that is sufficient for holding them ethically accountable for their creation.[46]

At this point, then, we can ask what account of interpretation best squares with the above-described features of *24*'s reception. Again, let me emphasize that the points I want to make here do not depend on exhaustive empirical analysis, and I do not deny that viewers have likely interpreted *24* in heterogeneous ways. Rather, I have merely been concerned to show that anyone who offers an ethical appraisal of *24* faces rational pressure to interpret the series with the aim of discerning work meaning, where that is conceived as higher-order meanings such as expressed attitudes that are, in fact, possessed by the work. Earlier I indicated that the identification of this interpretive goal counts as a strike against constructivism and relativism. If we now also consider that this interpretive goal is motivated by the desire to hold the series' creators ethically responsible, it is clear that neither constructivism nor relativism is able to account for this kind of case. For it makes little sense to hold 24's creators ethically accountable if the series' higher-order meanings are either constructed by viewers or not evaluable for truth or falsity. In other words, the practice of ethical criticism demands some sort of *realist* account of interpretation. By a "realist account," I mean an account which holds that meanings are really, objectively possessed by the work. Nothing other than a realist account of interpretation has the tools to make sense of and explain the common practice of ethical criticism or, for that matter, the parallel practice of ideological criticism.

However, the account of interpretation demanded by ethical criticism is also realist in another sense. To wit, it must necessarily make reference to real agents. In saying this, I mean to indicate that such an account must make reference to real people *and*, moreover, real people who have the capacities to exercise some degree of intentional agency in the creation of a television work. For ethical criticism involves, in part, judging the actions of real people. As we have seen, we need not assume that every action undertaken in the creation of a work is intentional or that semantic intentions are always successfully realized. But even in such cases, ethical criticism does presuppose that people successfully realize both present-directed intentions and proximal-future-directed intentions all the time in quotidian activities. In the absence of a fairly robust capacity for us to say and do what we mean, ethical criticism would appear incoherent.[47]

If this line of thought is correct, then we not only need a realist account of interpretation, but an intentionalist account. However, clearly not just any intentionalist account will do. Several varieties of intentionalism also provide inadequate accounts of interpretation in the context of ethical criticism. For example, fictionalist intentionalism is clearly a non-starter, because it makes no sense to ethically evaluate the actions of a fictional agent or such a construct itself. So, too, are certain varieties of hypothetical intentionalism, which, in a similar way as fictional intentionalism, take the relevant intentions to be those of a hypothetical, postulated, or implied agent. But again, ethical criticism demands a real agent because its objects are real agents, their actions, and their results.[48]

Jerrold Levinson's formulation of hypothetical intentionalism is a somewhat more complex case. In Levinson's view, "the core meaning of a [...] work is given by the best hypothesis, from the position of an appropriately informed, sympathetic, and discriminating reader of authorial intent to convey such and such to an audience through the [work] in question."[49] However, one important feature of this view is that Levinson cashes out the meaning of "appropriately informed" by specifying certain kinds of "interpretively admissible evidence," which is, in part, characterized by being essentially publicly available. This excludes authorial statements of intention in contexts such as private correspondence, diary entries, and the like. Among a variety of objections raised by critics of Levinson's hypothetical intentionalism, we should note here that the boundary between evidence that is essentially public and essentially private might be porous.[50]

Ethical criticism raises another problem for the way Levinson cordons off information that is not publicly available from what counts as "interpretively admissible evidence." Specifically, it seems that the public availability of the evidence is beside the point for the project of ethical criticism. Rather, we should want—and, I think, do want—*any* available evidence regarding authorial (or agential) intentions when the task at hand is to ethically assess a work, its creators, and their actions. Carroll makes a point along these lines that we can expand upon here.[51] He uses the example of Swift's "A Modest Proposal," but we can think here of satire more generally. Take any satirical work that, in light of all the structural and contextual evidence, seems to make a point or endorse an attitude that is ethically meritorious. Now suppose it happens that the private correspondence and diaries of the work's creators reveal that their actual intentions were not satirical at all; in fact, they intended to make a point or endorse an attitude that is ethically reproachable. A consequence of Levinson's view is that the creators would be ethically exculpated because such evidence would not be interpretively admissible.

But surely this is not the outcome we want or, indeed, would get in an actual case. Imagine, for example, that private correspondence or diaries indicated that Stephen Colbert was furious that *The Colbert Report* (Comedy Central 2005–2015) is widely interpreted as a satire of political conservatives. Suppose that all of the political positions he seemed to be mocking—opposition to gay marriage, opposition to legal abortions, opposition to regulation of the financial industry, and so forth—were positions that he actually intended to endorse.

In such a case, I submit, interpretations of *The Colbert Report* as satirical would be mistaken. For satire bears an essential link to intentionality; something cannot be satirical by accident or as the result of a failed intention to be earnest. Therefore, I suspect that the political and ethical evaluation of *The Colbert Report*, which splits along partisan lines, would be exactly the reverse of what it currently is: Conservatives would no longer find the show politically and ethically blameworthy, but meritorious; liberals would no longer judge the show politically and ethically praiseworthy, but reproachable. But this shift would not be a matter of "reinterpretation;" rather, it would be a recalibration of one's ethical appraisal in light of the revelation that the work did not mean what everyone thought it did. And this, I contend, reflects the fact that ethical criticism is essentially concerned with work meaning and the way in which actual intentions constrain it.

But it is not just satire that undermines hypothetical intentionalism in this way. Vince Gilligan, the show-runner of *Breaking Bad* (AMC 2008–2013), has been extremely vocal about his semantic intentions regarding the characters of Walter and Skyler White: "Walt has behaved at times in what could be regarded as an evil fashion, but I don't think he's an evil man. He is an extremely self-deluded man ... He can make himself believe, in the face of all contrary evidence, that he is still a good man." In the same interview, the following idea was posed to Gilligan: "Skyler White is seen by some as this henpecking woman who stands in the way of all of Walt's fun." To this, Gilligan replied, "Man, I don't see it that way at all ... I think the people who have these issues with the wives being too bitchy on *Breaking Bad* are misogynists, plain and simple ... She's got a tough job being married to this asshole." And, finally, it is worth noting that Gilligan was very explicit about his attitude toward violence on the show: "[H]opefully it goes without saying that moments like [the infamous box-cutter scene in Season 3, Episode 1] are meant to do the opposite of mak[ing] violence look attractive or sexy. They are meant to unsettle and upset."[52]

But now imagine an alternative universe in which *Breaking Bad* was exactly the same work, but the public statements of Gilligan and other relevant creators, such as Bryan Cranston and Anna Gunn, were significantly different. If you can, imagine no such public statements existed or, at least, that they were entirely ambiguous about the show's attitudes towards Walt and Skyler, such that they were of no help to the task of interpretation. Furthermore, suppose that private correspondence between Gilligan, Cranston, Gunn, writers, directors, and others revealed that all of the key creative agents were committed to the just *opposite* of what Gilligan has, in reality, publicly professed. That is, suppose that the private correspondence indicated that the creators' semantic intentions were to glamorize violence, to glorify Walt's escapades, and to vilify Skyler for being a killjoy.

The upshot of this fictitious scenario would be, I think, that we would—and should—revise our interpretation of *Breaking Bad*'s higher-order meanings and our ethical evaluation of it. We would—and ought to, in such a case—still agree with Emily Nussbaum that "some fans [had been] watching wrong." But the fans to which she refers would be those of us who had interpreted the show as expressing condemnation of Walt. And the interpretations of *Breaking Bad*'s "bad fans," as Nussbaum calls them, would be revealed to be *exactly right*.[53] Moreover, this shift in the meanings of *Breaking Bad* would underpin a parallel shift in our ethical evaluation of the series. It would be natural to no longer judge the series, as we commonly do now, to be ethically virtuous inasmuch as it expresses and attempts to elicit, on the part of viewers, a "merited response"—that of condemnation—for the deeply immoral character of Walt. Rather, we would judge the imaginary *Breaking Bad* as ethically flawed inasmuch as it expressed and attempted to elicit, on the part of viewers, an "unmerited response"—that of admiration and glorification—to the immoral character of Walt.[54] Hypothetical intentionalism, however, lacks the means to account for these kinds of situations, because it rules out private correspondence as not "interpretively relevant."

If this is right, some sort of actual intentionalism is needed to account for ethical criticism and the kind of interpretation that underpins it. We are still left with different strengths of actual intentionalism, including the extreme variety I mentioned previously, according to which work meaning is just whatever the work's creator(s) intended. As I also indicated previously, however, there are compelling reasons to think extreme actual intentionalism is untenable, and because I doubt there are any television studies scholars who aren't convinced of this, I won't provide further argumentation here. Thus, I submit, moderate actual intentionalism is the only account of interpretation that squares with the practice of ethical criticism.

There is at least one difficult question to address before setting the issue aside. As I have stressed, moderate intentionalism holds that it is only those intentions that are successfully realised in the structure of the work that play a role in determining work meaning. As Livingston puts it, "the minimal (and I should think default) standard of success being simply that the intentions are compatible with the linguistic and conventional meanings of the text or artefact taken in its target or intended context."[55] However, if we consider the nature of ethical judgment, it seems that this "success condition" might be too stringent, at least in the context of ethical criticism. In certain non-artistic contexts, individuals are ethically and legally culpable for actions they do not successfully realize, including, to mention an obvious example, attempted murder.

Perhaps there are parallel cases in artistic and specifically televisual contexts. Think again of the imaginary circumstances around *The Colbert Report*. Suppose Colbert privately declared that his actual intentions were to endorse various conservative viewpoints, but these intentions were so horribly botched that the success condition was not met. Would Colbert then be ethically exculpated? I suspect that, at least as far as his more extreme positions go—for example, opposition to equal rights for gay people—the answer would be no. Similarly, we could suppose of my imaginary *Breaking Bad* case that the creators' semantic intentions didn't successfully "mesh" with the structure of the work to warrant revising our interpretation of work meaning in the way I suggested. And yet, I suspect, we would feel that Gilligan and his team had done something ethically wrong merely by attempting to glorify Walt and vilify Skyler. That is, it intuitively seems that the imaginary Colbert, the imaginary Gilligan, and real artists may, in certain circumstances, still be subject to ethical criticism, even when their semantic intentions are not successfully realised in their creations. As far as ethical criticism goes, at least, it seems that in some cases the botched execution of intentions is still sufficient for ethical criticism.[56]

Puzzling though this may seem at first glance, I do not believe it threatens my analysis. The puzzle is explained, I think, by distinguishing various objects of our ethical criticism. The intuition we ought to respect is that the imaginary Colbert and the imaginary Gilligan would be ethically blameworthy despite not successfully realizing their intentions for their works to express particular attitudes. However, this is compatible with acknowledging that the works themselves are not, in fact, ethically flawed, because they do not endorse ethically flawed perspectives or solicit from viewers unmerited responses to ethically flawed perspectives. If this were the case, the works themselves would not be ethically blameworthy. Yet we would not thereby be precluded in any way from reproaching the imaginary Colbert or the imaginary Gilligan for what they tried to achieve in the works and for attitudes they themselves hold or endorse. And if this is right, the puzzle is merely apparent rather than a real one.

From Interpretation to Evaluation

Before proceeding to the final chapter, which discusses the evaluation of television art, it may be fruitful to make explicit the general connection between interpretation and evaluation that underlies the present chapter. To be sure, part of the argument for a moderate intentionalist account of the interpretation television artworks is that an artwork is a kind of communicative utterance, so one proper aim of interpretation in this context is to determine what the creator(s) intended to communicate. As Noël Carroll puts it, "Artworks have a communicative dimension. Consequently, all things being equal, we should try to engage them as we do the other communicative behaviors of our fellow humans—as sources of information regarding their intentions. Where interpretation comes into play, its point is arguably to discern the communicative intentions of the creator of the work."[57] Livingston refers to this sort of argument as a "conversational argument" for intentionalism, because it reasons that "intentionalist constraints on interpretation follow directly from basic norms of conversation and communication, said to be applicable to all (or at least most) appropriate art-interpretative projects."[58]

However, Livingston advances a distinct argument for intentionalism—what he calls an "axiological argument—that has been implicit in the account developed in this chapter. In his words, a moderate form of intentionalism "can also be justified in terms of an interest in some (but not all) kinds of artistic value—namely, values pertaining specifically to the work as an artistic accomplishment having determinate features, including semantic ones."[59] My claim in this chapter is that the appreciation of the ethical value of television artworks establishes, in at least some cases, work meaning as the proper aim of interpretation, because at least one commonly practiced variety of ethical criticism must necessarily make reference to what a work actually means. Furthermore, if the aim of interpretation is to discern work meaning for the purpose of ethically evaluating the work, this requires us to track the actual intentions of creators as they are successfully (or not!) realized in the work. For it is those successfully realized actual intentions that are at least partially constitutive of work meaning and, thus, the work's ethical value.[60]

However, ethical value is, arguably, just one component of a work's overall value *qua* art. Or, if one does not think there is such a thing as overall artistic value *per se,* then we can say ethical value is just one of a plurality of values artworks can manifest. In some appreciative contexts, appraisal of a television artwork's ethical value plays a central role; in other appreciative contexts, it plays a negligible role. That is to say, the appreciation of television involves tracking value in a broader sense than we have so far explored. In the closing chapter of this book, I will attempt to build upon the axiological argument for intentionalism. My ultimate goal is to show that there are important ways in which the evaluation of television artworks is a rational endeavour and in which artistic value obtains in television artworks in a real, objective sense. The starting point for this argument is the idea that the work meanings in television obtain in television works in a real, objective sense. And they result from the successful realization of semantic intentions, which is a particular kind of artistic achievement which can be objectively appraised. So, the successful realization of intentions in a work is a good-making feature in a real, objective sense. Or so I will argue.

Notes

1. Alan McKee, *Textual Analysis* (London: Sage, 2003), 2.
2. This is not to deny the existence of feedback loops, which afford viewers the opportunity to give feedback to creators, who may then decide to incorporate this feedback. In some cases, perhaps the incorporation of fan feedback in the creation of new episodes of a series may retrospectively alter the meanings of prior episodes. This is a complex metaphysical question to which there is no easy answer. I would only deny that it is viewers' interpretations *per se* that alter the properties of the work.
3. Robert Stecker argues, "If one is a relativist, it will be hard to impossible not to be a constructivist" (187). For a discussion of the relationship between relativism and constructivism, see Robert Stecker, *Interpretation and Construction: Art, Speech, and the Law* (Malden, MA: Blackwell, 2003), 186–87.
4. For example, see Ethan Thompson and Jason Mittell, "Introduction: An Owner's Manual for Television," in *How to Watch Television*, ed. Ethan Thompson and Jason Mittell (New York: New York University Press, 2012), 6; Jeremy Butler, *Television: Critical Methods and Applications*, 4th ed. (New York: Routledge, 2012), 10–12 and 359–363; Jonathan Gray and Amanda D. Lotz, *Television Studies* (London: Polity, 2012), 43–45.
5. In relation, also see the helpful critical review in Sonia Livingstone, *Making Sense of Television* 2nd ed., (London: Routledge, 1998), especially 33–50 and 171–191.
6. John Fiske, *Television Culture* (New York: Routledge, 1987), 15–16.
7. Ibid., 64.
8. Ibid., 80.
9. Ibid., 84.
10. This is to say nothing of the contestable semiotic assumptions that tacitly underpin the premise that television is read in the same way as a verbal text, thus admitting an equivalent degree of interpretive variation.
11. Stephen Davies, "True Interpretations," in *Philosophical Perspectives on Art* (Oxford: Oxford University Press, 2007), 191.
12. Beardsley, quoted in Davies, "True Interpretations," 192.

13. Butler, *Television: Critical Methods and Applications*, 363. Also see Livingstone, *Making Sense of Television*, 176, where she says: "Insofar as interpretations depend on the contingent contribution of the reader, they should be judged not as correct or mistaken but rather should be seen as a product of the reader's experience which generated them, or as more or less plausible given prevailing normative assumptions, or as more or less creative, critical, or interesting."
14. Davies, "True Interpretations," 196.
15. Stecker, *Interpretation and Construction*, 26.
16. Ibid., 57. Emphasis mine.
17. Alan McKee, "How to Tell the Difference between a Stereotype and a Positive Image: Putting *Priscilla, Queen of the Desert* into History" *Screening the Past* 9 (2000), n.p. Accessed March 15, 2016). http://www.screeningthepast.com/2014/12/how-to-tell-the-difference-between-a-stereotype-and-a-positive-image-putting%C2%A0priscilla-queen-of-the-desert%C2%A0into-history/.
18. Ibid.
19. Ibid.
20. I have borrowed the "chat" example from Paisley Livingston, whose views on the work/text distinction have also influenced my thinking about the matter in general. See Paisley Livingston *Art and Intention: A Philosophical Study* (Oxford: Oxford University Press, 2005), 112–34.
21. H. P. Grice, "Meaning," *The Philosophical Review* 66, no. 3 (July 1957): 377.
22. Michael Bratman, *Shared Agency* (Oxford: Oxford University Press, 2014), 15.
23. For statements regarding the "implied author" or "postulated author," see Wayne C. Booth, *The Rhetoric of Fiction*, 2nd ed. (Chicago, IL: University of Chicago Press, 1983); Alexander Nehamas, "The Postulated Author: Critical Monism as a Regulative Ideal," *Critical Inquiry* 8, no. 1 (Autumn 1981): 133–49. For statements of hypothetical intentionalism, see Jerrold Levinson, "Intention and Interpretation in Literature," in *The Pleasures of Aesthetics* (Ithaca, NY: Cornell University Press, 1996), 175–213; Jerrold Levinson, "Hypothetical Intentionalism: Statement, Objections, and Replies," in *Contemplating Art* (Oxford: Oxford University Press, 2006), 302–311. In the context of cinema specifically, Gregory Currie advances a view he calls "implied author intentionalism" in *Image and Mind: Film, Philosophy, and Cognitive Science* (Cambridge, UK: Cambridge University Press, 1995).
24. See, for a seminal account, E. D. Hirsch, *Validity in Interpretation* (New Haven, CT: Yale University Press, 1967). For a contemporary view, see William Irwin, *Intentionalist Interpretation: A Philosophical Exploration and Defense* (Westport, CT: Greenwood Press, 1999); and William Irwin, "Authorial Declaration and Extreme Actual Intentionalism: Is Dumbledore Gay?" *Journal of Aesthetics and Art Criticism* 73, no. 2 (Spring 2015): 141–47.
25. Irwin, "Authorial Declaration and Extreme Actual Intentionalism," 141.
26. Stecker, *Interpretation and Construction*, 42.
27. Paisley Livingston, *Cinema, Philosophy, Bergman: On Film as Philosophy* (Oxford: Oxford University Press, 2009), 93.
28. Livingston, *Art and Intention*, 142.
29. Ibid., 142–43.
30. Torin Monahan, "Just-in-Time Security: Permanent Exceptions and Neoliberal Orders," in *Reading 24: TV Against the Clock*, edited by Steven Peacock (London: I. B. Tauris, 2007), 111.
31. A seminal paper is Michael Walzer, "Political Action: The Problem of Dirty Hands," *Philosophy and Public Affairs* 2, no. 2 (Winter 1973): 160–80.

32. Paul Beston, "Getting Dirty in Real Time," *The American Spectator* (August 17, 2005). Accessed May 26, 2015. http://spectator.org/articles/48189/getting-dirty-real-time.
33. Timothy P. Carney, "I am Jack Bauer: What 24 Means for Homeland Security," *The National Review* (June 26, 2006). Accessed May 26, 2015. http://www.nationalreview.com/article/218042/i-am-jack-bauer-timothy-p-carney.
34. Richard Kim, "Pop Torture," *The Nation* (December 7, 2005). Accessed May 27, 2015. http://www.thenation.com/article/pop-torture.
35. Jon Wiener, "'24': Torture on TV," *The Nation* (January 15, 2007). Accessed May 27, 2015. http://www.thenation.com/blog/24–torture-tv.
36. Stephen Prince, *Firestorm: American Film in the Age of Terrorism* (New York: Columbia University Press, 2009), 239.
37. Ibid., 248.
38. John M. Parrish, "Defining Dilemmas Down: The Case of 24," *Essays in Philosophy* 10, no. 1, Article 7 (January 2009), n.p. Accessed May 27, 2015. http://commons.pacificu.edu/eip/vol10/iss1/7/.
39. Ibid.
40. For a study along these lines, see Keren Tenenboim-Weinblatt, "'Where Is Jack Bauer When You Need Him?' The Uses of Television Drama in Mediated Political Discourse," *Political Communication* 26, no. 4 (2009): 367–87. The article does not support my claim that interpretations of 24's higher-order meanings have tended to converge, while diverging along party lines with regard to the series' ethical standing. However, it seems to me that some of the empirical evidence that weighs against my claim—that is, the idea that some liberal journalists "interpret 24 as a direct criticism of the Bush administration and as a reality check" (378)—may not be statistically significant; for example, the author only identified two instances of this view in her study.
41. See Ted Nannicelli, "Moderate Comic Immoralism and the Genetic Approach to the Ethical Criticism of Art," *Journal of Aesthetics and Art Criticism* 72, no. 2 (Spring 2014): 169–79.
42. Jane Mayer, "Whatever It Takes: The Politics of the Man Behind '24'," *The New Yorker* (February 19, 2007). Accessed March 24, 2016. http://www.newyorker.com/magazine/2007/02/19/whatever-it-takes).
43. Lagouranis, quoted in J. Mayer, n.p.
44. The former sentiment has been expressed by prominent conservative talking-heads such as Rush Limbaugh, who moderated a panel as part of the conservative Heritage Foundation's symposium "24 and America's Image in Fighting Terrorism: Fact, Fiction, or Does It Matter?" The latter is clearly the tacit argument in Jane Mayer's article, "Whatever It Takes."
45. David Nevins, quoted in J. Mayer, "Whatever It Takes," n.p.
46. In practice, holding creators ethically accountable varies from case to case. I am not here endorsing a normative view of how the creators of ethically blameworthy artworks *should* be held accountable.
47. It is easy to see here that the problem of free will is not terribly far removed from this discussion, but it is clearly beyond the scope of this project.
48. See Noël Carroll, "Interpretation and Intention: The Debate between Hypothetical and Actual Intentionalism," in *Beyond Aesthetics* (Cambridge, UK: Cambridge University Press, 2001), 208–209.
49. Levinson, "Hypothetical Intentionalism," 302.

50. See Carroll, "Interpretation and Intention," 212–13; and Levinson's response in "Hypothetical Intentionalism," 310.
51. Carroll, "Interpretation and Intention," 209.
52. Lane Brown, "In Conversation: Vince Gilligan on the End of *Breaking Bad*," *Vulture* (May 12, 2013). Accessed May 29, 2015. http://www.vulture.com/2013/05/vince-gilligan-on-breaking-bad.html.
53. See, for example, Emily Nussbaum, "That Mind-Bending Phone Call on Last Night's 'Breaking Bad,'" *The New Yorker* (September 16, 2013). Accessed May 29, 2015. http://www.newyorker.com/culture/culture-desk/that-mind-bending-phone-call-on-last-nights-breaking-bad.
54. For a discussion of "merited response" arguments in the context of ethical criticism of art, see especially, Berys Gaut, *Art, Emotion, and Ethics* (Oxford: Oxford University Press, 2007), 227–51.
55. Livingston, *Art and Intention*, 155.
56. It might be interesting to think about this as a challenge to consequentalist moral theory, although it is clearly beyond the scope of my present project.
57. Noël Carroll, *On Criticism* (New York: Routledge, 2009), 139–140.
58. Livingston, *Art and Intention*, 150–151.
59. Ibid., 151–152.
60. My argument here closely follows Livingston's reasoning. Ibid., 152.

6 Evaluation

Introduction

As Alan McKee notes in a characteristically lucid paper, "One of Cultural Studies' most important contributions to academic thinking about culture is the acceptance as axiomatic that we must not simply accept traditional value hierarchies in relation to cultural objects."[1] One of McKee's aims in this essay is to counter the oft-encountered argument that poststructuralist theorizing results in "anything-goes relativism," because, he correctly points out, "Postmodern thinking, and the sociological turn in Cultural Studies informed by the work of Bourdieu, do not refuse all distinctions. Neither do they refuse all evaluation."[2] The move to which McKee objects is a bad inference from a true claim—"the Cultural Studies/postmodern turn denies absolute, universal value judgments"—to a false one: "This means that everything is relative, anything goes …"[3] For, as McKee and numerous other television studies scholars such as Charlotte Brunsdon have observed, even as these theoretical debates play out, "judgments are being made."[4]

Since the 1990 publication of Brunsdon's seminal essay, from which I quote, television studies has intermittently returned to "issues of judgment and value" (to borrow the title of another important paper on the topic)[5], seeking to more explicitly address the apparent gulf between the field's historical rejection of universal values and the undeniable fact that evaluative judgment is an ineluctable part of at least some modes of engagement with television. This chapter takes as a starting point the work of McKee and these other television studies scholars who have tracked a "return of value" in the field.[6] Whatever one thinks of this development, it seems uncontroversial to say that the place of evaluation and judgment in television studies depends in part upon the aims and purposes of the field's various projects and programs. A number of scholars have observed that evaluative matters have historically remained at the periphery of the field because of the weight placed on other concerns. My aim here is not to make a general argument for giving evaluation a more central role within the field. Rather, it is to call attention to the centrality of the apprehension of value in appreciative contexts.

As I indicated at the outset of the book, part of appreciating television as art simply is a matter of making evaluative judgments. For me, the question is not about the extent to which we should be concerning ourselves with evaluative matters. My impression is that television viewers take an appreciative stance toward television more often than not, suggesting that evaluation should be high on the agenda of television scholars. That aside, television scholars from a wide range of perspectives have observed that one of the challenges of conceptualizing television as an object of artistic appreciation—and, more specifically, of making evaluative judgments of television artworks—is that it is difficult to identify uncontroversial evaluative criteria.[7] In my view, therefore, the questions to address are rather about the nature and warrant of evaluative judgments of television.

Like McKee, I will begin by investigating an argument that starts from the premise that there are no universal principles of value—in this case, *artistic value*, specifically.[8] For the sake of argument, I will, like McKee, assume the truth of this premise, although I do not agree that it is "axiomatic" and think much depends on precisely how it is formulated. It is also important that this premise is assumed, because crucial to my purpose here is showing that one can simultaneously accept it *and* the arguments I will proceed to make—most controversially, that at least some judgments of artistic value in television are objectively grounded and evaluable for (approximate) truth.[9]

One preliminary matter before I begin: In discussions about the value of art, it is common to speak of aesthetic judgments and judgments of artistic value as if the two are synonymous. Oftentimes, commentators slide from speaking of aesthetic judgments of a given work to talking about the work's artistic value. In some cases, this is harmless. However, there is an important distinction here if one accepts the idea that art has a plurality of values—not just aesthetic, but political, cognitive, moral, spiritual, and so on.[10] Because I am a pluralist about the value of art, I do not want to use the terms interchangeably. As I indicated in the previous chapter, the appreciation of television art sometimes involves attending to and appraising the ethical value of a work, which plausibly interacts with its overall artistic value. Furthermore, it seems plausible that the artistic value of some forms of television art, such as documentaries and children's television, is bound up with cognitive value. So, I will just assume that the real issue in debates about the evaluative criticism of television is usually not merely television's aesthetic value, but its overall artistic value (of which aesthetic, ethical, and cognitive value may be constituent parts).

Expressivism in Television Studies

This chapter claims that some theorists have moved too quickly from the plausible premise that there are no universal principles of artistic value to the dubious idea that evaluative judgments of television can be neither objective nor evaluable for truth. My counterargument is that there is a bad inference in this argument and that there are positive reasons for thinking that at least some instances of evaluative judgment are objective and truth-evaluable.

Specifically, the argument I will critically examine is this: Because there are no universal principles of artistic value, evaluative television criticism has no objective basis and does involve objectively true (or false) judgments.[11] Therefore, in evaluative television criticism, what may seem to be (or purport to be) objective judgments of artistic value are, in fact, wholly subjective expressions of taste. Sometimes this conclusion is formulated slightly differently, such that "taste" is replaced by "opinion" or "emotion," but these variants seem to be less common. Their important, common feature is that they all posit evaluative television criticism as expressing subjective attitudes rather than rendering objective judgments that purport to be true. Call this *the expressivist argument*.

Although the expressivist argument is hardly specific to television studies,[12] it enjoys considerable popularity in the field. However, it seems to me that those television studies scholars who accept expressivism tend to assume it implicitly, rather than explicitly argue for it. Understandably, this is because, for many television scholars, the key point has not to do with the metaphysics of value. Rather, it is that artistic value is heterogenous, socio-historically contingent, and relative to particular interests or purposes. Work in television studies, cultural studies, and philosophy of art has advanced compelling arguments for this latter point, which I am happy to accept. My claim is that this point neither depends upon nor entails the further, logically separable claim that judgments of artistic value can be neither objective nor evaluable for truth or falsity. Perhaps some scholars of television hold no strong commitment to expressivism and will be happy to give it up if I can persuade them that doing so does not threaten what I take to be the key points about artistic value that they want to endorse.

For these reasons, in the critical portion of my discussion I shall focus closely upon explicit statements of the expressivist argument in television studies. For example, Michael Newman and Elena Levine offer a sociologically oriented statement of the expressivist argument in their recent book, *Legitimating Television*. With insufficient argumentation, they move from the plausible claim that "Judgments of taste ... are always products of social situations," to the contentious assertion that "taste ... is a system through which 'the social order ... is inscribed in people's minds.'"[13] Moreover, they claim, "this inscription is generally hidden from our direct perception, naturalized as true value and legitimate hierarchy."[14] This view of the nature of artistic value underpins Newman and Levine's overall project, which they describe as "analyzing patterns of taste judgment and classification [...] to unmask misrecognitions of authentic and autonomous value, bringing to light their political and social functions."[15] Thus, for Newman and Levine, evaluations that purport to be objective judgments of artistic value are rather entirely socially determined expressions of taste, because television *does not have* any objective (i.e., "true" or "authentic") artistic value. (I shall return to the more puzzling notion of "autonomous value" later.)

184 *Evaluation*

So, while expressivism may not often be explicitly endorsed in television studies, it is no straw man; neither, I hasten to add, is it naive. Its formulations in the context of cultural and television studies are likely well known to many readers, so here I will merely add that, in philosophical aesthetics, too, expressivism has a long history, which can be traced as far back as David Hume. Indeed, on at least some readings, Hume's conception of the difficulties raised by judgments of taste anticipates some of the claims of cultural studies.[16] Since then, expressivist (also known as emotivist) views have waxed and waned in popularity, but have never disappeared entirely.[17] In carefully developed formulations, expressivism has undeniable intuitive appeal and respectable arguments in its favor. So, my critique is grounded in the assumption that the expressivist argument in television studies is worthy of serious scrutiny.

Ultimately, however, I hope to show that the expressivist argument in television studies faces insurmountable problems. I shall discuss two, in particular, which as far as I can see have never been extensively addressed: If expressivism is correct, then what explains (1) the fact that in evaluative criticism we give reasons to justify our claims, and (2) the apparent normative force of evaluative criticism? Call (1) the problem of rationality, and call (2) the problem of normative force.

Let me briefly elaborate what these "problems" involve. There is no question that when we are confronted with works of television or any other art form, *some* of our evaluative claims *are* partly subjective in the sense that they involve the expression of attitude—an expression of taste. Often such claims are made upon an initial encounter with a work or as conversation starters; consider, for example: "*South Park* (Comedy Central 1997–present) is genius," "*Modern Family* (ABC 2009–present) is unbearable," "*Sesame Street* (PBS 1969–present) is brilliant," "*The Newsroom* (HBO 2012–2014) is puerile," "*Dora and Friends* (Nickelodeon 2014–present) is insipid," "*Bron* (SVT1/DR1 2011–present) is addictive," and "*Who Do You Think You Are?* (BBC2 2004–2006; BBC1 2006–present) is boring."

The problem of rationality arises because these sorts of claims do not exhaust our evaluative discourse. Rather, we often go on to distinguish our personal response to a work and its relative artistic merits or demerits. (Sometimes, of course, these are deeply entwined—as in comedic works.) Furthermore, and crucially, we usually give reasons in support of these more considered evaluations. For example, "The genius of *South Park* is its recognition that, as animation, it can satirize topic issues that would be too controversial for a live-action program like *Saturday Night Live* (NBC 1975–present)." Or: "I find *Modern Family* unbearable because it simply rehashes stereotypes that it purports to wink at knowingly." Or: "*Dora and Friends* is insipid, but there are few other programs that do a better job of introducing children to a second language." Moreover, the sorts of reasons we give usually involve objective (that is, mind-independent) properties. Once we start giving reasons in support of our evaluative claims, it is possible to debate our evaluations in a way that it isn't when two people don't see eye to eye about the flavor of coriander, chopped liver, or hops. We can, for example, debate whether *Dora and Friends* actually does a good job of introducing native English speakers to Spanish. Or debate whether *Modern Family* actually offers a substantive commentary on stereotypes or merely opportunistically rehashes them. (It is worth noting that in cases of the latter sort, such debates presuppose determinate work meaning, as I hinted in the previous chapter. More on this presently.)

This is *not* to say that such debates are always or even usually settled. Rather, the problem of rationality highlights a contrast between purely subjective expressions of taste and reason-giving evaluations. My wife thinks cookies-and-cream ice cream is disgusting, which I find baffling, but there is neither any need for her to go on to give reasons why, nor is there any sense in me giving her reasons to sway her otherwise. If the expressivist argument were right about the purely subjective nature of our evaluative claims, then it would be the same with all of our evaluative discourse about television: I think *Curb Your Enthusiasm* (HBO 2000–2011) is hilarious and that *Rastamouse* (BBC 2011–2015) is offensive, and you might feel just the opposite, but it would be irrational to give reasons in support of purely subjective expressions of taste. The problem for the expressivist argument is that we often do give reasons in support of our evaluative claims; we often strive to ground such claims with facts about the mind-independent, intersubjectively accessible properties of television artworks. The problem of rationality identifies an element of many evaluative claims that is reasoned rather than just felt. Such evaluative claims evidently aim towards truthfulness insofar as our reason-giving is a rational activity that typically involves objective features of the work.

The problem of normative force also identifies a feature of our evaluative discourse for which the expressivist argument seems unable to account. As I indicated above, if all evaluative claims about television artworks were analogous to subjective expressions of preference for various flavors or foods, debate and disagreement would be incoherent. Claims like "*Sesame Street* is a good children's show" would be equivalent to "In my opinion, *Sesame Street* is a good children's show." The latter is a descriptive claim; it simply describes my opinion. The former is a normative claim; it asserts that *Sesame Street* has merits that one's interlocuters *should* recognize. The problem for the expressivist argument is that while perhaps some evaluative discourse takes the descriptive form sketched above, most does not. For example, when David Bianculli of NPR calls *The Singing Detective* (BBC1 1986), "television's most polished, audacious masterpiece," and Steven Armstrong of *The Guardian* claims it is "one of the best pieces of TV you'll see in your life," these claims have normative force.[18] And this is true of some academic criticism as well. When Sarah Cardwell writes of a moment in *Perfect Strangers* (BBC2 2001) in which Stephen Poliakoff has "achieved something extraordinary in this sequence in terms of mood, through his manipulation of stylistic and formal elements," she is not simply expressing a favorable attitude towards what Poliakoff has done.[19] Rather, she is making the normative claims that his achievement is, *as a matter of fact*, extraordinary and that competent viewers should recognize this because it is *true*. Again, the problem for the expressivist argument is that it lacks the means to account for this feature of our evaluative discourse.

In the philosophy of art, the problems of rationality and normative force are familiar challenges for expressivist accounts of artistic value.[20] Because meta-theoretical debates are not the purview of television studies, television scholars who endorse the expressivist position typically do so tacitly, without mounting an argument for it or considering objections and counterarguments. This is understandable as a practical consequence of the field's purview, but it also allowed for some dubious theoretical claims to survive unchallenged. Therefore, at this point, I want to work with what I think is the most explicit and sustained statement of expressivism on offer in television studies, supporting it as much as possible with salient arguments from philosophical aesthetics. I have in mind Jason Mittell's recent account of television evaluation, which, if correct, could dissolve the problems of rationality and normative force.

Critical Communication

Evaluations of television, according to Mittell, do not "aspire to the status of fact or proof."[21] That is, in his view, evaluative judgments are not intended to be statements about what is true of a given television show. Rather, evaluative judgments are more like expressions of attitudes towards television programs *as we perceive them*. Evaluative criticism involves explaining why one perceives television shows as one does, as well as guiding others' perceptions so that they may see the show as the critic sees it. In Mittell's words, "I am inviting you to see the shows how I see them, hear how they are speaking to me."[22]

Yet why should we think that evaluative criticism is really a matter of explaining and fostering perceptions of a work? Mittell attempts to make the case by offering brief, comparative analyses of *Alias* (ABC 2001–2006), *24* (FOX 2001–2010), *The Wire* (HBO 2002–2008), and *Breaking Bad* (AMC 2008–2013), as well as an independent critique of *Mad Men* (AMC 2007–2015). In his analyses, he qualifies many of his claims. Rather than contending, "*Alias* is a far more effective series [than *24*]," he writes, "For me (as such evaluations are always draped in the cloak of personal caveat), *Alias* is a far more effective series [than *24*]."[23] Perhaps needless to say, this is hardly convincing evidence to suppose that, *by their nature*, evaluative judgments are more like explanations of how one perceives things than normative assertions. The issue is not only that Mittell has composed his examples for the specific purpose of supporting a broad, contestable claim about the very nature of evaluative criticism. Further problems include the fact that Mittell offers what look suspiciously like justifying reasons to support his claims and that he slides, quickly and often, from making qualified evaluative claims (e.g., "for me ...") to unqualified evaluative claims (e.g., "*24* takes its own ludicrousness way too seriously.")[24] These problems are, I think, indicative of the fact that Mittell is unsuccessful in his attempt to defend a moderate expressivism.

However, there are arguments to support Mittell's case if we look beyond television studies and cultural studies. In philosophical aesthetics, John Bender notes, "There is a long tradition of pragmatist/rhetorical theories of aesthetic justification, and it is often said that a critic's main function is to direct our attention over a work's features in such a way that we come to see the work as the critic does, i.e., to agree with his or her aesthetic ascriptions."[25]

The most sustained account of this position in the recent philosophical aesthetics literature is Arnold Isenberg's 1949 article, "Critical Communication." In this essay, Isenberg emphasizes the critic's role "as one who affords *new* perceptions and with them new values."[26] Specifically, his claim is this:

> ... it seems that the critic's *meaning* is "filled in," "rounded out," or "completed" by the act of perception, which is performed not to judge the truth of his description but in a certain sense to understand it. And if *communication* is a process by which a mental content is transmitted by symbols from one person to another, then we can say that it is a function of criticism to bring about communication at the level of the senses, that is, to induce a sameness of vision, of experienced content. If this is accomplished, it may or may not be followed by agreement, or what is called "communion"—a community of feeling which expresses itself in identical value judgments.[27]

According to Isenberg, then, criticism is essentially about inducing perceptions. As Joe Zeccardi summarizes in a recent defense of this position, "we do *not* describe artworks with an eye to arguing that they possess or lack certain properties that bear some relationship to aesthetic value or disvalue. [...] Rather, we describe artworks in order to help others see things the way that we see them."[28] It is here that the similarities to Mittell's account of evaluative criticism are evident.

Like expressivists in television studies, Isenberg takes issue with "a theory of criticism, widely held in spite of its deficiencies, which divides the critical process into three parts."[29]

> There is the value judgment or *verdict* (V): "This picture or poem is good—." There is a particular statement or *reason* (R): "—because it has such-and-such a quality—." And there is a general statement or *norm* (N): "—and any work which has that quality is *pro tanto* good."[30]

188 *Evaluation*

In this formulation, the norm is necessary because the verdict, which is a *value judgment*, does not follow directly from the reason, which is just a *description*, without additional support. In other words, it is not enough to say, "*The Wire* is good because it is narratively complex"; one needs to then explicitly or implicitly invoke a generalized norm—in this case: "and any work that is narratively complex is *pro tanto* good."

Expressed concretely, this "widely held theory of criticism" faces an obvious problem that television studies scholars have been quick to recognize. In the above example, the difficulty is that the generalized norm, "any work that is narratively complex is *pro tanto* good," is, at the very least, contentious and indeed probably false. In his writing on narrative complexity, Mittell has been at pains to make this point—to avoid "assuming universal or essential criteria of value"—so much so that he backs away from claiming narrative complexity is, objectively speaking, an artistic merit in all television shows.[31] And surely he is right that in certain contexts narrative complexity creates artistic disvalue. For example, in children's television programs, such as *Bob the Builder* (BBC 1998–2012) or *Fireman Sam* (BBC1 1987–1994; Channel 5 2003–present), narrative complexity would be likely to impede the target audience's enjoyment.

It is worth, however, pausing over the following consideration. As Zeccardi and other commentators have pointed out, the fact that a value judgment (or verdict) does not follow directly from a description (or reason) "still leaves open the possibility that descriptions can provide *inductive* support for verdicts."[32] True, for a value judgment to follow as the conclusion of a deductive argument, appeal to a universal value norm would seem to be necessary. But weaker, defeasible principles might nevertheless lend prima facie support to an inductive argument that has a value judgment as its conclusion. Here is an example modeled after one that Zeccardi gives[33]: A general (but non-universal and defeasible principle) along the lines of "children's television programs with significant amounts of repetition tend to be good" could offer prima facie support to the value judgment that *Blue's Clues* (Nickelodeon 1996–2007) and *Dora the Explorer* (Nickelodeon 2000–2015) are good—especially if we add that children's television programs are designed with the aim of eliciting particular responses (e.g., recall of previous narrative events) from a relatively well-defined target audience (i.e., novice appreciators of narrative fiction). Similarly, I think that the general approach of weakening and localizing principles to which value judgments appeal is the way forward, but I will make this argument in due course.

To return to the "widely held theory of criticism," however, the problem identified both by Isenberg and by the television studies expressivists is that any norm, that is, any statement like "any work that is narratively complex is *pro tanto* good" appears to be, in Isenberg's words, "a precept, a rule, a *generalized value statement*."[34] But there are no such rules or universal principles of artistic value (at least, that is, I accepted this "particularist" assertion for the sake of argument at the start). Although this is commonly claimed to be a lesson of poststructuralism or cultural studies, Isenberg (writing in 1949, it should be noted) is content to draw this conclusion from the putative fact that "there is not in all the world's criticism a single purely descriptive statement concerning which one is prepared to say beforehand, 'If it is true, I shall like that work so much the better.'"[35] As an aside, it is worth highlighting that this way of putting things conflates two distinct issues in a way that is understandable but erroneous. The onus is on the expressivist to demonstrate that evaluations of artistic value boil down to expressions of "liking" or "disliking"; even if one succeeds in this, it would not follow that artistic value simply *is* a matter of what one likes or doesn't. This claim would require a separate argument—one that would explain away the fact that there are plenty of artworks that I like that, prima facie, aren't very good (e.g., the original *Batman* (ABC 1966–1968) and others that I don't like but that I recognize are good (e.g., *Hannibal* (NBC 2013–2015)). Anyway, what I think Isenberg *should want* to say is that the absence of general principles of artistic value entails that, despite appearances to the contrary, the reasons given in support of evaluative claims do not (because they cannot) function as premises in arguments for the truth of verdicts or judgments of artistic value.

This conclusion, alongside the allied particularist premise I accepted for the sake of argument, is supposed to motivate Isenberg's alternative account of what is going on in evaluative criticism. As James Shelley helpfully summarizes, "R [the reason] functions not as a premise for V [the verdict] but as a guide to a perception of the work that allows for the value specified in V to be grasped directly. Since from this view it is an act of perception that mediates R and V, as opposed to an inference [...], there is simply no role for N [the norm] to play."[36] Here we see an important difference between Isenberg's original argument and the way it has frequently been appropriated by expressivists. Isenberg maintains that the absence of general principles of artistic value does *not* entail that evaluative criticism is in no way objective.[37] Rather, it seems to be Isenberg's view that evaluative criticism is intended to "induce a sameness of vision," in which case subjectivity and objectivity are somehow irrelevant.[38]

Despite the fact that Isenberg's conclusion is rather different from that of the expressivist, his argument can and has been marshalled in support of the expressivist's claims. A hybrid expressivist/Isenbergian argument comprises four theses:

1 the Isenbergian thesis that, because there are no general principles of artistic value, evaluative criticism cannot involve reasons that function like premises in arguments;
2 the Isenbergian thesis that, granted (1), it is plausible to conceive of reason-giving in evaluative criticism as intended to induce perceptions;
3 the expressivist thesis that, granted (1), there are no objectively true judgments of artistic value; and

190 *Evaluation*

4   the expressivist thesis that, granted (2) and (3), the point of inducing perceptions in evaluative criticism is to get the reader to see the work as the critic sees it, not because the critic's perception attends to something true about the work, but for some other reason.

Something like this argument is, I think, implicit in Mittell's work on evaluation. If I am wrong, and it is not, I would still maintain that this is the best way his work could be read and the most plausible version of expressivism in television studies.

Nevertheless, this formulation of the expressivist argument is unworkable. Point (3) is supposed to follow from (1), but it evidently does not and, in any case, I will argue that (3) is false. But because my criticisms of (1) and (3) will serve as a segue to my positive account of evaluative criticism, I want to focus on (2) and (4) for the moment. First, (2): the Isenbergian thesis that it is plausible to conceive of reason-giving in evaluative criticism as intended to induce perceptions. I think it is important here to distinguish between the idea that it is plausible to conceive of the *descriptions* of works involved in *some kinds* of criticism as intended to induce perceptions versus the notion that it is plausible to conceive of such descriptions as *reasons* that, in *evaluative criticism*, the critic gives in an attempt to engender a particular perception of the work.

The former claim seems cogent. In some critical contexts, the point of criticism surely is to bring about a particular perception of the work, and this is done through describing a work in such a way that calls attention to particular features or details. However, if the goal is to bring about a particular perception, then it is not at all clear that such descriptions can be functioning here as *reasons,* properly so called. In Frank Sibley's words, "an activity the successful outcome of which is seeing or hearing cannot, I think, be called *reasoning*. I may have reasons for thinking something is graceful, but not for seeing it is."[39] For example, I could describe elements of *Sesame Street* with the hope that my description might get you see the show as, say, satirical. Or I could give you reasons to *believe* the show is satirical. But it does not seem to make sense to say that my reasoning could engender a perception on your part because that does not seem to be how perception works.[40] Thus, the dilemma is, as Robert Hopkins puts it, "how to reconcile the rationality of critical discourse with its leading to perception. How can there be an argument with a perception as its conclusion?"[41]

Hopkins offers an interesting, admittedly tentative, argument to try to answer this question. However, he gives too much away at the outset by assuming that "the point of critical discussion is not the formation of belief but the engendering of perception."[42] For while it is plausible that inducing perception is the point of *some* critical discussion, there are good reasons to think that the point of evaluative criticism is in fact the formation of belief. Prima facie, the nature of our evaluative criticism indicates that the critic's goal is to move readers to accept a judgment that a show really is excellent, or terrible, or whatever. That is, the critic aims to persuade readers to *believe* that the show is how she or he claims. And *this* view seems to offer a more plausible account of the fact that evaluative criticism involves justifying reasons. Perhaps this is most clear in cases where artistic and ethical, political, and ideological values interact. For example, as we saw from the discussion in the previous chapter, it seems deeply implausible that critics who have harshly judged 24 because of its representation and endorsement of torture are merely inviting us to see the show as they did and feel as troubled as they did. Rather, they want us to accept as truthful and as correct the claim that 24 is flawed (artistically, politically, ethically) because it endorses torture (given some fairly non-controversial assumptions about the ethics of torture).

In sum, the second premise of the expressivist's Isenbergian argument faces two main problems. Although it is plausible that, in the context of non-evaluative criticism, the critic's goal is to engender perception, it does *not* seem plausible that this sort of criticism could involve reason-giving rather than simply describing things. Moreover, we have prima facie evidence to think that the goal of evaluative criticism, in particular, is not the engendering of perception but the formation of belief. So, the challenge to the second premise is this: It's neither clear how reasoning could engender perceptions nor that the engendering of perception is the end of *evaluative* criticism. A defender of the premise cannot forgo the latter claim without also abandoning the larger argument regarding the nature of evaluative criticism. But by drop[ing the former claim, the critic then owes a further account of the apparent rationality and normative force of evaluative criticism.

We find similar problems with premise (4), the expressivist thesis that, granted (2) and (3), the point of inducing perceptions in evaluative criticism is to get the reader to see the work as the critic sees it, not because the critic's perception attends to something true about the work, but for some other reason. This, it is worth noting, is not a view that would be endorsed by Isenberg or Hopkins. It is, however, a position that is maintained by Mittell. Two problems with this thesis carry over from the discussion of the second premise. First, there are good prima facie reasons to think that evaluative criticism is in the business of belief-formation (rather than perception-engendering) and *this* offers the most plausible explanation of both the normative force and rational nature of judgments of artistic value. These two matters become acute for the defender of (4), who also needs to reconcile them with the stronger claim that there is nothing objectively true about a given work that criticism aims at revealing. But it is unclear how this account of criticism could possibly explain the normative force that, prima facie, is part and parcel of evaluation. If this account of evaluative criticism were accurate, then our critical judgments would not even raise the problem of normative force that the account actually has to try to explain away.

The second problem relates to my objection to premise (2), which was that it is does not make sense to give reasons in an attempt to induce a

192 *Evaluation*

perception. The additional challenge for the proponent of premise (4) is that it is even *less* clear why television evaluation involves reason-giving if the perceptions induced do not reveal any objectively true features of the television show in question. For if there is no truth about a program that can be grasped by perceiving it in a particular way, then giving reasons to justify our claims seems to be incoherent.

The problem of rationality, like the problem of normative force, not only threatens premise (4) but also the overall expressivist argument. If there were no objective basis to evaluative judgments, such judgments would need no justification at all. We would simply assert how we felt and there would be no debate. But we do give reasons. We debate specific judgments such as "*Sesame Street* is a good program because it fosters an enjoyment of learning," and "Gratuitous violence against women mars the artistic achievement of *Game of Thrones* (HBO 2011–present)." As Daniel A. Kaufman points out, "The critic, when he or she makes such statements, intends the 'because' clauses to support the evaluative claims in a very particular way, namely, as support for their purported *truthfulness*."[43] In short, if we want to hold onto the idea that evaluative criticism is a rational and coherent activity, then it seems like we must accept the idea that judgments of artistic value aim for truthfulness.

Let us briefly return to Mittell's account of evaluation to see how these tensions play out. Glossing what he thinks evaluative criticism entails, Mittell writes:

> An evaluative critique does not aspire to the status of fact or proof. By claiming that a given program is good or that one series is better than another, I am making an argument that I believe to be true, but it is not a truth claim [...] Of course I do hope to convince readers that my evaluation is correct, and I certainly believe it to be true. But we do not make evaluations to make a definitive statement about the value of any given text; instead they are contingent claims lodged in their contextual moment that will almost undoubtedly be revised after future viewing and conversation.[44]

Despite my respect for much of Mittell's work and his attempt to talk about evaluation in a way that is still *verboten* in much of television studies, it must be said that this is a rather confused passage inasmuch as it runs together a number of quite distinct concepts—"fact," "proof," "truth," and "definitive statement." These need to be prized apart to get at what is relevant here. First, let's not worry at all about "proof," because it is unclear that anyone actually thinks the reasons she or he gives to justify an evaluative judgment constitute proof—at least if that concept is understood as involving verification or deduction. Similarly, there is a sense in which the idea of evaluative judgments having "the status of fact" is a straw man; who would claim that "*Mad Men* is an outstanding artistic achievement" reports a fact in the same manner as "*Mad Men* is set in the 1960s?" "Definitive statement" is yet another straw man; there is no reason to think evaluative judgments cannot be of objective facts or properties, aspire toward truthfulness, and remain open to revision. C. I. Lewis had a nice phrase for these: "non-terminating judgments."[45] The real issues, as I have tried to indicate, are whether evaluative judgments *aim* toward truthfulness, whether they are in any way objective and thus evaluable for proximate truth (or falsity).

Because of his skepticism about truth (at least with regard to the artistic value of television shows), Mittell holds that when he makes an argument he believes to be true, he nevertheless maintains "it is not a truth claim." But I doubt this is a coherent idea. Does it make sense to argue for a proposition, *p,* one believes to be true without claiming that *p* is true? It seems to me that if you are not claiming *p* is true, then you cannot be arguing that it is. This is one sense in which Mittell is being pulled between his commitment to expressivism and the rational, normative nature of our actual evaluative practices.

But the fact that Mittell describes his evaluative criticism as involving him "making an argument [he] believe[s] to be true," indicates his position is untenable. First, as we have seen, if Mittell's account of evaluative criticism as perception-guiding were correct, he should not *need* to make an argument at all. Indeed, it would not make any sense for him to be offering arguments because one cannot get someone to have a perception by arguing for it. Rather, one makes an argument in the hopes of getting someone to adopt a belief. And, in fact, Mittell admits as much in this passage: He does "hope to convince you that [his] evaluation is correct, and [he] certainly believe[s] it to be true." Here is the crux of the problem for Mittell: it is incoherent to try to convince someone that an evaluation is correct or to believe (yourself) that it is true if you hold the expressivist view that evaluations are not matters of objective fact.

Thus, what is somewhat odd about Mittell's chapter on evaluation is that despite admitting that he hopes to convince readers that his evaluations are correct and that he believes they are true, he concludes by explicitly embracing expressivism. At the end of the chapter, Mittell writes, "My negative reaction [to *Mad Men*] is ultimately analytically inexplicable, only pointing to my own personal preferences and tendencies."[46] Yet this conclusion, following a lengthy, close analysis that offers plausible reasons to believe *Mad Men* fails on its own terms and, thus, is not as good a show as is commonly thought, is deeply unsatisfactory if not incoherent. That is, whether *Mad Men* fails (or does not) on its own terms is not simply a matter of how Mittell or anyone else perceives the show. For there are facts, which are *in principle* discoverable, about what the show's creators intended to achieve and whether or not they succeeded. Thus, if Mittell's analysis is accurate, the correct conclusion to be drawn is *not* the one at which he arrives. Rather, it is that a negative evaluation of the show is *objectively* warranted to the extent that the creators' failure to achieve their aims constitutes a *pro tanto* artistic flaw.

In Defense of the Objectivity of Evaluative Judgments

Rehabilitating the idea that judgments of artistic value may be in some sense objective has not been a popular gambit in television studies. But if the preceding arguments are sound, then we ought to consider it within reach. The core idea, to which I have already alluded and upon which we ought to build, has been extensively developed in contemporary philosophy of art and, in fact, has a parallel with work in television studies. Roughly, the argument, goes like this: Television programs and other artworks are particular kinds of cultural artifacts. They are human creations which, in the overwhelming majority of cases, are intentionally designed for particular purposes, to fulfill particular functions. But of course art, including television, has a wide variety of purposes and a plurality of functions. The purposes and functions of any particular work depend on the *kind* of work it is, where "kind" encompasses things including medium, genre, mode, style, historical period, and so forth. So, evaluation is objective when it assesses the extent to which a particular work achieves its *specific* aims or purposes as well as fulfills the broader functions of the categories in which it is situated. Noël Carroll has dubbed this view "the plural category approach" to evaluation, but something like it has been independently argued for by various other philosophers, including Robert Stecker and Stephen Davies.[47] It should also sound familiar to film and television studies scholars, because it parallels points made by V. F. Perkins in *Film as Film* and Jason Jacobs, who has developed some of Perkins's ideas in the context of television studies.

I am not at all suggesting that, at our grasp, is a complete solution to difficult problems about artistic value and evaluation. For example, as Christine Geraghty has pointed out in response to the proposals of Carroll and Jacobs, there is a need to elaborate how this approach to evaluation could work in the context of television evaluation.[48] On the one hand, I want to emphasize that my intention is not to offer a complete account of television evaluation, but merely to establish that it does, in some instances, have an objective basis. On the other hand, I want to adumbrate a few ways in which television studies might build upon this rather general sketch of evaluation.

Let's begin with a broad, hopefully uncontroversial, point: Most cultural artifacts are created with the intention that they fulfill some particular function. Their value is, thus, as least partly a matter of how well they fulfill the function for which they are meant. For example, the goodness of a particular chair is relative to how well it fulfills the function of a chair to afford comfortable sitting. This is not to say that the fulfillment of this function exhausts the value of the chair; a chair that does not afford comfortable sitting may, for example, be valuable inasmuch as it is beautiful or expensive. However, a chair's value *as a chair* is a matter of how well it fulfills the primary function of chairs. It is important to see here that, assessed this way, a chair's goodness is a matter of objective fact. For the chair is good relative to how well it fulfills the function of a chair, and the function of a chair is an objective matter of fact. Daniel Kaufman puts it nicely: "objectivity with regard to function entails a commensurate objectivity of *value*. The function of a hammer is defined objectively, as the performing of a specific task, so the corresponding excellence of the hammer is likewise objective in nature."[49]

Note that this does not commit one to the claim that hammers or chairs have an unchanging, timeless function that could not be otherwise. On the contrary, as Amie Thomasson writes, "artifactual kinds are notoriously malleable and historical in nature."[50] But those functions still remain matters of objective fact: In a given socio-historical context, it either is or is not the case that the primary function of a chair is to afford comfortable sitting. In practice there may be a divergence of opinion regarding how well a given chair fulfills its function and, thus, how good it is. But this does not jeopardize the objective basis of evaluative judgment. Crucially, the evaluative criterion against which this debate plays out is objective: The debate is about *whether* or *to what extent* the chair fulfills its function. Furthermore, we can debate whether chairs actually have the function of affording comfortable sitting and we might even decide that a distinct function of chairs is to provide back support. But again, such debates do not threaten the objectivity of judgments regarding the fulfillment of a chair's function.

Now let's turn to television, bearing in mind Jacobs's and Geraghty's points about the importance of categories of television—genres, modes, and so forth. Although I acknowledge the difficulty of specifying purposes and functions of broad categories such as "television melodrama," there is no need to set our sights so high in the first instance. Instead, consider children's television, which plausibly has a more specific target audience and a narrower range of purposes and functions. Suppose, for the sake of argument, one of the purposes of children's television is to modestly exercise and develop children's cognitive skills without exhausting or frustrating them. If the artifact kind "children's television" has this (or any other) characteristic function, then an instance of children's television is objectively good *qua* children's television to the extent that it fulfills that function, which is an *objective* matter.

Here is a more formal presentation of the argument that makes clear how it overcomes the Isenbergian and expressivist challenges. First, here is the general argument.

1   Children's television programs are cultural artifacts.
2   Artifact kinds like "children's television" typically have particular functions.
3   Instances of children's television are good to the extent that they fulfill the particular functions of the artifact kind "children's television."
4   Features that aid in the realization of children's television's particular functions are good-making features.

5   Facilitating the exercise and development of children's cognitive skills (without resulting in exhaustion or frustration) tends to aid in the realization of (at least one of) children's television's particular functions.
6   Facilitating the exercise and development of children's cognitive skills is a good-making feature of children's television (*pro tanto*).

Now, here is how a practical application of the argument would look when plugged into the Isenbergian syllogism:

1a *Blue's Clues* is an instance of children's television. (Description 1a)
1b *Blue's Clues* facilitates the exercise and development of children's cognitive skills. (Description 1b)
2   Given the functions or purposes of children's television, instances of children's television that facilitate the exercise and development of cognitive skills are good (*pro tanto*). (General, but defeasible norm)
3   *Blue's Clues* is good (*pro tanto*). (Verdict or value judgment)[51]

Notice that rather than relying on a universal principle to connect the descriptions (1a and 1b) to the value judgment (3), this argument makes do with a general, *pro tanto* principle. That is, the argument accepts that the general claim made in (2) is defeasible. The claim of (2) is merely that owing to the purposes of children's television, exercising and developing children's cognitive skills tends to be a good-making feature.

Let me anticipate a few objections. First, some readers might be thinking that the function of exercising and developing cognitive skills might be a good-making feature of children's television, but it is not an *artistic* value. (This in turn might be related to the objection that children's television just isn't art.) But this objection ignores the overwhelming prima facie evidence that cognitive value is often a significant component of artistic value (consider "narratively complex" television serials, puzzle films, dense novels, cryptic poems, and so forth) and the extensive arguments that have been mounted in defense of this point.[52] Readers also might be thinking that children's television has a variety of other purposes and functions; it is a mistake to think that the cognitive value of children's television exhausts its overall artistic value. My response is that this is true and is not actually an objection. My claim is merely that a show like *Blue's Clues* has artistic merit to the extent that it fulfills this cognitive function. This is a *pro tanto* artistic merit that interacts with other artistic merits and flaws, which are, in turn, established by the extent to which the show achieves whatever other purposes we agree children's television has. This (or any other) *pro tanto* artistic merit may indeed be insufficient to warrant a positive judgment of the program's overall artistic value.

This, it should be clear, is the important move that secures the objectivity of the evaluative judgment without reliance upon universal principles of artistic value. If the argument is sound, then evaluative criticism need not be saddled with the problem Isenberg suggests it is. More importantly for the present purpose, it definitively refutes even the more plausible formulation of the television studies expressivist argument developed above. In particular, it does so by undermining both premise (1), the Isenbergian thesis that, because there are no general principles of artistic value, evaluative criticism cannot involve reasons that function like premises in arguments; and premise (3) the expressivist thesis that, granted (1), there are no objectively true judgments of artistic value.

It is worth mentioning a related argument in defense of the objectivity of judgments of artistic value. In the previous two chapters on interpretation (Chapters 4 and 5), I emphasized the ways in which creators of television artworks seek to realize various sorts of intentions about work meaning. In Chapter 4, I claimed they aim to realize categorical intentions about what sort of work to make, as well as lower-order semantic intentions about what fictional truths the work will embody or prescribe viewers to imagine. We can formulate a version of the above argument that preserves the objectivity of judgments of artistic value by relativizing evaluation to an appraisal of the creators' categorical intentions. That is, rather than stipulating the purposes of certain categories of television, we can invoke the creators' categorical intentions to make a work of a certain sort.

Recall the discussion of *The Colbert Report* from the previous chapter in which I asked readers to imagine that the apparent satire of the program was actually a failed intention to offer a straightforward political commentary. In this case, the imaginary, non-satirical *Colbert Report* would objectively have a *pro tanto* artistic flaw to the extent that its creators failed to realize their intention of making a straightforward political commentary. Of course, the inverse of this sort of imaginary case is more likely; sometimes people fail at things like satire and comedy. Comedy is a complicated case because of the response-dependent nature of humor. However, it seems plausible that a television program that is intended to be humorous, but which is not (on whatever account of humor one accepts), is *pro tanto* artistically bad. So, too, is a horror program intended to be frightening, but which instead elicits humor. So, too, is a putative suspense program that induces boredom. And so forth.

Such artistic flaws are, of course, defeasible. Plausibly, creators can fail to realize various categorical intentions to *some* degree (albeit perhaps not completely) and still find overall artistic success. Furthermore, the successful realization of categorical intentions, while a *pro tanto* artistic merit, does not guarantee overall artistic success. My successful realization of an intention to create a limerick constitutes a *pro tanto* artistic merit, but my creation is, on the whole, a rather poor artwork. Here an interlocutor might claim that, practically speaking, this is not a terribly helpful proposal. And I agree that, in practice, this local principle or criterion of artistic achievement needs to be supplemented with other considerations. But for the moment, the point is simply that this is another way in which judgments of artistic value can be objectively grounded.

Clearly, the scale of the creators' ambitions also seems relevant to our appraisal of what their works achieve. And here it may appear that we are leaving the realm of objectivity. By what criteria can we objectively judge that a television work—say, *Berlin Alexanderplatz* (1980)—is a "flawed masterpiece?" Or that the humble nature of creators' ambitions, no matter how successfully realized, results in a work of less artistic value than a putative flawed masterpiece? These are difficult questions that may admit of no entirely satisfactory answer. Nevertheless, it is not the case that we have no objective grounds for appraising the success of artistic intentions relative to ambition. Recall one of the central arguments of Chapter 2: Part of the medium's relevance to the appreciation of television as art is that it offers creators certain opportunities and presents certain challenges. This is the idea underlying Berys Gaut's thesis: "Some correct artistic evaluations of artworks refer to distinctive properties of the medium in which these artworks occur."[53] If one accepts this claim, then, *in principle*, differentiating features of the medium can lend objective grounds to judgments of artistic value relativized to the ambition of creators' intentions.

Here are some examples in which we are able to make objective judgments of artistic value with reference to the interaction of differentiating properties of the medium and artistic intentions. Let us start with a somewhat banal case: In the first episode of *Horace and Pete* (2016), a number of shots are slightly out of focus. There is little question this is a *pro tanto* artistic flaw; the creators wanted the shots to be in focus, but on several occasions they failed to execute. In most television works, attempting to get shots in focus is a very humble ambition. One of the reasons for this is that focused shots are a basic requirement for creating the conditions in which viewers can imaginatively engage with the fictional world represented. Another reason is that there is normally no good reason why the creators cannot re-shoot until they get the focus right. Here is the difference with *Horace and Pete*: Because the program is shot live (albeit not broadcast live), the camera team does not have the ability to set up individual shots in the way they would on a single-camera production. Neither do they have the ability to stop shooting and do another take if they make an error. Plausibly, the ambition to shoot live, with all of its attendant challenges, mitigates against the *pro tanto* flaw of soft-focus shots. That is, given the challenges of shooting live, soft-focus shots in *Horace and Pete* are not artistic flaws of the same magnitude as they are in single-camera television productions.

Here is one more example, related to television's differential feature of temporal prolongation: A common artistic intention underlying most fiction television is to create a coherent, unified narrative. Needless to say, this intention is realized with varying degrees of success. Once again, however, the ambition behind this intention seems relevant to artistic evaluation, because some instances of television demand that narrative threads be prolonged over several years. That is to say, the intention to create a coherent, unified narrative across a multi-season program is more ambitious than it is in the context of a single-season mini-series. Plausibly, the convoluted and incoherent narrative of *The X-Files* was a *pro tanto* artistic flaw in later seasons, including the most recent "re-boot." So, too, it is plausible that the assortment of loose narrative ends prevalent in the Season 1 finale of *True Detective* constitutes a *pro tanto* artistic flaw.

Nevertheless, these are flaws of different magnitudes because of their relationship to what the creators of each program attempted to achieve given the possibilities and constraints of the medium. The creators of the first season of *True Detective* limited their narrative to eight hour-long episodes and, therefore, had a relatively easier task in unifying the narrative. For this reason, several distracting plot holes in that series constitute a *pro tanto* artistic flaw that is greater than that from which *The X-Files* suffers. The severity of the artistic flaw comprised by the ultimate narrative incoherence of *The X-Files* needs to be weighed against the creators' intentions to create a complex story sustained over many years—to be precise, over more than two hundred episodes and two feature length films.

Again, one might object that this proposal is not specific enough to answer difficult questions about specific cases. It is true that what I have said here offers no details about how such comparative evaluations might be made in precise terms. But I think this is probably as it should be. It is unlikely we could ever come up with a precise method of tallying up the values of creators' ambitions relative to the challenges of the medium, weighing these against other *pro tanto* artistic merits or flaws, and come out with a decisive measure of artistic value. Nor should we want such a mechanism in my view. But this does not tell against my central claim here, which is that there is in fact an objective basis upon which we can ground appraisals of the ambition of creators' artistic intentions—namely, the fact that the medium affords artists particular possibilities and presents them with specific challenges.

Thus far I have been discussing the ways in which various sorts of artistic categories and categorical intentions undergird the objectivity of judgments of artistic value. At this point, I want to turn to the role of semantic intentions in this context. In Chapter 5, I claimed that television creators also attempt to realize various intentions regarding the higher-order meaning of their works, usually expressing or communicating attitudes or propositions. Furthermore, I claimed that despite the fact that creators do not always successfully realize those intentions, there are still good reasons to think that work meaning is determinate and indeed constrained by the intentions that *are* successfully realized. For example, one of the reason's Mittell's negative reaction to *Mad Men* is actually rationally warranted, despite his protestations, is this: He claims that the program sets out to critique the culture of 1960s Madison Avenue, but ends up glamorizing it. This is the way in which the show fails on its own terms.

We can extrapolate this claim to make a more general point. Suppose you accept the argument of the previous chapter, according to which the meanings a work actually has are partly determined by its creators (even if the work's *significance* for viewers is perpetually [re]constructed, contested, and so forth). If work meaning is determinate and at least partly determined by the successful realization of creators' intentions, then there are, *in principle,* objective grounds to decide three matters: (1) Whether or not the work's creators intended it to mean *p* or express *a*; (2) Whether or not the work means *p* or expresses *a*; (3) Whether the work's creators succeeded or failed in their efforts to have the work mean *p* or express *a* (if they so intended). Don't worry about the practical difficulties of ascertaining this information on a case-by-case basis. The point here is that if one accepts the arguments of the previous chapter and the uncontroversial premise that artists' success in realizing their intentions is a *pro tanto* artistic merit (and failure in realizing their intentions is a *pro tanto* artistic flaw), then it follows that there is another way in which evaluative judgments of television artworks can be objective.

In this context, the most obvious examples come from television programs that clearly assert propositions or attitudes—in particular nonfiction works. Plausibly, one of the achievements of a work like *Years of Living Dangerously* (2014) is its ability to compellingly and persuasively mount an argument that will spur viewers to action. In this case, the point, roughly, concerns the urgency of mitigating climate change. To the extent that the programs' creators successfully realized their intention to communicate the gravity of this issue and to convince viewers of the need to acknowledge and act upon human-influenced climate change, *Years of Living Dangerously* is *pro tanto* artistically good. But imagine a parallel program, *Years of Living Dangerously**, that was created with the exact same intentions, but with much less success. Imagine that, contrary to the intentions of the creators, *Years of Living Dangerously** actually expresses the attitude that it is too late to stop climate change, so we might as well just enjoy ourselves and not worry about our impact on the environment. To the extent that this imaginary program, *Years of Dangerously**, constituted a failure on the part of its creators to successfully realize their intentions to express a particular attitude, the program would be *pro tanto* artistically bad.

And once again, we must acknowledge that such *pro tanto* artistic merits and flaws are defeasible, rather than any sort of guarantee of a work's overall artistic value. So, too, we must admit that, practically speaking, evaluating the artistic success of a work in terms of how well it successfully realizes its creators' intentions to have some particular meaning or express some specific attitude, may not be as helpful a strategy as we might want. Perhaps this is especially true if we focus on works of fiction, from which it is plausibly more difficult to exact summary propositions or meanings. Anecdotally, however, it strikes me that we often appraise the artistic success of television programs, as Mittell does, in terms of the extent to which they successfully realize their aims, which usually include to express a particular attitude. In any case, once again, the important point for the present purpose is that this is yet another way in which judgments of the artistic value of television are based on objective grounds.

My final point on this topic again depends upon the previous chapter's arguments for the determinacy of meaning. Here is another way in which higher-order work meaning, especially the attitudes a work expresses or endorses, figures into our artistic evaluations. It is common to appraise a work not only in terms of how well it successfully realizes its aim to express a particular attitude but also in terms of the content of that attitude itself. Specifically, I have in mind cases in which a work's ethical (or ideological) content is relevant to our artistic appraisal of it. That is to say, in some cases the ethically or ideologically flawed character of the attitude a work (successfully) expresses constitutes a *pro tanto* artistic flaw.

Building upon the idea that artistic value interacts with and is constituted by other sorts of value, I want to suggest that ethical (or ideological) flaws in an instance of television may constitute artistic disvalue in an objective sense. Given the prevalent skepticism about "authentic" or "real" aesthetic and artistic value, clearly one contentious premise in this argument is that ethical (or ideological) value is real and that evaluations of such value have objective grounds and are evaluable for truth or falsehood. However, as the discussion in the previous chapter suggested, it seems unlikely that many television scholars are truly expressivists about ideological (and, one supposes, ethical) value. If the analyses of television that seek to expose sexism, racism, classism, and so forth have no objective basis and are not truth evaluable, then what's the point? If such work is coherent and meaningful in any sense, it *must* be because it aspires to truthfulness and objectively identifies *real* ideological (and ethical) merits or flaws. However, if one accepts this premise, along with the premise that artistic value is plural and partly constituted both other sorts of value, it follows that there is another way in which judgments of artistic value are also objectively grounded and evaluable for truth or falsity.

Suppose you accept the plausible claim that reality makeover programs, in the mold of *Extreme Makeover* (ABC 2002–2007), essentially police women's bodies and simultaneously subvert potential critiques of this function by couching it in neoliberal individualist rhetoric. There is significant support for this claim in a number of compelling feminist analyses of reality television. As the authors of one article put it, "This normalization of flawless femininity is obviously problematic for feminists, and the problem is compounded by a liberal logic that celebrates disciplinary practices of femininity as 'free' choice and individual pleasure … [T]he historical feminist insistence that disciplinary femininity is a symptom and effect of gender oppression is reshifted in this context as a denial of women's agency …"[54] If you accept all this, then something like the following thesis follows: The policing of women's bodies in reality makeover television series constitutes a form of gender oppression.

Add the plausible assumption that gender oppression is an ethical and ideological disvalue. Now it follows that if it can be shown that in certain instances of reality television (or any other sorts of television art) ethical and/or ideological value is a constituent of artistic value, then those instances of television that involve the policing of women's bodies have identifiable artistic flaws, the (dis)value of which can be *objectively* judged. To be clear, I am not suggesting there is a uni-directional relationship, by which ethical or ideological merits always constitute artistic merits, while ethical and ideological flaws always constitute artistic flaws.[55] Rather, what my argument requires and what I am claiming is merely that sometimes ethical or ideological flaws constitute artistic flaws or create artistic disvalue. There are a number of ways to argue for this position, but here I will merely sketch a simple one.

In just about any artistic context imaginable, including reality television, artistic success or value is partly a matter of creating sufficient interest or pleasure such that the beholder continues to engage the work—in the case of temporally organized works, through their completion. If the beholder is compelled to disengage the work, then the work plausibly has a *pro tanto* artistic flaw and in many cases could be regarded as an artistic failure, although of course there are exceptions to this. Reality television (and television more generally) is a kind of art that particularly depends upon viewer engagement for its artistic success because of its deep connections to commercial interests. Again, to be clear, there are significant degrees of variation here. Plenty of television programs are artistic successes despite low ratings. But if a program's target audience is compelled to disengage from the show, it has, evidently, failed to achieve one of its primary aims or purposes.[56]

Now consider a reality makeover series like *The Swan*, which aired for only two seasons on Fox in 2004. *The Swan* (which putatively turned "ugly ducklings" into "swans" through cosmetic surgery) was evidently so ethically and ideologically noxious—and recognizable as such to a wide variety of viewers—that people simply stopped watching it. That is, *The Swan* had the artistically disvaluable feature of being too troubling and offensive for (most of) its target audience to watch. And this feature resulted from its ideologically noxious and ethically reprehensible attitudes towards its contestants and women more generally.[57] In *The Swan*, we have a case in which political and ideological value interact with artistic value; the program's ideological flaws constituted artistic flaws. To avoid misunderstanding, let me emphasize that I am *not* claiming that the artistic value of *The Swan* or any other show can be measured in terms of popularity or audience ratings or even that cancellation due to lack of ratings is indicative of artistic disvalue. Rather, the claim is that driving the target audience to disengage from the work is a *pro tanto* artistic flaw, which, in the case of *The Swan*, is constituted by an ideological flaw. If this argument is right, then whoever wants to deny the reality of artistic value and disvalue will, in order to be consistent, be forced to deny the reality of political or ideological value and disvalue—more specifically, to deny that gender oppression is a real species of disvalue. Further, whoever denies that judgments of artistic value have objective grounds and are evaluable for truth will also, in order to be consistent, be forced to deny that judgments according to which gender oppression is a species of disvalue are in any sense objective or evaluable for truth.

Conclusion

To summarize, I have suggested that there are at least five ways in which judgments of the artistic value of television artworks are objectively grounded:

1 When they appraise a work in terms of how well it fulfills the characteristic aim(s) or purpose(s) of the category in which it is situated.
2 When they appraise a work in terms of the extent to which its creators successfully realized their categorical intentions to make a work of a particular kind.
3 When they appraise a work in terms of the extent to which its creators successfully overcame challenges posed by the medium.
4 When they appraise a work in terms of the extent to which its creators successfully realized their semantic intentions to make a work with a particular meaning or expressing a particular attitude.
5 When they appraise a work in terms of the extent to which its artistic value is affected by ethical (or ideological) value or disvalue that obtains in the work.

To my knowledge, nobody who has criticized the television aesthetics project has seriously entertained substantive claims for the objectivity for evaluative judgments. For example, according to Matt Hills, one of the lessons of poststructuralism is supposedly that the sort value judgments made by me and other advocates of the "television aesthetics" project "cannot ultimately and finally be sustained through critical argument."[58] This view, I have tried to show, is a common though erroneous one; what is interesting about Hills's essay is how he goes about criticizing those who he thinks have not accepted this "lesson." Such scholars stand accused of "pre-structuralism," which involves "assertions of inherent textual value which are supposedly objectively given 'in the medium' or 'in the text' …"[59] "Pre-structuralist invocations of TV aesthetics," Hills tells us, "are readily identifiable by virtue of the fact that they position aesthetic value as textually inherent (that is transcendent) rather than as textually and evaluatively relational."[60]

Now, one immediate reason for skepticism about Hills's objections to television aesthetics is that this description of "inherent value" is one that I think most contemporary philosophers of art would find puzzling.

Aestheticians (and moral philosophers) from Monroe Beardsley onwards have tended to follow C. I. Lewis in understanding "inherent value" as a species of *extrinsic* value.[61] For Lewis, "inherent value is an objective property of the thing to which it is attributable," which may *seem* like the view Hills wants to reject.[62] For Hills wants to deny that value is not a constituent or integral feature of "texts." But Lewis's view is subtle: In his view, inherent value "consists in a potentiality of the thing for conducing to realization of some positive value-quality in experience." That is, inherent value is not *intrinsic* to the "text" (or other object) but rather is "realizable through the presentation of it."[63] Lewis thus conceives of inherent value as objective but not intrinsic. Hills seems to think that value cannot be objective, because he assumes that if it cannot be intrinsic, then it cannot be objective.[64]

The problem is that few, if any, contemporary philosophers of art hold such a view; Hills is battling a straw man. Although Lewis himself distinguished inherent and instrumental value as two sorts of extrinsic value, subsequent philosophers of art and ethics have often thought about inherent value as a kind of instrumental value, because it is a value only insofar as it leads to another end—namely, a valuable experience.[65] And this is how many philosophers of art characterize artistic value, although they do not typically use the term "inherent" to describe it—no doubt in part because of the confusion the word is liable to generate. Indeed, one of the crucial points of George Dickie's study of theories of art evaluation is that most of the major contributions to the literature in the twentieth century (including Beardsley's "traditional" aesthetic theory of art) have advocated *instrumentalist* accounts of artistic value, according to which value does not obtain in the work itself. Rather, the work is valuable instrumentally to the extent that it affords a valuable experience.[66]

It is within this tradition that I have tried to situate my own modest proposal, according to which the artistic value of a given television program exists neither in the program (or "text") itself, nor its good-making features. On the contrary, I have emphasized that insofar as a given program is a cultural artifact, designed to fulfill a particular function or functions, its value is *instrumental*. I hope to have made some contribution to moving forward these debates in television studies and to have clarified some of the central concepts at stake in the appreciation of the art of television.

Notes

1. Usually this is phrased in terms of aesthetic value, but I will continue to use the term "artistic" in a broad sense that covers aesthetic value in art. See Alan McKee, "Which is the Best *Dr. Who* story? A Case Study in Value Judgements outside the Academy," *Intensities: The Journal of Cult Media* 1 (2001), n.p. Accessed March 15, 2016. http://intensitiescultmedia.wordpress.com/2012/12/11/intensities-1–springsummer-2001/ For a more recent statement of this claim, see Matt Hills,

"Television Aesthetics: A Pre-Structuralist Danger?" *Journal of British Cinema and Television* 8, no. 1 (2011): 102–103.
2. McKee, "Which Is the Best?," n.p.
3. Ibid., n.p.
4. Charlotte Brunsdon, "Problems with Quality," *Screen* 31, no. 1 (1990): 90.
5. Jason Jacobs "Issues of Judgement and Value in Television Studies," *International Journal of Cultural Studies* 4, no. 4 (2001): 427–47.
6. In addition to the above references, see John Caughie, *Television Drama: Realism, Modernism, and British Culture* (Oxford: Oxford University Press, 2000), 226–33; Jason Jacobs, "Television Aesthetics: An Infantile Disorder," *Journal of British Cinema and Television* 3, no. 1 (May 2006): 19–33; Sarah Cardwell, "Is Quality Television Any Good? Generic Distinctions, Evaluations, and the Troubling Matter of Critical Judgment," in *Quality TV: Contemporary American Television and Beyond*, ed. Janet McCabe and Kim Akass (London: I. B. Tauris, 2007), 19–34.
7. See, for example, Jacobs, "Issues of Judgement and Value"; Hills, "Television Aesthetics," 112; as well as Christine Geraghty, "Aesthetics and Quality in Popular Television Drama," *International Journal of Cultural Studies* 6, no. 1 (2003): 25–45; Jeremy G. Butler, *Television Style* (New York: Routledge, 2009), 19; Jason Mittell, *Complex TV: The Poetics of Contemporary Television Storytelling* (New York: New York University Press, 2015), 206–232.
8. For more recent statements of this premise in the context of television studies, see Hills, "Television Aesthetics"; and Mittell, *Complex TV*, 215.
9. The parenthetical here is intended to flag my assumption that evaluating claims for truth can be done in the absence of confirmation or verification. As I discuss later, I am happy to allow that objective judgments of value are always *theoretically* open to revision. For simplicity, however, I will, from this point, refer to "truth" rather than "(approximate) truth."
10. Arguments for the pluralism of value have, of course, been made in television and cultural studies, but they have also been made in the philosophy of art. See, for example, John Frow, *Cultural Studies and Cultural Value* (Oxford: Oxford University Press, 1995); George Dickie, *Evaluating Art* (Philadelphia, PA: Temple University Press, 1988); Robert Stecker, *Artworks: Definition, Meaning, Value* (University Park, PA: Pennsylvania State University Press, 1997); George Dickie, *Art and Value* (Malden, MA: Blackwell, 2001).
11. For an example of a recent endorsement of this premise, see Butler, *Television Style*, 19. According to Butler, "until television studies develops an aesthetic system that goes beyond taste and dominant culture norms, we must admit that semiotics, postmodernism, Foucault, and Bourdieu ... are correct to caution us about the hazards of television evaluation."
12. One can find different versions of expressivism in all sorts of different art contexts. For an excellent background discussion, see Robert Stecker, "Value in Art," in *The Oxford Handbook of Aesthetics*, ed. Jerrold Levinson (Oxford: Oxford University Press, 2003), 307–24.
13. Michael Z. Newman and Elena Levine, *Legitimating Television: Media Convergence and Cultural Status* (New York: Routledge, 2012), 6. In this passage, they are quoting Pierre Bourdieu, whose work I shall not address directly here, because the complexities within it and its reception in television studies demand a distinct paper. However, it is worth mentioning in passing that Bourdieu's

understanding of the aesthetic has been subject to devastating objections in both cultural studies and philosophy of art. See Frow, *Cultural Studies and Cultural Value*, 27–47; Richard Shusterman, *Pragmatist Aesthetics: Living Beauty, Rethinking Art* (Oxford: Blackwell, 1992), especially 169–200; and Nick Zangwill, *The Metaphysics of Beauty* (Ithaca, NY: Cornell University Press, 2001), 207–17.
14. Newman and Levine, *Legitimating Television*, 6.
15. Ibid., 7.
16. See, for example, Dabney Townsend, *Hume's Aesthetic Theory* (New York: Routledge, 2001), 210–15.
17. See, for example, A. J. Ayer, *Language, Truth, and Logic* (Hammondsworth, UK: Penguin, 1971 [1936]), 150.
18. David Bianculli, "25 Years Later *The Singing Detective* Still Shines," *Bianculli's Blog* (February 24, 2012). Accessed March 26, 2016. http://www.tvworthwatching.com/post/BIanculli-25-Years-Later-The-Singing-Detective-Still-Shines.aspx; Steven Armstrong, "*The Singing Detective:* Addictive and Avant Garde—Even 25 Years On," *The Guardian* TV and Radio blog (February 2, 2012). Accessed March 26, 2016. http://www.guardian.co.uk/tv-and-radio/tvandradioblog/2012/feb/02/singing-detective-addictive-bbc4.
19. Sarah Cardwell, "'Television Aesthetics' and Close Analysis: Style, Mood, and Engagement in *Perfect Strangers* (Stephen Poliakoff, 2001)," in *Style and Meaning: Studies in the Detailed Analysis of Film*, ed. John Gibbs and Douglas Pye (Manchester, UK: Manchester University Press, 2005), 193.
20. See, for a good recent discussion, Daniel A. Kaufman, "Normative Criticism and the Objective Value of Artworks," *Journal of Aesthetics and Art Criticism* 60, no. 2 (Spring 2002): 151–66.
21. Mittell, *Complex TV*, 207.
22. Ibid., 226.
23. Ibid., 208.
24. Ibid., 208.
25. John W. Bender, "Realism, Supervenience, and Irresolvable Aesthetic Disputes," *Journal of Aesthetics and Art Criticism* 54, no. 4 (Autumn 1996): 377.
26. Arnold Isenberg, "Critical Communication," *The Philosophical Review* 58, no. 4 (1949): 341.
27. Ibid., 336.
28. Joe Zeccardi, "Rethinking Critical Communication," *Journal of Aesthetics and Art Criticism* 68, no. 4 (Fall 2010): 370.
29. Isenberg, "Critical Communication," 330.
30. Ibid.
31. Mittell, *Complex TV*, 215, 217.
32. Zeccardi, "Rethinking Critical Communication," 369.
33. Ibid.
34. Isenberg, "Critical Communication," 332.
35. Ibid., 338.
36. James Shelley, "Critical Compatibilism," in *Knowing Art: Essays in Aesthetics and Epistemology*, ed. Matthew Kieran and Dominic McIver Lopes (Dordrecht, Netherlands: Springer, 2004), 126.
37. Isenberg, "Critical Communication," 338.
38. Ibid., 336.

39. Frank Sibley, "Aesthetic and Non-aesthetic," in *Approach to Aesthetics*, ed. John Benson, Betty Redfern, and Jeremy Roxbee Cox (Oxford: Oxford University Press, 2001), 40.
40. For a discussion, see Robert Hopkins, "Critical Reasoning and Critical Perception," in *Knowing Art*, ed. Matthew Kieran and Dominic McIver Lopes (Dordrecht, Netherlands: Springer, 2004).
41. Ibid., 138.
42. Ibid., 137.
43. Kaufman, "Normative Criticism," 151.
44. Mittell, *Complex TV*, 207–208.
45. C. I. Lewis, *An Analysis of Knowledge and Valuation* (La Salle, IL: Open Court, 1962 [1946]), 376.
46. Mittell, *Complex TV*, 232.
47. Noël Carroll, *On Criticism* (New York: Routledge, 2009), 180–89; Stecker, *Artworks: Definition, Meaning, Value*; Stephen Davies, "Replies to Arguments Suggesting that Critics' Strong Evaluations could not be Soundly Deduced," in *Philosophical Perspectives on Art* (Oxford: Oxford University Press, 2007), 207–224.
48. Geraghty, "Aesthetics and Quality."
49. Kaufman, "Normative Criticism," 156.
50. Amie Thomasson, "Artifacts and Human Concepts," in *Creations of the Mind: Artifacts and Their Representations*, ed. Eric Margolis and Stephen Laurence (Oxford: Oxford University Press, 2007), 62.
51. The structure of this argument is borrowed from the one developed in Carroll, *On Criticism*, 167.
52. See, for example, Nelson Goodman, *Languages of Art* (Indianapolis, IN: Hackett, 1976); Dickie, *Evaluating Art*.
53. Berys Gaut, *A Philosophy of Cinematic Art* (Cambridge: Cambridge University Press, 2010), 286.
54. Sarah Banet-Weiser and Laura Portwood-Stacer, "'I Just Want to Be Me Again!' Beauty Pageants, Reality Television, and Post-Feminism," *Feminist Theory* 7, no. 2 (August 2006): 269. Also see Alice Marwick, "There's a Beautiful Girl under All of This: Performing Hegemonic Femininity in Reality Television," *Critical Studies in Media Communication* 27, no. 3 (2010): 251–66.
55. Elsewhere I have argued that sometimes ethical flaws create artistic value. See Ted Nannicelli, "Moderate Comic Immoralism and the Genetic Approach to the Ethical Criticism of Art," *Journal of Aesthetics and Art Criticism* 72, no. 2 (Spring 2014): 169–79.
56. This discussion is particularly informed by Noël Carroll, "Moderate Moralism," *British Journal of Aesthetics* 36, no. 3 (July 1996): 223–38; and Marcia Muelder Eaton, *Merit, Aesthetic and Ethical* (Oxford: Oxford University Press, 2001). Feminist scholars, in particular, might be interested in an excellent discussion that my present argument parallels in some ways: A. W. Eaton, "Where Aesthetics and Ethics Meet: Titian's *Rape of Europa*," *Hypatia* 18, no. 4 (November 2003): 159–88.
57. See, for an example of discussion in the popular press, Lindy West, "*Celebrity Swan* is the Most Depressing Television Program Ever Conceived," *Jezebel* (February 20, 2013). Accessed February 1, 2016. http://jezebel.com/5985698/celebrity-swan-is-the-most-depressing-television-program-ever-conceived.

58. Hills, "Television Aesthetics," 100.
59. Ibid., 105.
60. Ibid., 99. The concern Hills expresses seems be the same sort of worry Newman and Levine have about "authentic and autonomous value.'" *Legitimating Television*, 6.
61. Monroe Beardsley, "Intrinsic Value," *Philosophy and Phenomenological Research* 26 (1965): 1–17.
62. C. I, Lewis, *An Analysis of Knowledge and Valuation* (LaSalle, IL: Open Court, 1962), 434.
63. Ibid., 432.
64. Hills, "Television Aesthetics," 111–12.
65. See, for example, the discussion of inherent value in Stecker, *Artworks: Definition, Meaning, Value*, 251–52.
66. Dickie, *Evaluating Art*.

Bibliography

Allen, Robert C. *Speaking of Soap Operas*. Chapel Hill: University of North Carolina Press, 1985.

———, ed. *To Be Continued: Soap Operas around the World*. London: Routledge, 1995.

Ang, Ien. *Watching Dallas: Soap Opera and the Melodramatic Imagination*. Translated by Della Couling. New York: Routledge, 1989.

Armstrong, Steven. "*The Singing Detective:* Addictive and Avant Garde—Even 25 Years On," *The Guardian* (TV and Radio Blog) (February 2, 2012). Accessed March 26, 2016). http://www.guardian.co.uk/tv-and-radio/tvandradioblog/2012/feb/02/singing-detective-addictive-bbc4.

Ayer, A. J. *Language, Truth, and Logic*. Hammondsworth, UK: Penguin, 1971 [1936].

Bacharach, Sondra, and Deborah Tollefsen. "We Did It: From Mere Contributors to Coauthors." *Journal of Aesthetics and Art Criticism* 68, no. 1 (Winter 2010): 23–32.

Bacon-Smith, Camille. *Enterprising Women: Television Fandom and the Creation of Popular Myth*. Philadelphia: University of Pennsylvania Press, 1992.

Baggini, Julian, and Peter S. Forsi. *The Philosopher's Toolkit: A Compendium of Philosophical Concepts and Methods*. Malden, MA: Blackwell, 2003.

Baker, Lynne Rudder. *Naturalism and the First-Person Perspective*. Oxford: Oxford University Press, 2013.

Banet-Weiser, Sarah, and Laura Portwood-Stacer. "'I Just Want to Be Me Again!' Beauty Pageants, Reality Television, and Post-Feminism." *Feminist Theory* 7, no. 2 (August 2006): 255–72.

Barthes, Roland. "From Work to Text." In *The Rustle of Language*. Translated by Richard Howard, 56–64. Berkeley: University of California Press, 1989.

Baum, Gary. "What Really Happened on HBO's *Luck*—And Why Nobody Was Held Accountable." *The Hollywood Reporter* (November 25, 2013). Accessed December 16, 2014. http://www.hollywoodreporter.com/feature/what-really-happened-on-hbos-luck-and-why-nobody-was-held-accountable.html.

Beardsley, Monroe. "Intrinsic Value." *Philosophy and Phenomenological Research* 26 (1965): 1–17.

Bender, John W. "Realism, Supervenience, and Irresolvable Aesthetic Disputes." *Journal of Aesthetics and Art Criticism* 54, no. 4 (Autumn 1996): 371–81.

Bennett, Tony. "Texts, Readers, Reading Formations." *Bulletin of the Midwest Modern Language Association* 16, no. 1 (1983): 3–17.

Berchini, Christina. "A Critical Scholar with a Dirty Little Secret (or Two)." *Inside Higher Ed* (September 25, 2015). Accessed March 3, 2016. https://

www.insidehighered.com/views/2015/09/25/scholar-says-academics-shouldnt-apologize-popular-entertainment-they-personally.

Beston, Paul. "Getting Dirty in Real Time." *The American Spectator* (August 17, 2005). Accessed May 26, 2015. http://spectator.org/articles/48189/getting-dirty-real-time.

Bianculli, David. "25 Years Later *The Singing Detective* Still Shines." *Bianculli's Blog* (February 24, 2012). Accessed March 26, 2016. http://www.tvworthwatching.com/post/BIanculli-25–Years-Later-The-Singing-Detective-Still-Shines.aspx.

Binkley, Timothy. "Piece: Contra Aesthetics." *Journal of Aesthetics and Art Criticism* 35, no. 3 (Spring 1977): 265–77.

Blanchet, Robert, and Margrethe Bruun Vaage. "Don, Peggy, and Other Fictional Friends? Engaging with Characters in Television Series." *Projections: The Journal for Movies and Mind* 6, no. 2 (Winter 2012): 18–41.

Bloom. Paul. "Water as an Artifact Kind." In *Creations of the Mind: Theories of Artifacts and Their Representation*, edited by Eric Margolis and Stephen Laurence, 150–56. Oxford: Oxford University Press, 2007.

Booth, Wayne C. *The Rhetoric of Fiction*. 2nd ed. Chicago, IL: University of Chicago Press, 1983.

Bordwell, David. "Convention, Construction, and Cinematic Vision." In *Post-Theory: Reconstructing Film Studies*, edited by David Bordwell and Noël Carroll, 87–107. Madison: University of Wisconsin Press, 1996.

———. *Making Meaning: Inference and Rhetoric in the Interpretation of Cinema*. Cambridge, MA: Harvard University Press, 1989.

———. *Narration in the Fiction Film*. Madison: University of Wisconsin Press, 1985.

Bourdon, Jérôme. "Live Television is Still Alive: On Television as an Unfulfilled Promise." *Media, Culture & Society* 22, no. 5 (2000): 531–56.

Bowers, Jeremy, Adam Cole, Danny DeBelius, Christopher Groskopf, and Alyson Hurt. "Previously, on *Arrested Development*." NPR.org. May 18, 2013. Accessed March 14, 2016. http://apps.npr.org/arrested-development/.

Bratman, Michael E. *Intention, Plans, and Practical Reason*. Cambridge, MA: Harvard University Press, 1987.

———. "Reflection, Planning, and Temporally Extended Agency." *The Philosophical Review* 109, no. 1 (January 2000): 35–61.

———. *Shared Agency*. Oxford: Oxford University Press, 2014.

———. "Shared Cooperative Activity." In *Faces of Intention: Selected Essays on Intention and Agency*, edited by Michael E. Bratman, 93–108. Cambridge, UK: Cambridge University Press.

Brown, Lane. "In Conversation: Vince Gilligan on the End of *Breaking Bad*." *Vulture* (May 12, 2013). Accessed May 29, 2015. http://www.vulture.com/2013/05/vince-gilligan-on-breaking-bad.html.

Brunsdon, Charlotte. "Problems with Quality." *Screen* 31, no. 1 (1990): 67–90.

———. "Text and Audience." In *Remote Control: Television, Audiences, and Cultural Power*, edited by Ellen Seiter, Hans Borchers, Gabriele Kreutzner, and Eva-Maria Warth, 116–29. New York: Routledge, 1989.

Buckingham, David. *Public Secrets: East Enders and its Audiences*. London: BFI, 1987.

Budd, Malcolm. *The Aesthetic Appreciation of Nature*. Oxford: Oxford University Press, 2002.

Bury, Rhiannon. "Praise You Like I Should: Cyber Fans and *Six Feet Under*." In *It's Not TV: Watching HBO in the Post-Television Era*, edited by Marc Leverette, Brian L. Ott, and Cara Louise Buckley, 190–208. New York: Routledge, 2008.

Butler, Jeremy G. *Television: Critical Methods and Applications*. 4th ed. New York: Routledge, 2012.

———. *Television Style*. New York: Routledge, 2009.

Caldwell, John Thornton. "Authorship Below-the-Line." In *A Companion to Media Authorship*, edited by Jonathan Gray and Derek Johnson, 347–69. Malden, MA: Wiley-Blackwell, 2013.

———. "Convergence Television: Aggregating Form and Repurposing Content in the Culture of Conglomeration." In *Television After TV: Essays on a Medium in Transition*, edited by Lynn Spigel and Jan Olsson, 41–74. Durham, NC: Duke University Press, 2004.

———. *Televisuality: Style, Crisis, and Authority in American Television*. New Brunswick, NJ: Rutgers University Press, 1995.

———. *Production Culture: Industrial Reflexivity and Critical Practice in Film and Television*. Durham, NC: Duke University Press, 2008.

Cardwell, Sarah. *Andrew Davies*. Manchester, UK: Manchester University Press, 2005.

———. "Is Quality Television Any Good? Generic Distinctions, Evaluations, and the Troubling Matter of Critical Judgment." In *Quality TV: Contemporary American Television and Beyond*, edited by Janet McCabe and Kim Akass, 19–34. London: I.B. Tauris, 2007.

———. "Television Aesthetics." *Critical Studies in Television* 1, no. 1 (2006): 72–80.

———. "Television Aesthetics: Stylistic Analysis and Beyond." In *Television Aesthetics and Style*, edited by Jason Jacobs and Steven Peacock, 23–44. London: Bloomsbury, 2013.

———. "'Television Aesthetics' and Close Analysis: Style, Mood, and Engagement in *Perfect Strangers* (Stephen Poliakoff, 2001)." In *Style and Meaning: Studies in the Detailed Analysis of Film*, edited by John Gibbs and Douglas Pye, 179–94. Manchester, UK: Manchester University Press, 2005.

———. "Television amongst Friends: Medium, Art, Media." *Critical Studies in Television* 9, no. 3 (Autumn 2014): 6–21.

Carney, Timothy P. "I am Jack Bauer: What 24 Means for Homeland Security." *The National Review* (June 26, 2006). Accessed May 26, 2015. http://www.nationalreview.com/article/218042/i-am-jack-bauer-timothy-p-carney.

Carroll, Noël. "Anglo-American Aesthetics and Contemporary Criticism: Intention and the Hermeneutics of Suspicion." In *Beyond Aesthetics*, 180–90. Cambridge, UK: Cambridge University Press, 2001.

———. "Art, Creativity, and Tradition." In *Art in Three Dimensions*, 53–73. Oxford: Oxford University Press, 2010.

———. "Art, Practice, and Narrative." In *Beyond Aesthetics*, 63–75. Cambridge, UK: Cambridge University Press, 2001.

———. *Comedy Incarnate: Buster Keaton, Physical Humor, and Bodily Coping*. Malden, MA: Blackwell, 2009.

———. "Defining the Moving Image." In *Theorizing the Moving Image*, 49–74. Cambridge, UK: Cambridge University Press, 1996.

———. "Engaging Critics." *Film Studies: An International Review* 8 (Summer 2006): 161–69.
———. "Film, Attention, and Communication: A Naturalistic Account." In *Engaging the Moving Image*, 10–58. New Haven, CT: Yale University Press, 2003.
———. "Forget the Medium!" In *Engaging the Moving Image*, 1–9. New Haven, CT: Yale University Press, 2003.
———. "Identifying Art." In *Beyond Aesthetics* (Cambridge, UK: Cambridge University Press, 2001), 75–100.
———. "Interpretation and Intention: The Debate between Hypothetical and Actual Intentionalism." In *Beyond Aesthetics*, 197–213. Cambridge, UK: Cambridge University Press, 2001.
———. "Moderate Moralism." *British Journal of Aesthetics* 36, no. 3 (July 1996): 223–38.
———. *On Criticism*. New York: Routledge, 2009.
———. *A Philosophy of Mass Art*. Oxford: Clarendon Press, 1988.
———. *The Philosophy of Motion Pictures*. Malden, MA: Blackwell, 2008.
———. "TV and Film: A Philosophical Perspective." In *Engaging the Moving Image*, 265–80. New Haven, CT: Yale University Press, 2003.
Caughie, John. *Television Drama: Realism, Modernism, and British Culture*. Oxford: Oxford University Press, 2000.
Cavell, Stanley. "The Fact of Television." *Daedalus* 111, no. 4 (Fall 1982): 75–96.
———. "A Matter of Meaning It." In *Must We Mean What We Say?*, updated ed., 213–37. Cambridge, UK: Cambridge University Press, 2002.
Cohen, Ted. "Television: Contemporary Thought." In *Encyclopedia of Aesthetics*, vol. 4, edited by Michael Kelly, 369–70. Oxford: Oxford University Press, 1998.
Conor, Bridget. *Screenwriting: Creative Labor and Professional Practice*. New York: Routledge, 2014.
Couldry, Nick. *Inside Culture: Re-imagining the Method of Cultural Studies*. London: Sage, 2000.
Creeber, Glen. "The Joy of Text? Television and Textual Analysis." *Critical Studies in Television* 1, no. 1 (2006): 81–88.
———. *Serial Television: Big Drama on the Small Screen*. London: BFI, 2005.
———. *Small Screen Aesthetics: From Television to the Internet*. London: BFI, 2013.
Curran, Angela. "Medium-Involving Explanations and the Philosophy of Film." *British Journal of Aesthetics* 52, no. 2 (April 2012): 191–95.
Currie, Gregory. *Image and Mind: Film, Philosophy, and Cognitive Science*. Cambridge, UK: Cambridge University Press, 1995.
Cutting, James, and Manfredo Massironi. "Pictures and Their Special Status in Perceptual and Cognitive Inquiry." In *Perception and Cognition at Century's End*, edited by Julian Hochberg, 137–68. New York: Academic Press, 1998.
D'Addario, Daniel. "Aaron Sorkin Gets More Sexist Every Year." *Salon* (September 10, 2013). http://www.salon.com/2013/09/09/aaron_sorkin_gets_more_sexist_every_year/.
Danto, Arthur C. *The Transfiguration of the Commonplace*. Cambridge, MA: Harvard University Press, 1981.
Davies, David. "Against Enlightened Empiricism." In *Contemporary Debates in the Aesthetics and Philosophy of Art*, edited by Matthew Kieran, 6–36. Malden, MA: Blackwell, 2006.
———. *Art as Performance*. Malden, MA: Blackwell, 2004.

———. "Categories of Art." In *The Routledge Companion to Aesthetics*. 3rd ed., edited by Berys Gaut and Dominic McIver Lopes, 224–34. New York: Routledge, 2013.

———. "Ontology." In *The Routledge Companion to Philosophy and Film*, edited by Paisley Livingston and Carl Plantinga, 217–26. New York: Routledge, 2009.

Davies, Stephen. *Definitions of Art*. Ithaca, NY: Cornell University Press, 1991.

———. "Ontology of Art." In *The Oxford Handbook of Aesthetics*, edited by Jerrold Levinson, 155–80. Oxford: Oxford University Press, 2005.

———. "Replies to Arguments Suggesting that Critics' Strong Evaluations Could Not Be Soundly Deduced." In *Philosophical Perspectives on Art*, 207–24. Oxford: Oxford University Press, 2007.

———. "True Interpretations." In *Philosophical Perspectives on Art*, 191–97. Oxford: Oxford University Press, 2007.

Devitt, Michael, and Kim Sterelny. *Language and Reality*. 2nd ed. Cambridge, MA: MIT Press, 1999.

Dewey, John. *Art as Experience*. New York: Penguin, 2005 [1934].

Dhoest, Alexander, and Nele Simmons. "Still TV: On the Resilience of an Old Medium." *European Journal of Media Studies* 2, no. 1 (2013): 19–34.

Dickie, George. *Art and Value*. Malden, MA: Blackwell, 2001.

———. *The Art Circle*. New York: Haven Publications, 1984.

———. *Evaluating Art*. Philadelphia, PA: Temple University, 1988.

Dowler, Kevin. "Television and Objecthood: The 'Place' of Television in Television Studies." *Topia: Canadian Journal of Cultural Studies* 8 (Fall 2002): 43–60.

Eaton, A. W. "Where Aesthetics and Ethics Meet: Titian's *Rape of Europa*." *Hypatia* 18, no. 4 (November 2003): 159–88.

Eaton, Marcia Muelder. *Merit, Aesthetic and Ethical*. Oxford: Oxford University Press, 2001.

Eco, Umberto. "Towards a Semiotic Inquiry into the Television Message." Reprinted in *Television: Critical Concepts in Media and Cultural Studies*, vol. 2, edited by Toby Miller, 3–19. New York: Routledge, 2003.

Egan, Andy. "Projectivism without Error." In *Perceiving the World*, edited by Bence Nanay, 68–96. Oxford: Oxford University Press, 2010.

Ellis, John. *Visible Fictions*. London: Routledge, 1982.

Feuer, Jane. "The Concept of Live Television: Ontology as Ideology." In *Regarding Television: Critical Approaches*, edited by E. Ann Kaplan, 12–22. Los Angeles, CA: American Film Institute, 1983.

———. "Reading *Dynasty*: Television and Reception Theory." In *Classical Hollywood Narrative: The Paradigm Wars*, edited by Jane Gaines, 275–93. Durham, NC: Duke University Press, 1992.

Fiske, John. "Moments of Television: Neither the Text Nor the Audience." In *Remote Control: Television, Audiences, and Cultural Power*, edited by Ellen Seiter, Hans Borchers, Gabriele Kreutzner, and Eva-Maria Warth, 56–78. New York: Routledge, 1989.

———. *Television Culture*. New York: Routledge, 1987.

Fiske, John, and John Hartley. *Reading Television*. London: Methuen, 1978.

Foucault, Michel. "What Is an Author?" In *Language, Counter-Memory, Practice: Selected Essays and Interviews*, edited by Donald F. Bouchard. Translated by Donald F. Bouchard and Sherry Simon, 113–138. Ithaca, NY: Cornell University Press, 1977.

Frow, John. *Cultural Studies and Cultural Value*. Oxford: Oxford University Press, 1995.
Gaut, Berys. *Art, Emotion, and Ethics*. Oxford: Oxford University Press, 2007.
———. "'Art' as a Cluster Concept," in *Theories of Art Today*, edited by Noël Carroll 25–44. Madison, WI: University of Wisconsin Press, 2000.
———. "Film Authorship and Collaboration." In *Film Theory and Philosophy*, edited by Richard Allen and Murray Smith, 149–72. Oxford: Oxford University Press, 1997.
———. *A Philosophy of Cinematic Art*. Cambridge, UK: Cambridge University Press, 2010.
———. "Replies to Ponech, Curran, and Allen." *British Journal of Aesthetics* 52, no. 2 (April 2012): 201–8.
Genette, Gérard. *Paratexts: Thresholds of Interpretation*. Translated by Jane E. Lewin. Cambridge, UK: Cambridge University Press, 1997.
Geraghty, Christine. "Aesthetics and Quality in Popular Television Drama." *International Journal of Cultural Studies* 6, no. 1 (2003): 25–45.
———. *Women and Soap Opera: A Study of Prime Time Soaps*. Cambridge, UK: Polity, 1991.
Gombrich, E. H. *Art and Illusion: A Study in the Psychology of Pictorial Representation*. New York: Pantheon, 1960.
———. *The Image and the Eye: Further Studies in the Psychology of Pictorial Representation*. London: Phaidon, 1982.
Goodman, Nelson. *Languages of Art*. Indianapolis, IN: Hackett, 1976.
———. *Ways of Worldmaking*. Indianapolis, IN: Hackett, 1978.
Gorton, Kristyn. *Media Audiences: Television, Meaning, and Emotion*. Edinburgh: Edinburgh University Press, 2009.
Gracyk, Theodore. *Listening to Popular Music: Or, How I Learned to Stop Worrying and Love Led Zeppelin*. Ann Arbor: University of Michigan Press, 2007.
Grant, James. *The Critical Imagination*. Oxford: Oxford University Press, 2013.
Gray, Jonathan. "New Audiences, New Textualities: Anti-Fans and Non-Fans." *International Journal of Cultural Studies* 6, no. 1 (2003): 64–81.
———. *Show Sold Separately: Promos, Spoilers, and Other Media Paratexts*. New York: New York University Press, 2010.
———. *Watching with The Simpsons: Television, Parody, and Intertextuality*. New York: Routledge, 2006.
———. "When Is the Author?" In *A Companion to Media Authorship*, edited by Jonathan Gray and Derek Johnson, 88–111. Malden, MA: Wiley-Blackwell, 2013.
Gray, Jonathan, and Amanda D. Lotz. *Television Studies*. London: Polity, 2012.
Gregory, R. L. *Eye and Brain: The Psychology of Seeing*. 5th ed. Princeton, NJ: Princeton University Press, 1997.
Grice, H. P. "Meaning." *The Philosophical Review* 66, no. 3 (July 1957): 377–88.
Gripsrud, Jostein. *The Dynasty Years: Hollywood Television and Critical Media Studies*. London: Routledge, 1995.
Grodal, Torben. "Agency in Film, Filmmaking, and Reception." In *Visual Authorship: Creativity and Intentionality in Media*, edited by Torben Kragh Grodal, Bente Larsen, and Iben Thorving Laursen, 15–36. Copenhagen, Denmark: Museum Tusculanum Press, 2005.
Hall, Stuart. "Encoding/Decoding." Reprinted in *Television: Critical Concepts in Media and Cultural Studies*, vol. 4, edited by Toby Miller, 43–53. New York: Routledge, 2003.

———. "Reflections upon the Encoding/Decoding Model: An Interview with Stuart Hall." In *Viewing, Reading, Listening: Audiences and Cultural Reception*, edited by Jon Cruz and Justin Lewis, 253–74. Boulder, CO: Westview Press, 1994.

Hall, Stuart, and Paddy Whannel. *The Popular Arts*. London: Hutchinson Educational, 1964.

Harrington, C. Lee, and Denise D. Bielby. *Soap Fans: Pursuing Pleasure and Making Meaning in Everyday Life*. Philadelphia: Temple University Press, 1995.

Hartley, John. *A Short History of Cultural Studies*. London: Sage, 2003.

———. *Television Truths: Forms of Knowledge in Popular Culture*. Malden, MA: Blackwell, 2008.

Hatfield, Gary. "Perception as Unconscious Inference." In *Perception and Cognition: Essays in the Philosophy of Psychology*, 124–52. Oxford: Oxford University Press, 2009.

Hayward, Jennifer. *Consuming Pleasures: Active Audiences and Serial Fictions from Dickens to Soap Opera*. Lexington: University of Kentucky Press, 1997.

Heath, Stephen. "Representing Television." In *Logics of Television: Essays in Cultural Criticism*. edited by Patricia Mellencamp, 267–302. Bloomington: Indiana University Press, 1990.

Henze, Donald F. "Is the Work of Art a Construct? A Reply to Professor Pepper." *The Journal of Philosophy* 52, no. 16 (1955): 433–39.

Herman, David. *Storytelling and the Sciences of Mind*. Cambridge, MA: MIT Press, 2013.

Hick, Darren Hudson. "A Reply to Paisley Livingston." *Journal of Aesthetics and Art Criticism* 66, no. 4 (2008): 393–98.

———. "When Is a Work of Art Finished?" *Journal of Aesthetics and Art Criticism* 66, no. 1 (2008): 67–76.

Hills, Matt. "Cult TV, Quality and the Role of the Episode/Programme Guide." In *The Contemporary Television Series*, edited by Michael Hammond and Lucy Mazdon, 190–207. Edinburgh: Edinburgh University Press, 2005.

———. *Doctor Who: The Unfolding Event—Marketing, Merchandising, and Mediatizing a Brand Anniversary*. Basingstoke, UK: Palgrave Macmillan, 2015.

———. "Television Aesthetics: A Pre-Structuralist Danger?" *Journal of British Cinema and Television* 8, no. 1 (April 2011): 99–117.

———. "Television and Its Audience: Issues of Consumption and Reception." In *Tele-Visions: An Introduction to Studying Television*, edited by Glen Creeber, 93–106. London: BFI, 2006.

———. *Triumph of a Time Lord: Regenerating Doctor Who in the Twenty-First Century*. London: I. B. Tauris, 2010.

Hilpinen, Risto. "On Artifacts and Works of Art." *Theoria* 58 (1992): 58–82.

Hirsch, E. D. *Validity in Interpretation*. New Haven, CT: Yale University Press, 1967.

Hochberg, Julian. "The Perception of Pictorial Representations." *Social Research* 51, no. 4 (Winter 1984): 841–862.

Hopkins, Robert. "Critical Reasoning and Critical Perception." In *Knowing Art: Essays in Aesthetics and Epistemology*, edited by Matthew Kieran and Dominic McIver Lopes, 137–53. Dordrecht, Netherlands: Springer, 2004.

———. *Picture, Image, and Experience: A Philosophical Inquiry*. Cambridge, UK: Cambridge University Press, 1998.

Irwin, William. "Authorial Declaration and Extreme Actual Intentionalism: Is Dumbledore Gay?" *Journal of Aesthetics and Art Criticism* 73, no. 2 (Spring 2015): 141–47.

———. *Intentionalist Interpretation: A Philosophical Exploration and Defense*. Westport, CT: Greenwood Press, 1999.
Iseminger, Gary. "Aesthetic Appreciation." *Journal of Aesthetics and Art Criticism* 39, no. 4 (Summer 1981): 389–97.
———. *The Aesthetic Function of Art*. Ithaca, NY: Cornell University Press, 2004.
Isenberg, Arnold. "Critical Communication." *The Philosophical Review* 58, no. 4 (1949): 330–44.
Jacobs, Jason. Body Trauma TV: The New Hospital Dramas (London: BFI, 2003).
———. *Deadwood*. London: BFI, 2012.
———. *The Intimate Screen: Early British Television Drama*. Oxford: Oxford University Press, 2000.
———. "Issues of Judgement and Value in Television Studies." *International Journal of Cultural Studies* 4, no. 4 (2001): 427–47.
———. "Television Aesthetics: An Infantile Disorder." *Journal of British Cinema and Television* 3, no. 1 (2006): 19–33.
———. "Television, Interrupted: Pollution or Aesthetic?" In *Television as Digital Media*, edited by James Bennett and Nicki Strange, 255–80. Durham, NC: Duke University Press, 2011.
———. "*True Detective* and Practical Criticism." *CST Online* (April 11, 2014). Accessed February 18, 2015. http://cstonline.tv/true-detective-and-practical-criticism.
Jacobs Jason and Steven Peacock, eds., *Television Aesthetics and Style*. New York: Bloomsbury, 2013.
James, William. *Pragmatism*. New York: Longmans, Green, and Co., 1907.
Jarrett, James L. "More on Professor Pepper's Theory of the Aesthetic Object." *The Journal of Philosophy* 49, no. 14 (1952): 475–78.
Jenkins, Henry. *Textual Poachers: Television Fans and Participatory Culture*. New York: Routledge, 1992.
Johnson, Richard. "What Is Cultural Studies, Anyway?" *Social Text* 16 (1986–1987): 38–80.
Jones, Sarah Gwenllian. "The Sex Lives of Cult Television Characters." *Screen* 43, no. 1 (Spring 2002): 79–90.
Jullier, Laurent. "Specificity, Medium II." In *The Routledge Encyclopedia of Film Theory*, edited by Edward Branigan and Warren Buckland, 442–45. New York: Routledge, 2014.
Kaufman, Daniel A. "Normative Criticism and the Objective Value of Artworks." *Journal of Aesthetics and Art Criticism* 60, no. 2 (Spring 2002): 151–66.
Kieran, Matthew. "The Vice of Snobbery: Aesthetic Knowledge, Justification, and Virtue in Art Appreciation." *The Philosophical Quarterly* 60, no. 239 (April 2010): 243–63.
Kim, Richard. "Pop Torture." *The Nation* (December 7, 2005). Accessed May 27, 2015. http://www.thenation.com/article/pop-torture.
Kornhaber, Spencer, Christopher Orr, and Amy Sullivan. "The *True Detective* Finale: That's It?" *The Atlantic* (March 10, 2014). Accessed February 19, 2015. http://www.theatlantic.com/entertainment/archive/2014/03/the-em-true-detective-em-finale-thats-it/284312/.
Krausz, Michael. *Rightness and Reasons: Interpretation in Cultural Practices*. Ithaca, NY: Cornell University Press, 1993.
Kulvicki, John. *Images*. New York: Routledge, 2014.
———. *On Images: Their Structure and Content*. Oxford: Oxford University Press, 2006.

Kutz, Christopher. "Acting Together." *Philosophy and Phenomenological Research* 61, no. 1 (July 2000): 1–31.

Lamarque, Peter. "The Death of the Author: An Analytical Autopsy." *British Journal of Aesthetics* 30, no. 4 (1990): 319–31.

———. *Work and Object: Explorations in the Metaphysics of Art*. Oxford: Oxford University Press, 2010.

LaMarre, Heather L., Kristen D. Landreville, and Michael A. Beam. "The Irony of Satire: Political Ideology and the Motivation to See What You Want to See in *The Colbert Report*." *The International Journal of Press/Politics* 14, no. 2 (April 2009): 212–31.

Laycock, Joseph. "*True Detective* vs. H. P. Lovecraft's 'Cosmic Horror.'" *Salon.com* (March 17, 2014). Accessed February 19, 2015. http://www.salon.com/2014/03/16/the_dangerous_mythology_of_true_detective_partner/.

Levinson, Jerrold. "Artworks as Artifacts." In *Creations of the Mind: Artifacts and Their Representation*, edited by Eric Margolis and Stephen Laurence, 74–82. Oxford: Oxford University Press, 2007.

———. "Defining Art Historically." In *Music, Art, and Metaphysics*, 3–25. Ithaca, NY: Cornell University Press, 1990.

———. "Extending Art Historically." In *The Pleasures of Aesthetics*, 150–71. Ithaca, NY: Cornell University Press, 1996.

———. "Hypothetical Intentionalism: Statement, Objections, and Replies." In *Contemplating Art*, 302–11. Oxford: Oxford University Press, 2006.

———. "Intention and Interpretation in Literature." In *The Pleasures of Aesthetics*, 175–213. Ithaca, NY: Cornell University Press, 1996.

———. "Refining Art Historically." In *Music, Art, and Metaphysics*, 37–59. Ithaca, NY: Cornell University Press, 1990.

———. "What a Musical Work Is, Again." In *Music, Art, and Metaphysics*, 231–47. Ithaca, NY: Cornell University Press, 1990.

Lewis, C[larence] I. *An Analysis of Knowledge and Valuation*. LaSalle, IL: Open Court, 1962 [1946].

Lewis, David. "Truth in Fiction." *American Philosophical Quarterly* 15, no. 1 (January 1978): 37–46.

Livingston, Paisley. *Art and Intention: A Philosophical Study*. Oxford: Oxford University Press, 2005.

———. "Authorship." In *The Routledge Companion to the Philosophy of Literature*, edited by Noël Carroll and John Gibson. New York: Routledge (forthcoming).

———. *Cinema, Philosophy, Bergman: On Film as Philosophy*. Oxford: Oxford University Press, 2009.

———. "From Text to Work." In *After Post-Structuralism: Interdisciplinarity and Literary Theory*, edited by Nancy Easterlin and Barbara Riebling, 91–104. Evanston, IL: Northwestern University Press, 1993.

———. "History of the Ontology of Art." *Stanford Encyclopedia of Philosophy*, edited by Edward N. Zalta (Summer 2013 edition). Accessed July 24, 2014. http://plato.stanford.edu/entries/art-ontology-history/.

———. *Literary Knowledge: Humanistic Inquiry and the Philosophy of Science*. Ithaca, NY: Cornell University Press, 1988.

———. "On Authorship and Collaboration." *Journal of Aesthetics and Art Criticism* 69, no. 2 (Spring 2011): 221–25.

———. "When a Work Is Finished: A Response to Darren Hudson Hick." *Journal of Aesthetics and Art Criticism* 66, no. 4 (2008): 393–98.

Livingstone, Sonia. *Making Sense of Television: The Psychology of Audience Interpretation*. 2nd ed. London: Routledge, 1998.

Logan, Elliott. *Breaking Bad and Dignity: Unity and Fragmentation in the Serial Television Drama*. Basingstoke, UK: Palgrave Macmillan, 2016.

Loofbourow, Lili. "Marty, the Monster." *Los Angeles Review of Books* (March 11, 2014). Accessed February 19, 2015. http://lareviewofbooks.org/essay/true-detective-finale.

Lopes, Dominic McIver. *Beyond Art*. Oxford: Oxford University Press, 2014.

———. "True Appreciation." In *Photography and Philosophy: Essays on the Pencil of Nature*, edited by Scott Walden, 210–30. Malden, MA: Blackwell, 2008.

Lotz, Amanda. *The Television Will Be Revolutionized*. New York: New York University Press, 2007.

Lyons, Margaret. "*The Newsroom* Is Incredibly Hostile toward Women." *Vulture* (July 17, 2012). Accessed March 8, 2016. http://www.vulture.com/2012/07/newsroom-aaron-sorkin-women-hostile-misogyny.html.

Maras, Steven. *Screenwriting: History, Theory, and Practice*. London: Wallflower, 2009.

Margolis, Joseph. *Art and Philosophy*. Atlantic Highlands, NJ: Humanities Press, 1980.

Marriott, Stephanie. *Live Television: Time, Space, and the Broadcast Event*. London: Sage, 2007.

Martinez, Isabel Cecilia. "The Cognitive Reality of Prolongational Structures in Tonal Music. Ph.D. diss, Roehampton University, 2007. Accessed March 11, 2016. http://roehampton.openrepository.com/roehampton/bitstream/10142/107557/1/Isabel%2520Martinez%2520PHD%2520Thesis.pdf.

Marwick, Alice. "There's a Beautiful Girl under All of This: Performing Hegemonic Femininity in Reality Television." *Critical Studies in Media Communication* 27, no. 3 (2010): 251–66.

May, Larry. "Collective Inaction and Shared Responsibility." *Noûs* 24 (1990): 269–278.

Mayer, Jane. "Whatever It Takes: The Politics of the Man behind '24.'" *The New Yorker* (February 19, 2007). Accessed March 24, 2016. http://www.newyorker.com/magazine/2007/02/19/whatever-it-takes.

Mayer, Vicki. *Below the Line: Producers and Production Studies in the New Television Economy*. Durham, NC: Duke University Press, 2008. http://www.vulture.com/2012/07/newsroom-aaron-sorkin-women-hostile-misogyny.html.

McKee, Alan. "How to Tell the Difference between a Stereotype and a Positive Image: Putting *Priscilla, Queen of the Desert* into History." *Screening the Past* 9 (2000). Accessed March 15, 2016. http://www.screeningthepast.com/2014/12/how-to-tell-the-difference-between-a-stereotype-and-a-positive-image-putting%C2%A0priscilla-queen-of-the-desert%C2%A0into-history/.

———. *Textual Analysis*. London: Sage, 2003.

———. "Which is the Best *Dr. Who* story? A Case Study in Value Judgements outside the Academy." *Intensities: The Journal of Cult Media* 1 (2001). Accessed January 20, 2013. http://intensitiescultmedia.wordpress.com/2012/12/11/intensities-1–springsummer-2001/ Accessed January 20, 2013.

Mele, Alfred R. "Conscious Intentions and Decisions." In *Effective Intentions: The Power of Conscious Will*. Oxford: Oxford University Press, 2009.

Mele, Alfred R., and Paul K. Moser. "Intentional Action." *Noûs* 28, no. 1 (1994): 39–68.

Meskin, Aaron. "Authorship." In *The Routledge Companion to Philosophy and Film*, edited by Paisley Livingston and Carl Plaintinga, 12–28. New York: Routledge, 2008.
Messaris, Paul. *Visual Literacy: Image, Mind, and Reality* Boulder, CO: Westview Press, 1994.
Mittell, Jason. *Complex TV: The Poetics of Contemporary Television Storytelling*. New York: New York University Press, 2015.
———. "True Disappointment." *Just TV* (March 10, 2014). Accessed February 19, 2015. https://justtv.wordpress.com/2014/03/10/true-disappointment/.
Monahan, Torin. "Just-in-Time Security: Permanent Exceptions and Neoliberal Orders." In *Reading 24: TV Against the Clock*, edited by Steven Peacock, 109–18. London: I. B. Tauris, 2007.
Morley, David. *The "Nationwide" Audience*. London: BFI, 1980.
Nannicelli, Ted. "Moderate Comic Immoralism and the Genetic Approach to the Ethical Criticism of Art," *Journal of Aesthetics and Art Criticism* 72, no. 2 (Spring 2014): 169–79.
———. "Ontology, Intentionality, and Television Aesthetics." *Screen* 53, no. 2 (Summer 2012): 164–79.
———. *A Philosophy of the Screenplay*. New York: Routledge, 2013.
Nannicelli, Ted, and Malcolm Turvey. "Against 'Post-Cinema.'" *Cinéma & Cie: International Journal of Film Studies* (forthcoming).
Neale, Steve, and Frank Krutnik. *Popular Film and Television Comedy*. London: Routledge, 1990.
Nehamas, Alexander. "The Postulated Author: Critical Monism as a Regulative Ideal." *Critical Inquiry* 8, no. 1 (Autumn 1981): 133–149.
Neisser, Ulric. *Cognitive Psychology*. New York: Appelton-Century-Crofts, 1967.
Nelson, Robin. *TV Drama in Transition: Forms, Values, and Cultural Change*. Basingstoke, UK: Palgrave Macmillan, 1997.
Newall, Michael. *What Is a Picture? Depiction, Realism, Abstraction*. Basingstoke, UK: Palgrave Macmillan, 2011.
Newman, Michael Z., and Elena Levine. *Legitimating Television: Media Convergence and Cultural Status*. New York: Routledge, 2012.
Norman, Joel. "Two Visual Systems and Two Theories of Perception: An Attempt to Reconcile the Constructivist and Ecological Approaches." *Behavioral and Brain Sciences* 25 (2002): 73–144.
Novitz, David. *The Boundaries of Art: A Philosophical Inquiry into the Place of Art in Everyday Life*. Philadelphia, PA: Temple University Press, 1992.
Nussbaum, Emily. "Broken News." *The New Yorker* (June 25, 2012). Accessed March 8, 2016. http://www.newyorker.com/magazine/2012/06/25/broken-news.
———. "Cool Story, Bro." *The New Yorker* (March 3, 2014). Accessed February 18, 2015. http://www.newyorker.com/magazine/2014/03/03/cool-story-bro.
———. "The Disappointing Finale of *True Detective*." *The New Yorker* (March 10, 2014). Accessed February 19, 2015. http://www.newyorker.com/culture/culture-desk/the-disappointing-finale-of-true-detective.
———. "That Mind-Bending Phone Call on Last Night's 'Breaking Bad.'" *The New Yorker* (September 16, 2013). Accessed May 29, 2015. http://www.newyorker.com/culture/culture-desk/that-mind-bending-phone-call-on-last-nights-breaking-bad.
Olsen, Stein Haugom. "Criticism and Appreciation." In *Philosophy and Fiction: Essays in Literary Aesthetics*, edited by Peter Lamarque, 38–51. Aberdeen, UK: Aberdeen University Press, 1983.

———. "Value Judgments in Criticism." *Journal of Aesthetics and Criticism* 42, no. 2 (Winter 1983): 125–36.

O'Regan, Tom. "Transient and Intrinsically Valuable in Their Impermanence: Television's Changing Aesthetic Norms." *LOLA* (December 2012). Accessed March 8, 2016. http://www.lolajournal.com/3/tv.html.

Parrish, John M. "Defining Dilemmas Down: The Case of 24." *Essays in Philosophy* 10, no. 1, Article 7 (January 2009). Accessed May 27, 2015. http://commons.pacificu.edu/eip/vol10/iss1/7/.

Paskin, Willa. "The Horrible Things That Men Do to Women." *Slate* (February 23, 2014). Accessed February 18, 2015. http://www.slate.com/articles/arts/television/2014/02/true_detective_the_women_on_the_show_are_treated_badly_but_there_s_a_good.html.

Peacocke, Christopher. "Depiction." *The Philosophical Review* 96, no. 3 (July 1987): 383–410.

Pepper, Stephen. *The Work of Art*. Bloomington: Indiana University Press, 1955.

Perkins, V. F. *Film as Film: Understanding and Judging Movies*. Harmondsworth, UK: Penguin, 1972.

Petranovich, Sean. "How to Philosophize with a 5 Wood." In *Curb Your Enthusiasm and Philosophy*, edited by Mark Ralkowski, 173–88. Chicago: Carus Publishing, 2012.

Pettersson, Anders. "P. F. Strawson and Stephen Davies on the Ontology of Art: A Critical Discussion." *Organon F: International Journal of Analytic Philosophy* 16, no. 4 (2009): 615–31.

Prince, Stephen. "The Discourse of Pictures: Iconicity and Film Studies." In *Film Theory and Criticism*. 6th ed. Edited by Leo Braudy and Marshall Cohen, 87–105. Oxford: Oxford University Press, 2004.

———. *Firestorm: American Film in the Age of Terrorism*. New York: Columbia University Press, 2009.

Putnum, Hilary. "Is There a Fact of the Matter about Fiction?" In *Realism with a Human Face*, edited by James Conant, 209–13. Cambridge, MA: Harvard University Press, 1990.

Redvall, Eva Novrup. *Writing the Producing the Television Drama in Denmark*. Basingstoke, UK: Palgrave Macmillan, 2013.

Repp, Charles. "What's Wrong with Didacticism?" *British Journal of Aesthetics* 52, no. 3 (July 2012): 271–85.

Robinson, Tasha. "*Firefly*: The Complete Series." *The A.V. Club* (January 12, 2004). Accessed March 22, 2016. http://www.avclub.com/review/firefly-the-complete-series-11623.

Rock, Irvin. *The Logic of Perception*. Cambridge, MA: MIT Press, 1983.

Rudner, Richard. "The Ontological Status of the Esthetic Object." *Philosophy and Phenomenological Research* 10, no. 3 (March 1950): 380–88.

Sadek, José Roberto. *Telenovela: Um olhar do cinema*. São Paulo, Brazil: Summus, 2008.

Saito, Yuriko. *Everyday Aesthetics*. Oxford: Oxford University Press, 2007.

Sandvoss, Cornel. "The Death of the Reader? Literary Theory and the Study of Texts in Popular Culture." In *Fandom: Identities and Communities in a Mediated World*, edited by Jonathan Gray, Cornel Sandvoss, and C. Lee Harrington, 19–32. New York: New York University Press, 2007.

Sarris, Andrew. "Notes on the Auteur Theory in 1962." In *Auteurs and Authorship: A Film Reader*, edited by Barry Keith Grant, 35–45. Malden, MA: Blackwell, 2008.

Scannell, Paddy. *Television and the Meaning of "Live": An Enquiry into the Human Situation*. London: Polity, 2014.
Schier, Flint. *Deeper into Pictures*. Cambridge, UK: Cambridge University Press, 1986.
Schwartz, Robert. "The Role of Inference in Vision." In *Visual Versions*, 95–105. Cambridge, MA: MIT Press, 2006.
Sconce, Jeffrey. "What If? Charting Television's New Textual Boundaries." In *Television After TV*, edited by Lynn Spigel and Jan Olsson, 93–112. Durham, NC: Duke University Press, 2004.
Seaman, William R. "Active Audience Theory: Pointless Populism." *Media, Culture, and Society* 14 (1992): 301–11.
Segal, Lynne. *Straight Sex: Rethinking the Politics of Pleasure*. Berkeley: University of California Press, 1994.
Sellors, C. Paul. "Collective Authorship in Film." *Journal of Aesthetics and Art Criticism* 65, no. 3 (Summer 2007): 263–71.
———. *Film Authorship: Auteurs and Other Myths*. London: Wallflower, 2010.
Sepinwall, Alan. *The Revolution Was Televised: From Buffy to Breaking Bad—The People and the Shows That Changed TV Drama Forever*. Carlton, Australia: Black Inc., 2013.
Shattuc, Jane M. "Television Production: Who Makes American TV?" In *A Companion to Television*, edited by Janet Wasko, 142–54. Malden, MA: Blackwell, 2006.
Shelley, James. "Critical Compatibilism." In *Knowing Art: Essays in Aesthetics and Epistemology*, edited by Matthew Kieran and Dominic McIver Lopes, 125–36. Dordrecht, Netherlands: Springer, 2004.
Shusterman, Richard. "Pragmatism." In *The Routledge Companion to Aesthetics*, 3rd ed., edited by Berys Gaut and Dominic McIver Lopes, 96–105. New York: Routledge, 2013.
———. *Pragmatist Aesthetics: Living Beauty, Rethinking Art*. Oxford: Blackwell, 1992.
Sibley, Frank. "Aesthetic and Non-Aesthetic." In *Approach to Aesthetics*, edited by John Benson, Betty Redfern, and Jeremy Roxbee Cox, 33–51. Oxford: Oxford University Press, 2001.
Smith, Anthony N. "*True Detective* and the Pleasures of Genre Uncertainty." *CST Online* (April 11, 2014). Accessed February 18, 2015. http://cstonline.tv/true-detective-and-the-pleasures-of-genre-uncertainty.
Smith, Greg M. *Beautiful TV: The Art and Argument of Ally McBeal*. Austin: University of Texas Press, 2007.
Stanley, Alessandra. "So Sayeth the Anchorman." *The New York Times* (June 21, 2012). http://www.nytimes.com/2012/06/22/arts/television/the-newsroom-an-hbo-series-from-aaron-sorkin.html.
Stecker, Robert. *Artworks: Definition, Meaning, Value*. University Park: Pennsylvania State University Press, 1997.
———. "Definition of Art," in *The Oxford Handbook of Aesthetics* edited by Jerrold Levinson, 136–154. Oxford: Oxford University Press, 2003.
———. *Interpretation and Construction: Art, Speech, and the Law*. Malden, MA: Blackwell: 2003.
———. "Value in Art." In *The Oxford Handbook of Aesthetics*, edited by Jerrold Levinson, 307–24. Oxford: Oxford University Press, 2003.
Strawson, P. F. *Individuals: An Essay in Descriptive Metaphysics*. London: Methuen, 1959.

Sutrop, Margit. "The Death of the Literary Work." *Philosophy and Literature* 18 (1994): 38–49.

Swirski, Peter. *Literature, Analytically Speaking*. Austin: University of Texas Press, 2010.

Szczepanik, Petr, and Patrick Vonderau, eds. *Behind the Screen: Inside European Production Cultures*. Basingstoke, UK: Palgrave Macmillan, 2013.

Tenenboim-Weinblatt, Keren. "'Where Is Jack Bauer When You Need Him?' The Uses of Television Drama in Mediated Political Discourse." *Political Communication* 26, no. 4 (2009): 367–87.

Thomasson, Amie. L. "Artifacts and Human Concepts." In *Creations of the Mind: Artifacts and Their Representation*, edited by Eric Margolis and Stephen Laurence, 52–73. Oxford: Oxford University Press, 2007.

———. "The Ontology of Art and Knowledge in Aesthetics." *Journal of Aesthetics and Art Criticism* 63, no. 3 (Summer 2005): 221–229.

Thompson, Ethan, and Jason Mittell. "Introduction: An Owner's Manual for Television." In *How to Watch Television*, edited by Ethan Thompson and Jason Mittell, 1–10. New York: New York University Press, 2013.

Thompson, Kristin. *Storytelling in Film and Television*. Cambridge, MA: Harvard University Press, 2003.

Townsend, Dabney. *Hume's Aesthetic Theory*. New York: Routledge, 2001.

Travers, Ben. "*True Detective* Finds the Light in a Truly Surprising Season Finale." Indiewire.com (March 10, 2014). Accessed February 19, 2015. http://www.indiewire.com/article/television/true-detective-finds-the-lights-winning-in-a-truly-surprising-season-finale.

Truffaut, François. "A Certain Tendency of the French Cinema." In *Auteurs and Authorship: A Film Reader*, edited by Barry Keith Grant, 9–18. Malden, MA: Blackwell, 2008.

Tucker, Ken. "*Firefly* Came Back: This Is the Role Nathan Fillion Was Born to Play: A Flawed Leader of Men and Women." *EW* (March 7, 2011). Accessed March 22, 2016. http://watching-tv.ew.com/2011/03/07/firefly-nathan-fillion-joss-whedon/.

Turvey, Malcolm. "Familiarity Breeds Contempt: Why Repeat Exposure Does Not Necessarily Turn TV Characters into Friends." In *Screening Characters*, edited by Johannes Riis and Aaron Taylor (forthcoming).

Vaage, Margrethe Bruun. *The Antihero in American Television*. New York: Routledge, 2016.

Vassallo de Lopes, Maria Immacolata, Silvia Helena Simões Borelli, and Vera da Rocha Resende. *Vivendo com a telenovela: mediações, recepção, teleficcionalidade*. São Paolo, Summus, 2002.

Velleman, J. David. "What Happens When Someone Acts?" *Mind* 101, no. 403 (July 1992): 461–81.

Walton, Kendall L. "Categories of Art." Reprinted in *Marvelous Images: On Values and the Arts*, 195–220. Oxford: Oxford University Press, 2008.

———. *Mimesis as Make-Believe*. Cambridge, MA: Harvard University Press, 1990.

Walzer, Michael. "Political Action: The Problem of Dirty Hands." *Philosophy and Public Affairs* 2, no. 2 (Winter 1973): 160–80.

Weiner, Jonah. "The Man Who Makes the World's Funniest People Even Funnier." *New York Times Magazine* (April 19, 2015). Accessed March 8, 2016. http://www.nytimes.com/2015/04/19/magazine/the-man-who-makes-the-worlds-funniest-people-even-funnier.html?_r=0.

West, Lindy. "*Celebrity Swan* Is the Most Depressing Television Program Ever Conceived." *Jezebel*. (February 20, 2013). Accessed February 1, 2016. http://jezebel.com/5985698/celebrity-swan-is-the-most-depressing-television-program-ever-conceived.
Wiener, Jon. "'24': Torture on TV." *The Nation* (January 15, 2007). Accessed May 27, 2015. http://www.thenation.com/blog/24–torture-tv.
Wilson, George. "On Film Narrative and Narrative Meaning." In *Film Theory and Philosophy*, edited by Richard Allen and Murray Smith, 221–38. Oxford: Oxford University Press, 1997.
Wimsatt, W. K., Jr., and M. C. Beardsley. "The Intentional Fallacy." *The Sewanee Review* 54, no. 3 (July–September 1946): 468–88.
Woledge, Elizabeth. "Decoding Desire: From Kirk and Spock to K/S." *Social Semiotics* 15, no. 2 (August 2005): 235–50.
Wollheim, Richard. *Art and Its Objects*, 2nd ed. Cambridge, UK: Cambridge University Press, 1980.
Woodward, Richard. "Truth in Fiction." *Philosophy Compass* 6, no. 3 (2011): 158–67.
Zangwill, Nick. *Aesthetic Creation* (Oxford: Oxford University Press, 2007).
———. *The Metaphysics of Beauty*. Ithaca, NY: Cornell University Press, 2001.
Zeccardi, Joe. "Rethinking Critical Communication." *Journal of Aesthetics and Art Criticism* 68, no. 4 (Fall 2010): 367–77.
Zillmann, Dolf. "The Psychology of Suspense in Dramatic Exposition." In *Suspense: Conceptualizations, Theoretical Analyses, and Empirical Explorations*, edited by Peter Vorderer, Hans J. Wulff, and Mike Friedrichsen, 199–232. Mahwah, NJ: Lawrence Erlbaum Associates, 1996.

Index

24 164, 166–172, 186–7, 191

Adorno, T.W. 1
Adventures of Captain Marvel, The 74
Adventures of Priscilla, Queen of the Desert, The 164
aesthetic judgment 8–9, 99, 182–4, 186–7
aesthetic value 3–9, 182, 201, 203–4
agency: compared to authorship 18–20, 41–5; definition of 20
Alias 186
Alive Day Memories: Home from Iraq 167
All in the Family 127
Angels in America 167
anti-intentionalism 21–2, 144, 167
appreciation: 5–10; aesthetic 82, 99, 162, 182; and agency 17–18, 25–7; of television art 41–5, 58–68, 182, 198
Arrested Development 68, 79–80
art: definition of 2–5; television as 67–81
authorship: attributional conception of 19; causal conception of 18–19, 41; and responsibility 18, 25, 42–5
L'Avventura 74

Back to the Future 73, 75
Back to the Future II 75
Barthes, Roland 93–4, 96–7, 126
Batman 189
Beardsley, Monroe 161, 204
Berlin Alexanderplatz 42, 198
Black Ice 62
Blanchet, Robert 69–73, 77
Blue's Clues 188, 196
Bob the Builder 188
Bordwell, David 100, 138–9

Bourdieu, Pierre 181
Bratman, Michael 20–1, 32–6, 167
Breaking Bad 21, 26–7, 38, 68, 71, 75–77, 173–5
Bron 184
Brunsdon, Charlotte 181
Butler, Jeremy 152, 158, 161

Caddyshack 78
Caldwell, John Thornton 25, 29, 49, 53, 91–2
Cardwell, Sarah 10, 14–15, 17, 48, 82, 85, 185
Carroll, Noël 1, 3, 53, 55–62, 64–7, 81–2, 151, 166–7, 173, 176, 194
categories of television 58–9, 130–6, 194–199
Cavell, Stanley 15, 47, 85, 132
Charmed 107
Cheers 142
Chimes at Midnight 58
Colbert Report, The 135, 173, 175, 197
College 78
Collingwood, R.G. 2
Columbo 72
Creeber, Glen 46, 53, 55, 90–1
critical judgment: see *judgments of value*
critical pluralism: see *interpretation, pluralism about*
Curb Your Enthusiasm 68, 79, 185

Damages 36, 70
Davies, David 59–60, 63, 105–6, 130, 135
Davies, Stephen 160, 162, 194
Deadwood 21, 112
Decalogue, The 42
Dewey, John 98–9
Dickie, George 15–16, 204–5

226 Index

Doctor Who 95
Dora the Explorer 188
Dora and Friends 184–5
Downton Abbey 60
Duck Soup 78

Eco, Umberto 95
Empire 139
E.R. 110
evaluation: see *judgments of value*
expressivism 182–193
Extreme Makeover 201

Family Guy 128
Fanny and Alexander 42
Fantômas 74
fictional truth 136–145, 148–151
Firefly 112–13
Fireman Sam 188
Fiske, John 90, 96–8, 101–3, 116–17, 153, 159–160
Flash Gordon 74
Foucault, Michel 45, 205
Friday Night Lights 20–1, 26
Friends 68, 72, 137, 143

Game of Thrones 55, 64, 192
Gaut, Berys 23–9, 51, 60, 62, 66–8, 81, 198
General, The 78
Geraghty, Christine 194–5
Gilligan's Island 131
Girls 29
Godfather, The 147
Gombrich, E.H. 100
Good Wife, The 29, 68
Gracyk, Theodore 9, 17
Grant, James 9
Gray, Jonathan 92–5, 101, 106, 126–8
Greenberg, Clement 2
Green Hornet, The 74
Grice, H.P. (Paul) 31, 165

Hall, Stuart 96
Hannibal 189
Harry Potter 75
Hartley, John 54, 56, 158
Hills, Matt 92–5, 101, 106, 126, 128, 158, 203–4
Hirsch, E.D. 22, 123, 128, 137
Homeland 68, 76, 137
Horace and Pete 198
Horkheimer, Max 2

House of Cards 72
Hunger Games, The 64

I, Claudius 139
I Love Lucy 139
intentionalism: actual 167, 175; extreme actual 167, 175; hypothetical 172–4; moderate 144, 149, 156, 166–8, 175–6
intentions: categorical 108–110, 112–13, 122, 130, 197–9, 203; definition of 20–2; executive 35–40, 44–5, 89; future-directed 21, 167, 172; 20–1, 172; present-directed 20–1, 172; semantic 109–110, 113, 122, 130, 157, 167, 171–7, 197, 203; subsidiary 35–8, 44–5
interpretation: constructivist approaches to 124–128; pluralism about 13, 124, 157, 162; realism about 166–68, 172, 175–6; relativist approaches to 124, 128–9, 134–6, 158–166
Iseminger, Gary 7–8
Isenberg, Arnold 187–191

Jacobs, Jason 10–11, 55, 58–9, 91, 110, 146, 194–5
Jaws 71
Judex 74
judgments of value 8–9, 13–14, 58, 99, 110, 133–4, 163, 168–170, 181–204

Kaufman, Daniel A. 192, 195
Krausz, Michael 98, 101–3
Kutz, Christopher 35

Laramie Project, The 33
Levine, Elena 41, 183
Levinson, Jerrold 105, 109, 172–3
Lewis, C.I. 193, 204
liveness 52–3, 56, 66–7, 81–2
Livingston, Paisley 18–19, 24–7, 30–5, 40–1, 61, 91, 109, 142, 148, 166–8, 175–6
Lotz, Amanda D. 53, 126–8
Louie 19
Luck 44

M*A*S*H 68, 72, 103
MacDonald, Dwight 2
Mad Men 71–2, 160, 186, 192–3
Margolis, Joseph 98, 101–2, 160
Marty 33

Index

McKee, Alan 125–6, 157–8, 164–6, 181–2
meaning: see *interpretation*
medium: definition of 61–4; essentialism and anti-essentialism 52–6, 66; materialism 57–9; specificity of television 65–7
Mittell, Jason 19, 23, 134, 158, 186–88, 190–6, 199–200
Modern Family 184–5

Neighbors 58, 62
neo-pragmatism: see *pragmatism*
Newman, Michael Z. 41, 183
Newsroom, The 28, 30, 164, 184
Normal 33
North by Northwest 144
Nussbaum, Emily 131, 174

objectivity in interpretation and evaluation 123–4, 126, 134, 156–7, 161–3, 182–5, 188–203
One Life to Live 68
ontology of television: constructivist approaches to 92–103; characterized by concern with identifying and individuating properties 64, 89–92, 104–5, 108–9, 112–13; determined by successfully realized artistic intentions 88–90, 108–113

Patterns 33
Pepper, Stephen C. 98–101
Perkins, V.F. 18, 23, 26, 58, 194
philosophical aesthetics 2, 6, 67, 88–90, 98, 105, 160, 184–7
pragmatism 98–101, 124
Pratt, Henry John 69, 72–3
Psycho 71

Rastamouse 185
Requiem for a Heavyweight 33
Rome 139

Saraband 33
Saturday Night Live 58, 62, 184
Seinfeld 142
Sellors, C. Paul 30–5, 40–1
Serbian Film, A 43
Sesame Street 184–5, 190, 192
Sex and the City 142
Sibley, Frank 190
significance 123, 128, 137
Simpsons, The 73, 94, 132

Singing Detective, The 185
Six Feet Under 105
Sixth Sense, The 71
Sopranos, The 33, 38–9, 70, 140, 143–8
South Park 36, 110, 132, 184
St. Elsewhere 137
Star Trek 141, 149–150
Star Trek: The Next Generation 72
Star Wars 74
Stecker, Robert 124, 127–9, 137, 162, 166–8
Strawson, P.F. 105
sufficient control 23–5, 29–35, 37, 39–40, 43–5
Swan, The 202
Swirski, Peter 136, 138

television aesthetics 10–11, 110, 113, 203
temporal boundaries: see *ontology*
temporal prolongation 37, 65, 67–73, 77–82, 132, 137, 198
Thomasson, Amie L. 106–7, 195
Too Big to Fail 33
Top Chef 81
Top of the Lake 42
Transparent 19
True Detective 42, 131–6, 199
truth: in evaluative judgment 182–5, 191–3, 201–3; in fiction, see *fictional truth*; in interpretation 123–5, 129, 134–5, 161–3, 172
Twin Peaks 133

Usual Suspects, The 71

Vaage, Margrethe Bruun 69–73, 77
value: aesthetic 3–4, 7–9, 99, 182, 201; appreciation of 6–9; artistic 68–9, 81–2, 176–7, 182–3, 188–9, 191–4, 196–204; ethical 168–9, 176–7, 191, 201–2; interaction 182, 191, 196, 201–2; pluralism 142, 168, 177, 182, 194, 201
value judgments: see *judgments of value*
Vampires, Les 74
Veep 29
vehicular media 4, 56, 60–5, 80–2, 98

Walking Dead, The 34
Walton, Kendall L. 58, 130–1, 134–6, 139, 141, 149

War, The 81
When the Levees Broke 167
Who Do You Think You Are? 184
Who Wants to Be a Millionaire? 110
Wire, The 36, 39, 72, 111, 186, 188
WWE Raw 3

X-Files, The 19, 133, 137, 143, 199
X-Men 75

Years of Living Dangerously 200

Zeccardi, Joe 187–8